BOBBY MOORE

The authorised biography

The author and the publisher thank Terry O'Neill for his considerable help with the illustrations, especially his telling portrait of Bobby Moore for the front cover.

The back cover shows Moore and Pele exchanging shirts after the classic England-Brazil duel in Mexico in 1970.

BOBBY MOORE

The authorised biography

Jeff Powell

EVEREST BOOKS LIMITED
4 Valentine Place, London SE1

Published in Great Britain by Everest Books Ltd, in association with Ken Adam, 1976.

ISBN 0905018 206

Copyright © Jeff Powell 1976

Printed and bound in Great Britain by
REDWOOD BURN LIMITED
Trowbridge & Esher

Contents

CHAPTER ONE

Under the Influences

Bobby Moore was 17 the night he nerved himself to walk into West Ham's first team across the debris of Malcolm Allison's broken dreams.

The anguish behind the eyes of Allison's bold handshake is the image burned deepest into Moore's memory of that autumn evening in 1958 when the roar of a huge crowd first prickled his spine, when he first sniffed the addictive aroma of stardom.

It is not the new boy's thrill of playing the Manchester United legend off Upton Park which fidgets with Moore's mind during his long, insomniac nights.

Through solitary hours spent counting shadows on bedroom ceilings, Moore still nurses the guilt that his own precocious arrival on the central stage of English Soccer denied Allison the fulfillment of his own playing career. In the moment of Moore's accession to the No. 6 shirt, Allison lost his forlorn chance of playing just once in the First Division for West Ham United.

Allison, the man who taught Moore all he knew. Allison, his idol. Allison, friend. Allison, inspirational fighter against the gasping corrosion of tuberculosis. Allison, having put young Bobby on the road from West Ham's worst apprentice to England's most-capped international, turned from his protegee to walk heavily from the dressing room.

For that one night only, Big Mal was a beaten man. Yet of everything he gave Moore, that unwilling sacrifice was the most important. Bobby watched him go through a confusion of emotions, elation at his own imminent debut bruised by pity for the man whose teaching had made it possible. His own future was at the mercy of his feelings.

Many an adolescent might have collapsed under the weight of the guilt. Instead, Moore's boyhood went out into the corridor with Allison. As the door closed, Bobby shut out his feelings, locked away in some hidden corner of his private self all the dangerous turmoil of excitement, fear, passion and compassion.

Before he even kicked a ball, he was being forged into the haughty captain of England. The immaculate Bobby Moore was conceived out of Allison's most grievous disappointment.

He went out and wowed them.

West Ham, newcomers to the First Division, beat Manchester United 3-2. The Press telephones chattered acclaim for a new young master of the defensive arts.

Moore smiles at that 'I just hit a couple of balls straight. Nothing really.'

The Allison connection can only be dredged up from the bottom of a long, long glass. Even then, Moore probes gingerly at the memory.

'Malcolm had been battling for months to recover from tuberculosis. I'd even seen him the day he got the news of his illness. I was a groundstaff boy and I'd gone to Upton Park to collect my wages. I saw Malcolm standing on his own on the balcony at the back of the stand. Tears in his eyes. Big Mal actually crying.

'He'd been coaching me and coaching me and coaching me but I still didn't feel I knew him well enough to go up and ask what was wrong.

'When I came out of the office I looked up again and Noel Cantwell was standing with his arm round Malcolm. He'd just been told he'd got T.B.

'It's not like Malcolm to give up. By the start of that '58 season we were battling away together in the reserves, Malcolm proving he could still play, me proving I might be able to play one day.

'West Ham had just come up. They went to Portsmouth and won. They beat Wolves at home in their second game. After three or four matches they were top of the First Division, due to play Manchester United on the Monday night, and they had run out of left halves. Billy Lansdowne, Andy Nelson, all of them were unfit. It's got to be me or Malcolm.

'I'd been a professional for two and a half months and Malcolm had taught me everything I knew. For all the money in the world I want to play. For all the money in the world I want Malcolm to play because he's worked like a bastard for this one game in the First Division.

'It would have meant the world to him. Just one more game, just one minute in that game. I know that on the day Malcolm with all his experience would probably do a better job than me. But maybe I'm one for the future.

'It somehow had to be that when I walked into the dressing room and found out I was playing, Malcolm was the first person I saw. I was embarrassed to look at him. He said "Well done. I hope you do well." I knew he meant it but I knew how he felt. For a moment I wanted to push the shirt at him and say "Go on, Malcolm. It's yours. Have your game. I can't stop you. Go on, Malcolm. My time will come."

'But he walked out and I thought maybe my time wouldn't come again. Maybe this would be my only chance. I thought: you've got to be lucky to get the chance, and when the chance comes you've got to be good enough to take it.

'I went out and played the way Malcolm had always told me to play. Afterwards I looked for him back in the dressing room. Couldn't find him'

It goes very quiet all over Moore's big house when he tells the story. He sits surrounded by the plush rewards of all the football years which followed, right hand holding a lager up to the light of a crystal chandelier, left forefinger tracing patterns in condensation on the expensive glass.

It is the sort of silence you are afraid to break with a cough.

Moore shatters the rare and brittle moment himself, snapping the top off another beer. He gulps down the merest hint of embarrassment. This man is accustomed to betraying as much emotion as the Post Office Tower.

Allison taught him that 'Be in control of yourself. Take control of everything around you. Look big. Think big. Be big. Tell people what to do.'

The words hummed in Moore's schoolboy ears. He says: 'I was a boy, training at West Ham on Tuesday and Thursday evenings. Malcolm was in charge, always the commanding figure. For me it was an adventure. Malcolm was the hero.

'Now I see that for him I was the first of a long line of players who he looked on as his own creation. Malcolm's always had one special player close to him.

'What a challenge it was for him to take an older player like Tony Book up from Bath and Plymouth to Manchester City. Then there was Mike Summerbee, then Colin Bell. He bought Rodney Marsh for City to be like a son he could adore. At Crystal Palace he had Don Rogers and then Peter Taylor. Malcolm has to have one.

'Well I was the first, when Malcolm was coaching schoolboys. He took a liking to me when I don't think anyone else at West Ham saw anything special in me. Just for that, I would have done anything for him. Every house needs a foundation and Malcolm gave me mine.

'It went beyond that. He was the be-all and end-all for me. I looked up

9

to the man. It's not too strong to say I loved him.'

Behind that rush of sentiment lies Moore's undying gratitude for the simple philosophy which is the basis for his reputation as a player of vision, as the best reader of a football match in the world.

Moore's capacity for detecting the subtlest shifts and eddies of the highest quality play was the priceless gift handed down to him in one sentence by Allison.

Moore explains: 'Malcolm said one simple thing which was to stay in my life forever. We sometimes used to get the same bus from the ground and we were sitting upstairs one day when Malcolm said very quietly: "Keep forever asking yourself If I get the ball now, who will I give it to?" He told me that was di Stefano's secret at Real Madrid.

'So simple. So real. So easy. I've carried that with me into the middle of Wembley, Maracana, Hampden Park, Every great stadium.

'Wherever it was, I would always know that maybe the left back was free, the right winger running, the inside left dropping off his man into space for me.

'There's nothing complicated about vision. It's pictures in your mind, put there purely and simply by looking around yourself. It's good because it's so simple. The bad players are the players who make the game difficult. I've passed that piece of Malcolm on down to one or two players I believed could benefit.

'I gave it to Les Strong at Fulham and I can't describe the pleasure it gave me in return to see an absolutely immediate change in his manner of play.

'I'll always be in Malcolm's debt for that insight. It was like suddenly looking into the sunshine.'

The vision, however, did not blind Moore to the imperfections in Allison's life style. Bobby swallowed Malcolm's football philosophy, ran in many of the same social circles, but always held back something of himself, refusing to dive headfirst into the whirlpool of self-indulgence.

In his later years as captain of West Ham and England, Moore was probably more aloof from the majority of his fellow players than was Allison as manager of Manchester City and Crystal Palace.

Far from curbing the social habits of his players, Allison more often led them gaily into the night clubs and up to the bars. There is a swagger about such behaviour. It has style, It has dash. But it has dangers, and not only in Manchester's Piccadilly or London's Park Lane.

Even in the sunshine of a 1973 Summer in South Africa, Allison caught a cold. In a country where sport and the social life are the white man's haven from political criticism, Malcolm's high octane mixture of the two brought trouble to his touring team.

Moore says: 'Malcolm's had a great life but he has left some question marks behind him *en route*. As a manager I would still want to be part of my players. But only up to a point. I wouldn't even think about taking them out to night clubs. I would like to feel that after a game I could go round to the local pub and have a drink with them.

'Come seven o'clock I would say "I'm going home." I might be going out somewhere later myself. But not with the lads. How else could I hope to discipline people? I would have told Mike Summerbee he had it in him to be the greatest winger in the world and to go out and prove it to me every game. If he failed, he would have to get in the reserves and prove he was still in good physical condition. I don't know if Malcolm leaves himself the right to do that.

'Look at South Africa. I went there, had a marvellous time and I know they would have me back any time I wanted to get on a plane. Malcolm went there with a team of great players: Rodney Marsh, Frank McLintock, Don Rogers.

'Yet they got diabolical publicity and I ask myself why? Why do it, Malcolm? He's no different from me in that whatever he does is going to get blown up by the publicity. We know that, and it's happened to me once or twice, yet I've managed to stay clear of day-to-day troubles.

'Malcolm should have conquered South Africa but the truth is that he has a streak in him which makes him abuse people or a situation. I appreciate life and don't want to spoil it for myself. If people put themselves out for me I won't abuse them.

'That's the difference between us and that difference is why I can't support Malcolm blindly in everything he does. Much as I love him as a man, much as I respect his knowledge of football, I still have to question him in my mind.'

That process of clinical reappraisal was digging to the very roots of Allison's teaching 15 years later, in Bobby's last season at West Ham.

Like a reliable computer, Moore's mind sifts its imput of information absolutely on merit, aloof from the apparent importance of the source.

Hence the impact of one Lenny Heppell, ballroom dancer and night club proprietor who strictly belongs no closer to football than a distant relative. He is father-in-law to Bryan 'Pop' Robson, regular scorer of goals with Newcastle, West Ham and Sunderland.

Heppell had been loosely involved with West Ham for the best part of a year before he secured a firm introduction to Bobby Moore.

He moved south from Durham in the wake of his son-in-law's transfer from Sunderland and began to work with a handful of West Ham players on their balance and timing. Moore remembers thinking: 'What the hell's he doing? I can't believe in that nonsense.'

For months they exchanged no more than a good morning nod. The more appearances Heppell made at Upton Park, the more remote England's captain seemed. Moore has no problem presenting a forbidding exterior when he senses someone fidgeting to get into his company.

Heppell got no further than 'hullo' until one day in February 1974 Moore went into a local steak house for lunch and found a spare chair at a table with Robson, Trevor Brooking and Lenny Heppell. Moore admits he had enjoyed a lager or two after a hard morning's training and sat relaxed and easy in his chair.

Heppell looked across and said: 'I'm glad you're sitting like that.' Moore, on the defensive said: 'What do you mean?'

'I'm glad to see you relaxed and round shouldered. I never thought you could relax.' 'You don't know me. Maybe it's because I've had a lager.'

It was not the friendliest start to a relationship. Yet the seeds of interest were sown.

Moore says: 'I had a few sessions with him after that and he made simple common sense. He made me question the very first thing Malcolm ever told me: Stand big.

'Lenny told me I ran like a coat hanger. Upright. I looked at myself on television and saw he was right. It was what Malcolm had told me 15 years earlier. It made me look big alright but it made my running harder and slower. Lenny talked me into rolling my shoulders but not my body.

'West Ham went to play up at Newcastle and I knew Lenny was watching so I ran out the way he wanted. We lost, so it sounds crazy to say it, but it worked. I made one long run, the sort of run that would have had me blowing hard a few weeks earlier, and this time I was fresh and ready to go again.

'I watched myself on TV the next day, the Sunday. I looked terrific. It made me want to get out there and play, the way watching Tom Mix at the Saturday morning pictures made you want to go out and play cowboys and indians.

'Lenny got on at me then about turning. He told me to turn like the ballroom dancers – head first. It was logic when he made you think about it. He told me to turn my head and my body would follow. He made me notice that when I crossed the road I leaned forward head first. My feet followed. I started throwing my head and instead of falling flat on my face, my feet would follow.

'Simple? To me it was magic. It was something I wished I had heard years before. My turning and speed of movement had improved one hundred per cent. It was a bit late for me. But Lenny was helping the others. He told Trevor Brooking exactly the opposite to me. Trevor was too relaxed. Easy-ohsy, flopping here, flopping there. Lenny tensed him up. Put some oomph in him. Next thing Trevor's in the England team.

'Makes you realise that too many people in football think they know everything and don't want to listen to people outside the game.'

Nevertheless, Moore still needs a conscious effort to resist Allison's indoctrination. Unthinking, he stands erect at his private bar dispensing the drinks. Shoulders back.

The house is named with head-high pride: Morlands. In some distant corner the au pair is putting the children to bed. The latest in a succession of fast cars sits crouched and ready in the drive. Tina, the blonde model wife, completes the image, curled deep into quiet cushions.

By road, it is perhaps ten miles from the chimneys of industrial Barking to the charm of stockbroker Chigwell. Essex is a county of sharp contrasts. Materially, Moore's progress can scarcely be measured. Mentally, he has also come a long way; able now to turn a wry phrase around his origins.

'Ordinary street, ordinary people, ordinary home, a few ordinary factories in the back garden.'

Robert Frederick Moore, only son of Robert and Doris Moore. Born in Upney Hospital on April 12, 1941. Bred in the whimsically misnamed Waverley Gardens, a terraced tributary of Barking's lorry-laden River Road. As destiny would have it, reared no more than a loud cheer from Alf Ramsey's native Dagenham.

Unlike Ramsey, unlike in fact so many local boys made good, Moore shows no desire to cut the umbilical cord which links us all to our heritage. Stretch the ties, yes. Sever them, never.

The voice remains unmistakeably working-class-London as Moore recalls: 'I lost my first cup final 3-1 at the age of 12. I couldn't get home fast enough. To my Mum and Dad. To cry my eyes out. They made me see it wasn't the end of the world.

'I thought it was. I thought I was a failure. Deep down I had wanted to play for England way back, when I was a baby in the Barking Primary School team.

'When I passed the 11-plus I went to Tom Hood Grammar School in Leyton. The first two months were murder. I was the only boy from my district. Up at seven a.m., on my own on the bus from home to Barking station, train to Wanstead, trolleybus to Leyton, long walk to the school. I was sick with it. I went to the doctor pining for any sort of school in

Barking and got a certificate for a transfer on the grounds of travel sickness.

'The same week, though, I got picked for the district at football. Played for them. Got into that first cup final but didn't realise I'd been spotted.'

The West Ham ground is now thick with people willing to claim first sighting of Moore's talent. Between them, they talked Bobby into training at Upton Park.

It is a significant pointer to his personality that he remembers being overawed more vividly than he recalls most of his early triumphs.

'I was,' he says, 'the 13th player on the groundstaff. I was ordinary. I was lucky to be there. And every time I looked at one of the other lads I knew it.

'Every one of them had played for Essex or London, and at least been for trials with England Schoolboys. I had nothing. All around me were players with unbelievable ability. They were the same age as me and I was looking up at them and wishing I was that good, that skilful.

'The first time I got a representative game I played for Essex over-15s because they needed a makeshift centre forward. I kept lumbering down the middle until our keeper hit a big up-and-under clearance which their keeper caught as I bundled him into the net. Very classy.

'The referee was weak – there's a familiar thought – and gave the goal for Essex. Everyone knew it was a joke. Most of all, the lads who knew they were better than me.'

Inferiority was not a complex Moore enjoyed. The longer it lasted, however, the more it became a spur to improvement. 'The best quality I had was wanting to succeed.'

For a time, Moore was a better cricketer than footballer. As a young batsman with a quick eye and characteristic willingness to stand in the line of fire, he captained South of England Schoolboys against the North.

'Colin Milburn was their skipper but I won the toss, we batted, I opened. I'd just reached double figures when I got an edge and Ollie caught me in the slips.

'He said "On your way, Mooro." I was sick. But half an hour later it rained. The match was abandoned. At least I got my innings.'

Essex wanted Moore to take a lot more knocks for them. The County Cricket Club were interested in several other West Ham boys, Geoff Hurst and Martin Peters among them. They knew in which sport the real money was to be made.

Bobby was still a long way from being a perceptive footballer, but he was already a penetrating student of the game. The giants of England football in the early Fifties will be somewhat less than delighted to learn what the young Moore thought of them as he peered down from the terraces.

'When I first started playing, the England team was full of legends. Billy Wright. Stan Matthews. But there was no-one, not one player in the England team I idolised.

'It seemed to me to be full of the wrong players. I used to go to Charlton Athletic a lot when they were in the First Division and they always seemed to be playing West Bromwich Albion in front of 70,000 people.

'West Brom, a magic side. Ronnie Allen, Johnny Nicol, Frank Dudley. Above all, Ray Barlow. He was my idol, a great left half. So calm, played it so easy, just knocked it about.

'Don't talk to me about Wright and Matthews. How often did Ray Barlow play for England?'

The answer: Just once, a token cap against Northern Ireland in the 1955 Home Championship. 'Diabolical,' says Moore. Barlow has never met Bobby and has no clue to the profound influence he had on young Moore's career. Unsolicited and unexpected, Moore's words come as an overdue tribute to an underrated craftsman of the cloth cap age.

Not until Manchester United's young Duncan Edwards emerged as the brightest of all the Busby Babes for a brief and brutally truncated international career did Moore identify with a hero in the England team.

'I played truant from school to watch Duncan play at White Hart Lane. He put two past Tottenham. He was the Rock of Gibraltar at the back, dynamite coming forward.

'There will never by another player like him. Duncan's death was the greatest tragedy of the United plane crash. I cried when I heard. I was visiting Malcolm at the time, I'd just been signed on by West Ham and I'd gone down to the T.B. convalescence home at Midhurst in Surrey with Noel. We all sat there crying. Two grown men and me.'

The exact passes of Johnny Haynes wiped away the tears. Never beginning to presume that one day they would be close friends, Moore stood and watched Fulham and England as Haynes gave a never-ending exhibition of how to hit the right pass, at the right moment, with just the right weight on the ball.

'Once you got used to watching that perfection, you realised the rest of the secret. John is always available, always hungry for the ball, always wanting to play.

'I say "is" because if I was picking a team now, right now in the mid-seventies,, Johnny Haynes would be in. So he's 40-odd. So he's the

15

master. I loved watching the player and since then I've learned to love the man.

'The two go together. I couldn't feel that close to anyone I did not respect.'

The economy of Barlow, the majesty of Edwards, the artistry of Haynes. The fragments of influence were coming together, waiting to be given their final push into place by Malcolm Allison and his own best friend at West Ham, Noel Cantwell.

'When Malcolm was looking finished as a player I looked to Noel on the pitch. That first year West Ham were back in the First Division, before my game against United, I went to Tottenham to watch them play.

'Noel Cantwell was left back, Noel Dwyer in goal. It was the best display of defending and goalkeeping I'd ever seen. They drew 2-2 but without the two Noels it would have been Spurs by a distance.' By then, West Ham manager Ted Fenton was convinced young Bobby was ready. The debut against United was giddy confirmation. The first, sobering fall was already on its way.

'Three days later, on the Saturday, we went up to Nottingham Forest. They were a good team. They'd been to the Cup Final and just then were running third in the League.

'I should have been warned but I was full of myself. I thought it was a doddle. I got the roasting of my life. I've never since been turned over like that.

'A little Scots feller called Johnny Quigley did everything to me. Turned me inside out. There was a big crowd – crowds were big then – and as we came back up the tunnel for the second half they were all shouting "Play on the left half, that's the weak link".

'I thought: "What the hell am I doing here?" We lost 4-0 and the way Quigley took me apart it could have been forty. Embarrassment.

'That night I was having my first date with Tina. I had the paper in my pocket saying how I got roasted. I ripped it up. If I'd had the money I'd have bought every evening paper in London and torn them all up.

'I got dropped. Dropped? I was lucky to ever play again.'

For the rest of that season, Bobby's romance with Tina made better progress that his career. By the summer he had played only a handful of first team games but was holidaying in the South of France with his Ilford girl friend and her family.

On leaving their beach in St. Aygulf, he was required to join West Ham's tour in Austria. 'I got the train to Nice where I was to catch a plane to Austria. How did I know where they kept the airport? For hours

I walked up and down the seafront there. The Promenade des Anglais. Like an idiot. Suitcase on my head. I didn't have a penny on me. Finally, someone took pity and directed me down the coast road to the airport.'

Like coming up against Johnny Quigley, it was an instructive experience. 'I vowed I'd never let myself get in such a state again. I now find it unbelievable that so many senior players can't get themselves through customs unless the club secretary is there with the tickets and passports.'

A few hours later, Moore was vowing never to go abroad again. 'I thought club tours were supposed to be glamorous. When I got to Baden Baden we were in an antique hotel and every time a door creaked open an old boy came through it in a wheelchair. They were all there to be cured by the waters.

'Ted Fenton said if I didn't like it I needn't bother to go on another trip.' Moore could smile at the memory 15 years, countless flying hours and endless miles later. At that point, however, he was still a long way from first team regularity. Even now, he doubts he would ever have broken through had West Ham not sold John Smith to Tottenham.

Smith was the white hope of West Ham. Moore was one of the players-in-waiting when Smith considered Tottenham's money worth the risk of fighting Dave Mackay and Danny Blanchflower for a first team place at White Hart Lane.

Moore emerged from the shadows. Smith went into the sort of frustrated decline Bobby feels might have been his own destiny. He says: 'You've got to be lucky even if you know you're good enough to take the chance if it comes. If John hadn't gone to Spurs I might have been a reserve footballer who threw in the towel, gave up the game.'

Moore was pushing 20 when he finally began a full season in the West Ham team. In 1960, that was still young. But for Bobby it had been a long wait.

That season was something less than a riotous success.

'We went to Wolves in the first game, Noel Cantwell at left half and me at left back. We were playing the way the players wanted...4-2-4 with plenty of good football. We played well and lost 4-2.

'It went that way for a few games. Playing well but no breaks. Then the manager had his say. He wanted us to hit long through balls from the half way line. We became the world's best hitters of long through balls to nobody from the half way line. We seemed to lose every match 4-0.'

Moore's basic education was complete. That flash of contempt for Ted Fenton was the beginning of an irreverence for most managers.

17

It bred an artificial relationship with Alf Ramsey, made him fret for transfers to Bill Nicholson at Spurs, Brian Clough at Derby and Malcolm Allison at Crystal Palace, and finally pushed him into the unlikely arms of Alec Stock at Fulham.

Above all it fostered ten years of mutual suspicion between Moore and one comparably complex, influential and private person.

Ron Greenwood

CHAPTER TWO

The Gospel According to St. Ron

The end of the 747's heavy climb out of Heathrow was signalled by the snapping release of three seat belts. Bobby Moore, Jimmy Greaves and Freddie Harrison were first up the stairs, racing for the sanctuary of the bar high in the dome of the Jumbo. The only way to travel to New York.

The winter of 1970, although meteorologically unremarkable, blew hard through the littered streets of Upton Park. It seemed one more cold blast would be enough to dump the local First Division football team in the gutter with the rest of the garbage. By way of escapism, watching West Ham that season was as much a relief from the Cockney working week as cementing the back yards.

Moore's team were in retreat, momentarily forsaking the trauma of the relegation struggle for the tinsel of a prestige friendly against Pele's team, Santos of Brazil.

Yet Moore and Greaves were still very much names to impress the American public. Harrison, who lurched from the East End into business on his own wits and the coat-tails of Moore's reputation, was staying close to his partner. Moore: 'By the end of the runway we were in the bar. Totting.'

Down in the body of the aircraft, as befitted the older God-fearing man, Ron Greenwood sat through the formalities, the nasal blandishments of the air hostess, the permission to loosen the seat belt. He is invariably unobtrusive. That day he was an even quieter study in distant thought. Arguably England's foremost authority on Soccer, Ron Greenwood was now manager of the most tattered team in the First Division.

That Saturday, West Ham had lost 4-1 at Newcastle United, again travelling as badly as old wine. Greenwood had hoped that game would be their salvation. Instead, the result reeked of relegation.

If ever a non-drinker needed a drink...

19

But that was not Greenwood's way. Especially not near his players. He went forward and upward in search of nothing stronger than a throat-cooling Coke.

Harrison obliged. And kept obliging – lacing Greenwood's innocuous order with Bacardi, loosening the worried tongue with rum. Moore enjoyed what he knew to be a juvenile joke. There had been years of restrained animosity between him and Greenwood.

Within an hour the spiked drinks put Greenwood where Moore had wanted him for so long – at his mercy. He savours the moment still. 'I knew the pressure was on him. West Ham were struggling again. The Newcastle result looked a killer. Freddie kept slipping him the Bacardis and he cracked somewhere out over the Atlantic.

'He just blurted it out: "I'm going to resign." And he looked at me.' Moore sensed he could have crushed Greenwood then. One savage sentence telling him it was about bloody time would have applied the final push. The respect of his most famous player would have been publicly torn away.

Moore felt like doing it. Twirled his own glass. But said: 'No, Ron. Be bigger than resigning.'

Greenwood was spared by Moore's feeling of debt for their early association. In those days he had lapped up all the knowledge the man had to offer and begged for more.

The young Bobby first fell under Greenwood's persuasive influence as an impressionable sixteen-year-old. In October 1957 Moore was recruited to the England Youth team where Greenwood, then earning his living as assistant manager of Arsenal, was flexing the more progressive of his ideas.

Greenwood briefed the boy on how to handle Holland in Amsterdam's daunting Olympic Stadium and Moore's representative career began with a 3-2 away win. He says: 'I was magic that first night and I loved Ron for helping me. Coming home on the plane I grabbed the seat next to him and cross-questioned him wicked about football, football, football.

'For a long time it was the same. I followed him around like a puppy, being a pest to him. Picking his brains. It went on when he was manager of the England under-23 team and then when he came to West Ham to take over from Ted Fenton.

Moore, even now, glows with the compliment Greenwood paid him at that time: 'Ron told me one of his major reasons for coming to West Ham was that he knew he had me there to start building his team around.'

The metaphorical flirtation during those meetings for junior international matches was now on a close and regularised club footing. As in many a marriage, the first rows were about money. 'There was a time,' says Moore, 'when we were having what is politely called a dispute over £2 a week. God knows I needed it. I couldn't believe Ron when he said the club couldn't afford it.'

'That was the start. All through I didn't earn good money at West Ham. I wasn't badly off, but I was not the monster money-earner everyone seems to think. All over the First Division, footballers were always earning more than I got at West Ham.

'I believe Ron resented the benefits I did get as a young man coming into the game at a time when they were abolishing the maximum wage. Yet playing in some of the teams he put out for West Ham I had to earn every penny. I was lucky other things happened for me in football.'

In any relationship, growing disenchantment is a difficult process to reverse. Between Moore and Greenwood, it was accelerated every time they strayed outside the narrow confines of pure football strategy and technique.

Moore recalls an early disappointment with Greenwood's handling of men. 'Not long after he came to Upton Park we had to play Arsenal, Ron's old team. I knew how much it meant to him for us to do well but we were paralysed. Lost 4-0. Yet it was one of the best games I ever played for West Ham. He knew I'd done everything for him and I needed him to swallow his own disappointment and thank me. He just crept up to me and whispered: "Well played." I wanted him to say I was magnificent. I wanted him to tell the world that he didn't know what we would have done without Mooro. Then I could have slept that night. Ron has never understood that footballers need that gee-up.'

Still, at that time, West Ham were on the upswing and the depth of Greenwood's knowledge was the overpowering consideration.

Moore was still impressed by the way Greenwood had used him and Johnny Byrne in a prophetic partnership to dominate an under-23 international match. In May of 1961, Young England went to Tottenham's White Hart Lane ground to face West Germany amid the chaotic administration which seemed to be the order of the day for representative teams at that time.

Greenwood was advised late by the Football Association staff that he was short of players and even had to call Mike Harrison away from the end of a full day's training at Chelsea to play on the wing. Yet the Germans were thrashed 4-1. Moore says: 'Budgie (Johnny Byrne) must have had 100 touches of the ball, 75 of them from my passes, most of that one-touch, all down to Ron's organisation.

'I can't deny his brilliance. The man is the encyclopedia of football. At international level, with international players, he was fantastic.

'Without question he would have made a tremendous England manager. Perhaps an even better manager of England than Alf Ramsey.

'Put Ron on a World Cup level and every player in the squad would understand him and benefit from him. Ron has been involved in every FIFA report and analysis that has mattered. He sees things in football which are beyond the comprehension of many players and coaches in the game.

'That was one of his problems at West Ham. Ron talks about the game at such a high level, sometimes in such a complicated way that it goes straight over the head of the average player.'

That realisation dawned on Moore one Saturday in the early Sixties when he glanced around the West Ham dressing room during a Greenwood team talk and saw ten other heads nodding agreement, but eight pairs of eyes glazed over. He says: 'Some days I believe there were only a couple of us who understood a word he was on about. He never seemed to realise that he should have been talking down to more than half the team. In his way he was guilty of what I was always being falsely accused of: not adjusting to the need to play bread-and-butter club football.'

The irony of that will not be lost on Greenwood, who more than once summarised Moore's apparent disdain for the more humdrum matches by saying: 'Bobby should play every game at Wembley.'

Greenwood mirrored Moore's professional respect by saying: 'Bobby is one of the few truly great players who can make the game look simple. For a long time I rated him the best player in the world.' He also reflected: 'Ask me to tell you about Bobby Moore the footballer and I will talk for days. Ask me about Bobby Moore the man and I will dry up in a minute.'

Moore says: 'I know very litle of Ron as a man. I have a picture in my mind of him sitting at home with his wife Lucy on a Friday night discussing picking his team and how we would play. That's where we are different. Tina doesn't know what 4-2-4 means. If she did, there's no way I would ask her to pick my team. We have a lot of enjoyment outside the game but I don't know if Ron has much of a life outside football.'

There was the essence of the eventual conflict. Moore's character and life-style assumed its own, more flamboyant proportions as he emerged from the professional shadow of Greenwood, a churchgoing man dedicated to the sanctity of his family life and purity in football.

Moore and Byrne became almost as good at cracking bottles as at splitting opposing defences. The pair became very much the hub of a social whirl involving most of West Ham's most successful team. Jim Standen, John Bond, Ken Brown, Eddie Bovington, Alan Sealey, Geoff Hurst, Peter Brabrook, and later Martin Peters. Only Jack Burkett and John Sissons were on the fringe.

What Moore regarded as an engaging life style which promoted· an irresistible team spirit, Greenwood suspected to be a social problem rooted in drink and compounded by hangers-on. By way of illustration, there is Moore's recollection of the train journey home from Hillsborough in 1964 in the wake of what he believes to be the finest performance in West Ham's history, the F.A. Cup semi-final victory over Manchester United.

'It was the only time I ever knew Ron to be emotional. And it was all wrong to me. The train was packed, a madhouse. Singing, sinking a few beers. So Ron just burst out crying. He was slumped over a table in the dining car sobbing. Budgie and I went and asked him what was up. He said: "We've got this far without all these hangers-on. We don't need these people".

'I said: "Ron, please God we've got these people for the next five years. They used to hang on to Tottenham. Now they're hanging on to us. As long as they're with us, we know we're winning something."

'He said: "We don't need them." and he wanted the punters out of the bar.'

Even before they got to Wembley, that divergence of opinion led Greenwood to deliver what Moore received as a crushing blow to their relationship.

The Members of the Football Writers' Association elected Bobby to the elite company of Footballers of the Year, which required his attendance at the presentation banquet on the Thursday evening before the Cup Final. The winner of the award is traditionally supported at that annual gathering of soccer people by all those close to him at his club. At 23, Bobby also had the distinction of being the youngest ever Footballer of the Year. Greenwood, however, regarded the function as too close to Wembley.

'I made my way over from our hotel alone,' says Moore. 'Yet even though Ron had refused to let the lads come I couldn't believe the club wouldn't support me. I looked round the Cafe Royal and I couldn't see a soul from West Ham. Not a single face. Not Ron himself, not even a director. Did the Directors think *they* were playing on Saturday? That hurt, deep down. I still left early enough to help win the bloody Final for them.'

Two days later Moore made what he regarded as a conciliatory gesture, probably his last, and felt rebuffed. 'We were a bit lucky against Preston in that Final but when we won I felt it was lovely for Ron most of all, achieving something by sticking to his principles. I went to cuddle him at the end but he didn't want that from me.

'Ron felt deeply about people without showing it on the outside. I knew then that although he respected me, he didn't like me. I believe he had every reason to respect me and no reason to dislike me. But there it was.'

Thereafter even the Soccer discussions grew less frequent. 'Ron asked me why I didn't go to him any more, to ask about the game. He took it as a sign that I was turning against him.'

Moore still listened as intently as ever in team talks but made less effort to encourage concentration by the others, looking at the ceiling, out of the window, anywhere except at the manager. 'Once Ron called me to his office and said: "I know you take in what I'm saying, but will you please also look as if you're listening. How else can I make the rest pay attention?" Yet it wasn't my intention to undermine him.'

Greenwood was now experiencing almost as much trouble as everyone else in getting through to his captain. Moore insists he does not consciously erect barriers but admits to recognising the effect of his instinctive and somewhat aloof withdrawal from the herd. It is an indication of how his ego expanded in company with his stature in the game that Moore tells this anecdote, without a hint of surprise that he should have been the focal point of the story. 'Alan Ball highlighted to me how people had trouble getting close to me. The first time he got picked for England he went back to Everton, his club at the time, and all the players there asked him what Bobby Moore was like. He told them: "Just like the rest of you." They said: "Don't believe you."

'Once you're put on a pedestal where no-one thinks you're touchable then you can't convince people you're the same sort of person as themselves.

'I have noticed that people sometimes seem nervous about coming up to me and talking to me but I can't believe that was the problem for Ron. I think, instead, he wanted me to go to him as his captain. Perhaps I was at fault, but that was not my way.

'Perhaps I should have been a go-between. Perhaps it would have helped when things started to go wrong. But I looked on myself as one of thirty professionals, one of the chaps. I didn't want the people I had to play with thinking I was one of THEM, picking the team. Budgie was

much closer to Ron, always in and out of his office. But he had a bubbling personality and could get away with it. Nobody would accuse
Budgie of getting them dropped.'

That aloof position – a shade superior to many of the team, deliberately distant from the management – was maintained by Moore until West
Ham's cup-winning years of 1964 and 1965 paled into the long depression of relegation strife and humiliating failure in the knock-out com-
petitions.

Moore felt he knew the answer to the problem and went to press his
solution on Greenwood, urging the manager to buy Maurice Setters, the
one-time Manchester United and Coventry defender whose more recent
battles were fought in the courtroom over his dismissal as manager of
Fourth Division Doncaster Rovers.

Moore: 'I begged Ron to sign Maurice. He was tough and could play
a bit and we needed to be harder at the back. Ron said: "No, he's a
rebel. A problem."

'I said: "With Maurice we can win the world. Don't let it all go."

'He said: "Don't worry, I've got one for us. A nice boy. Been to
college. Got a long body and short legs."

Moore walked out. A few days later John Cushley walked in from
Celtic. 'John's strength when he came was that he was a hard Scottish
boy,' says Moore. 'Ron knew in his heart that we needed someone to do
some kicking. He knew I was professional enough to do it, even though
I'm not a physical person. I've hammered people on a very few occasions
when its been absolutely necessary.

'Ron tried to close his eyes to it. In John Cushley he was buying a
compromise which satisfied his conscience. A nice lad who could get
stuck in. But he couldn't expect everyone to be like me and win by intelligence...or by deciding when to kick people.

'Ron was in a right quandary. He'd bought someone to put some stick
about but couldn't bear watching. One of John's first games was a
friendly in Germany in 1967. We were playing against Dortmund and
Siggi Held, their old World Cup forward, started making runs
everywhere. John had the answer to that: whack, whack, whack.
Everywhere Siggi ran John put him flat on his face. In the end Siggi ran
up the white flag. Surrendered.

'We were all saying "Nice one Cush. You'll do for us." But when we
got in at half time Ron pulled him to one side and said: "John, I've
bought you to be tough but sometimes you've got to take it easy."

'As we walked out for the second half John came up to me looking
puzzled and said: "I'm playing it too hard. The manager doesn't like

me." John Cushley never made another tackle for West Ham.

'The same thing happened after he bought Alan Stephenson from Crystal Palace. After a game or two I heard Ron saying to Stevo: "Alan, you can't get stuck in like that all the time. Sometimes you've got to read it, hold off, use your brain." Ron was looking for perfection, but it was another centre half ruined.'

Greenwood, however, was encouraged by the team's development. Cushley's arrival came at a time of much shuffling of the playing staff and in that same 1967, West Ham undertook one of their periodic jaunts to America. Moore says: 'Ron and I were talking in one hotel room about how pleased he was to have got rid of what he called the nasty characters in the team. He was worried about the nasty people. He was telling me even though I'm sure he thought I was one of them, a dodge-pot. So was Budgie but the difference with me and Budgie was that we could kick the ball in the right direction.

'Ron said he felt we were getting a team of nice lads together. I sat and wondered who the hell had ever won anything in football with eleven nice people. And in the next room John Cushley and John Charles, two of his nice boys, were falling off their beds at three in the afternoon.'

Moore already felt he could never influence a change in Greenwood. That belief was rooted in one early conversation in which Greenwood had recounted an incident from his own playing career to illustrate the importance of staying true to one's principles. Moore recalls: 'Ron was talking about playing centre half for Chelsea against Matt Busby's great old Manchester United team and I asked how he had coped with that terrific centre forward of theirs, Tommy Taylor.

'Taylor was tremendous in the air but Ron said he went into the match believing he could beat him in an honest jump for the headers. The first cross came in and he got a clear sight of the ball and went up expecting to head it away. Taylor timed his jump in front of him and got the touch and United nearly scored. A few minutes later the same thing happened and Taylor scored from the header.

'So it went on through the game. Ron never changed his tactics, never tried to block Taylor's run or nudge him off his jump, not even when Taylor stuck in United's third with his head. He believed he was doing the right thing and when the last high ball of the game came into Chelsea's penalty area he went up just the same. Still trying to win his first header of the afternoon, fair and square.'

Those principles guided Greenwood through his coaching and management and won him the respect and admiration of hundreds of people deeply involved in the game. The flowing, open football which

Greenwood's beliefs demanded of West Ham also earned him the gratitude of tens of thousands of football-loving spectators who relished watching his team.

At times West Ham stood alone against the violence, brutality and intimidation which, in the late Sixties and early Seventies, threatened to bludgeon all the enchantment out of English football. When the tide turned again towards skill, soccer was in many ways in Greenwood's debt.

That was small consolation for Moore, who had felt the years slipping by with no club honours to reward his individual genius. He makes no bones about it: 'What sickens me is that I was not successful at club level. When we won the two cups Ron had a good team because he had a majority of good players. With the right management we could have gone on to dominate the game for a period the way Leeds did later.

'I never won a League Championship medal. For that, I cannot forgive Ron. It wasn't just this business of not enough so-called steel. The man's man-management was bad. I could see through him and I knew he was hurt when we lost another bad cup tie to another poor team. I was hurt. A lot of us were hurt. He should have let himself show it. The lads would come in the dressing room with their heads down and he would say we would talk about it on Monday. Why wait? Tell me what I did wrong. Tell another one he can't bloody play. Tell that player he bottled it. He knew, alright. No man ever saw so much in a game as Ron Greenwood. But he could not motivate people.

'Some games I would love to have done it. Perhaps he wanted me to. But it wasn't my job. Not even as captain. It wasn't up to me to slag another player, and by Christ I've played with enough who aren't good enough.

'At Fulham, for example, they have to make do with what they've got. But Ron kept on buying for West Ham. One or two buys have come off for him for a season. They've won the cup again and a lot of his disastrous buys have been forgotten.

'Look at Bobby Ferguson. Came down from Kilmarnock as a record fee for a goalkeeper at the time. Helluva nice lad, but he can't have been a good buy for West Ham. Alright, he helped the club out for a few games here and there but later Ron couldn't even see the sense of cutting his losses. Bobby went to Sheffield Wednesday on loan with a view to a transfer. I heard that Ron asked £40,000, they offered £35,000. It looks as if Ron's silly little mind wouldn't let him go even though he would be getting £150 off the weekly wage bill as well as helping out a lovely lad who'd done him a turn.

'Like Ron, I might have bought Tommy Taylor from Orient. When he first came in alongside me at centre half I thought he could be a world beater. I would have loved the same ability for age that young Tommy had. But it's not working out as well as it should.

'His best buy was Pop Robson. And he should never have let him go. After Pop got twenty-eight goals one season he should have told him he was the greatest in the world and sent him out to get even more next season. That was all Pop needed. A boost. Ron never said a thing to him. You could never go to Ron for inspiration.'

Yet the paradox remains that if Moore needed counsel on a football problem, Greenwood is the man to whom he would turn 'It's true I would feel cut off if I badly needed advice on something about football and could not go to Ron. No-one in the world knows more about the game.'

It remained, then, the difference in life-style, rather than any lack of professional respect, which put such severe strain on a relationship which both parties were at pains to present to the outside world as untroubled.

Once, when they were discussing the social whirl, Greenwood preached: 'If the individual takes care of himself, the whole will of the team puts itself together.'

Yet the day still came when Bobby Moore was one of several individuals caught in an indiscretion which seemed to the public to have undermined the West Ham team.

That was in a northern seaside resort which has lured many footballers into the quicksands of scandal.

CHAPTER THREE

Blackpool:
Or how our hero stopped worrying and learned to love the booze.

Blackpool lights up a stub of coastline with the stuff impoverished dreams are made of: candyfloss and carousels, fish and chips, one-arm bandits and bingo, brittle rock and hard drinking, slap and tickle, day trippers and daft hats, two weeks and to hell with the cost.

Above all, there are the illuminations.

Lancashire textile workers and Yorkshire miners come up for sea air and flutter moth-like around that neon Tower. Blackpool is as sophisticated as pie and peas. Which is precisely why, in what might loosely be termed The Northern Season, its population multiplies beyond the bursting limits of its boarding houses.

Bobby Moore would choose Blackpool for a holiday after almost anywhere from Benidorm to Barbados. Yet he will make the most of the place, knowing that the Soccer season, unlike the holiday season, makes no allowances for such quirks of personal preference.

Blackpool also has a football team, who tend to hover optimistically between the Second and First Divisions. West Ham were drawn away to Blackpool in the third round of the F.A. Cup. Irrevocably. The tie was to be played on January 2 1971.

Even in deep winter, even with seas and collars up in unison, Blackpool holds on to an element of unreality. Some of the lights never go out. Those survivors are reinforced at Christmas by a festive flicker of the main switch.

New Year's Day is no easy day to take a professional team to Blackpool in the hope of doing a professional job. Bobby Moore will acknowledge that 'Let's face it, no matter what you tell them, most footballers will go out somewhere to celebrate New Year's Eve. That year was no different but everyone felt up to light training on the Friday morning.

'Then we had that long and tedious train journey to Blackpool. We arrived about five o'clock and dinner was at 7.30 and even in that time we heard plenty of people suggesting the next day's game would be off because the pitch was iced up. The boredom was bad enough even without thinking we may have wasted the trip.'

Before dinner a group of West Ham players drank a lager each as they sat watching children swim in the heated indoor pool of the Imperial Hotel. Moore later sipped two glasses of wine during dinner and then, *en route* to an intended early night, stopped in the foyer 'just to sit for half an hour and watch the families who were up for the Christmas holiday.'

Moore sat in the company of Jimmy Greaves, Brian Dear and Clyde Best. They were joined by two members of a television crew come to Blackpool to film the match. Talk and time slipped by until 11 p.m. when the T.V. men upped and said they were off to take in another of the Blackpool sights: Brian London.

London, he of the lantern jaw and looping punches, had retired from heavyweight prizefighting into the equally colourful business of night club proprietorship. He was happily installed in the 007 Club, an archetypal rendezvous for those nocturnal beings among us who have trouble surviving the small hours without the help of a drink, a few friends and some background music.

Two taxis arrived at the hotel entrance, one for the television crew, the other ordered in error and therefore left vacant, waiting, available. The trap was laid and baited.

In some such moments Moore has as much resistance to the heat of temptation as a snowflake in a desert 'I couldn't even tell you the names of the television people but I'd met Brian London on many occasions and thought it would be nice to look him up. The transport was there. We just joined them. On the spur of the moment.'

Even at the peak of his career, Greaves never saw anything wrong in a beer or two before a match. Dear never needed his arm twisting to go for a drink. Best, the big young Bermudian, was swept along by the senior players towards an hour's devillment which was to mushroom into the biggest disciplinary incident Ron Greenwood had to handle.

The four of them were in London's club for little more than an hour. Moore, Greaves and Dear drank about four bottles of lager each. Best sat with them at the bar but did not drink, making his own compromise between personal friendship and professional discipline. They were back in the hotel foyer a few minutes before 1 a.m....ordering coffee and sandwiches.

Moore says: 'I suppose we all realised at the time that we were leaving ourselves vulnerable. People will throw up their hands in horror at the thought of professional sportsmen going for a drink the night before a game. But it was hardly a diabolical liberty. In fact we thought very little about it. We were in bed by one-thirty and got up about ten o'clock the next morning. That's a good night's sleep by anyone's standards.'

For Moore, Greaves and Dear, a few lagers and two glasses of wine during a long evening represented a very modest consumption of alcohol. Moore: 'Not one of us felt we had jeopardised the team's chances. No player would do that on purpose. If a player did I would consider him warped, I wouldn't want him in my team, he shouldn't be part of any team.

'The problem was not the drinking. It was the result.'

The afternoon after the early morning before, West Ham walked into one of their familiar defeats by a lesser team. Moore and Greaves both played. Dear was substitute. Ironically the non-drinker, Best, was not picked. Blackpool won 4-0.

'There was only one winner from the start.' says Moore. 'We were totally outplayed. The pitch was bony with the ice. They were steamed up to have a go and West Ham were never in it. We were left once again with the feeling of utter disappointment at being beaten by a team from lower down the League.

'Our position in the First Division didn't mean much at the time and everything that season hinged on a good Cup run. But those results had become a regular occurrence. Ron Greenwood was upset with the per-formance because it was hardly a performance at all. It was a sick trip home but nothing much was said and that seemed to be the end of it.'

It was, in fact, the beginning. On the Monday Greenwood was con-fronted in his office by an irate supporter who had travelled to Blackpool, heard that players were in a night club and been sickened by the result.

'Normally,' says Moore, 'Ron would have dismissed that sort of thing. From that aspect Ron was too big a man to have truck with people phon-ing in or calling to tell tales on players just because the team had a bad result.'

This time, however, club chairman Reg Pratt walked into the manager's office in the middle of the heated discussion and the midst of his own disappointment with the Cup defeat. He demanded to know what the fuss was about.

The supporter also contacted several Fleet Street newspapers and on Monday afternoon Brian Dear received two phone calls from journalists seeking confirmation of the story. Dear denied everything and telephon-ed Moore to warn him that the newspapers were making enquiries.

An hour later Dear answered another phone call, this time from Greenwood, and admitted the indiscretion to his manager. Again he telephoned Moore with the news.

Moore drove early to Upton Park on Tuesday morning and at once sought out Greenwood in the manager's office.

'I understand there's something you want to see us about.'

'No, not really. I don't want to talk about anything.'

'Well, you've obviously heard. I know you have. It is true. I've come to apologise. We know we did wrong but it wasn't done with any ill intent. All we can do now is apologise.'

'You've hurt me. Let me down. I don't want to talk about it any more. It will be dealt with in due course.'

Greenwood, whose habit was to keep all West Ham affairs as private as possible, was confronted by a scandal already breaking in the Press. He felt obliged to name the guilty players to journalists in order to protect the reputation of the innocent members of his team.

While Greenwood plunged into a round of meetings with the club's directors, BBC television were making their usual secretive arrangements for that Wednesday night's *This is your Life* programme, with Moore as the surprised subject. West Ham delayed announcing their verdict on Moore and company until Thursday, thereby allowing the BBC to go ahead with their programme unembarrassed. Moore: 'One night I'm a T.V. star. Next day, the big hammer.'

The punishment was a two week suspension for Moore, Greaves and Dear, plus a fine of a week's wages, in Moore's case £200. Best, rightly, was treated more leniently.

The repercussions were considerable. Greaves was hastened towards retirement. Dear ran out of clubs willing to take a chance that goals would keep coming despite a merry life style and expanding waist line.

Not only was Moore's golden image somewhat tarnished, but the suspension kept him from being match fit to lead his country against Malta in the European Championship. So Alan Mullery, with whom Moore was later to team up at Fulham, was given the honour of England captaincy for that one match.

All for what? At the risk of shattering whatever schoolboy illusions remain about this great game of ours, it is necessary to record that the fuss was over nothing at all unusual.

It would take a very naive or a somewhat dishonest manager to insist that his players never take a drink the night before a big game. The crime in Blackpool was getting caught, compounded by losing the match.

Greaves did not turn farther away from the game that made him famous out of a sense of shame. He was disgusted with the fuss made by holier-than-thou critics. Moore made no excuses – not even mentioning the rumours that the match would be off – because he did not believe any were necessary: 'Greavesy and I were sickened by the way Blackpool was blown up out of all proportion. Whether people like it or not, whether they care to admit it, footballers are always doing what we did in Blackpool.

'It's been done many times before, both abroad and in England. I remember when I was first picked for the England team being a bit surprised to see that Greavesy always popped out for a couple of pints of beer the day before a big game. When you first get your chance you wouldn't dream of doing it but Greavesy didn't think anything of it and in fact it was what he needed.

'After I moved to Fulham and we had our long run of matches to the 1975 F.A. Cup Final, we used to go to the local after training every Friday for a lager before travelling to the cup-ties. Nobody complained because we kept winning.

'It happens all the time. Our visit to Brian's club made not the slightest difference to the result in Blackpool. Perhaps it was exaggerated by my involvement. I know that when you are England captain people are always looking for little chinks in your armour, little slip-ups that they can cash in on, so I try not to give them the chance.'

Like most of his contemporaries, Moore resents the extreme reaction of the media and large sections of the public every time a player is known to have sampled the demon drink. Personally, he has a high tolerance to lager, his favourite poison, and wine, which he enjoys with most meals. He is also a more relaxed individual after the first couple of drinks and even after a heavy night has a remarkable power of recovery which enable him to cope comfortably with strenuous training early the next day.

Although some of his acquaintances damage his reputation by telling exaggerated stories of his social life – even though he and I have swum through a few liquid evenings together – Bobby usually keeps his alcoholic indulgence within reasonable bounds.

Moore sums up his attitude to drink in a neat phrase of his own: 'A car needs petrol.' Elaborating: 'Of course some players have damaged themselves by too much social life. Two of the best players I knew, Jim Baxter and Budgie Byrne himself, did themselves no favours. But everyone is different. A drink helps me unwind the way it obviously helped Dave Mackay. You were always hearing stories of Dave being picked up off the pavement up and down Tottenham High Road every night of the week. It didn't stop him being a great player for Spurs every time he went out on to the pitch.

'As long as you don't regularly drink to excess, the problem is mental rather than physical. When I first started out as a young professional I wouldn't dream of taking a drink after Thursday.

'I wasn't really used to it because my dad never drank at all. Yet you saw the senior pros going for a couple of beers on a Friday and slowly it dawned on you that the whole business is just an attitude of mind. At first you think you mustn't do certain things in case it affects you. Then you realise everyone is different and its an individual decision.

'I like a drink and as long as it's not to excess I feel better for it. But if you're seen holding a lager in this country people start shaking their heads and asking whatever happened to the clean-living sportsmen.

'That's not the case anywhere else. I've seen the Italian and the Brazilian national teams, for example, sit down to lunch before a big evening game with wine on the table. They say it helps the digestion. Here people make you think you shouldn't be doing it and create another problem in the player's mind.'

Discipline was left to the individual at West Ham. Greenwood wanted to treat his players like responsible men, wanted to trust them. Sometimes the response was good, often he was let down.

Yet, invariably, the football was entertaining.

During the 1965-66 European Cup Winners' Cup campaign they travelled to Greece for a return match against Olympiakos two weeks after establishing a 4-0 lead in the first leg of the tie in London.

Moore recalls: 'One or two of the lads were getting stuck into the bevy on the plane and we had to make a stopover in Switzerland. Before we took off again the pilot came through and asked Budgie how much more champagne he was likely to need. Budgie said: "Just one more crate."

'When we got to Greece they had to put Budgie to bed for two days. Two more of the lads went out on the booze the night we arrived in Greece and they were falling about with stomach cramp and all sorts.

'That was often the way in our European ties. For me, that was over-doing it. These were some of the most important games a lot of the West Ham lads played in their lives. When it's that big, I'll leave it to the night after the match to go totting. And I love life as much as anyone.

'Yet Budgie was incredible the way he got away with it. It was a struggle to get him out of bed on the day of that match in Greece, yet he was brilliant. He murdered them again. We drew 2-2 and skated through on aggregate.'

The temptation to let pleasure interfere with the business of winning football matches had required Moore, Byrne and several more stars to salvage their distinguished names in more dramatic fashion on an even larger stage in the early summer of 1964.

Fresh from their triumph in the F.A. Cup, Moore and Byrne were key members of Alf Ramsey's England squad selected to travel to Lisbon for a prestige international match against Portugal on Sunday May 17, 1964.

As usual the players gathered under Ramsey at the rather anonymous Whites Hotel, near the Football Association offices in Lancaster Gate, four days before the match.

Again as usual, Ramsey took them training on the smooth turf of the Bank of England sports ground at Roehampton. The manager then suggested they should spend half an hour in the bar with the club staff and members who always gave the England team whole-hearted co-operation.

Ramsey, as was his practice whenever he drank with his players, bought the round and then ushered his squad on to the coach back to central London in time for dinner at the hotel.

It was a warm evening and after dinner Moore and those closest to him took a stroll along the Bayswater Road. They were a distinguished company; Moore, Byrne, Gordon Banks, Jimmy Greaves, George Eastham, Bobby Charlton, Ray Wilson.

It was still very warm. They jumped at the suggestion of a drink in the West End.

Again it was nothing too outrageous. The match was still four days away. Even the multiple distractions of the West End of London did not keep that elite company of footballers out later than a few minutes after midnight.

But Ramsey was not a trusting soul like Greenwood. At 11.30 he and his staff patrolled the hotel corridor to check the rooms. One of his assistants, Harold Shepherdson, discovered the empty beds.

Ramsey and Shepherdson simply placed each missing individual's passport on his pillow. To players accustomed to team officials keeping all travel documents, the inference was obvious. They were lucky still to be making the trip.

Alf then let them sweat. Moore: 'As soon as we saw the passports we knew we'd been rumbled. We flew out on the Thursday morning thinking we would be for it sometime that day. Alf said nothing. Friday, nothing. Then we had a meeting after training on the Saturday and right at the end he let us have it.'

As he dismissed the squad, England's manager said: 'There are seven players who I think would like to stay and see me.' One by one the rest of the squad walked out looking questioningly at the seven, who had kept the incident to themselves.

Ramsey said: 'If I had enough players in the squad none of you would be in the side. In fact, I don't think you would be here at all. But I haven't enough players. And I don't think you will do it again. Because I think you now realise it would not be worth the risk.'

Ramsey then named all seven in the side to play Portugal next day, as if daring them to fail. The public, unaware of the drama, thrilled to a dramatic match which England won 4-3. Johnny Byrne rose to the challenge with a brilliant hat-trick. Bobby Charlton scored the fourth goal.

Still Moore felt it was a storm in a beerglass. 'It would have been ridiculous if some of those great players had not gone on to the 1966 World Cup just because we had a few beers fours days before a match.'

For Moore, in fact, it had been something of an achievement to get to sleep not long after midnight. His insomnia has often led him to seek refuge in a long night's socialising and he has played all the better for not spending several hours tossing and turning in bed.

Between Fulham's F.A. Cup semi-final and final he was seldom in bed after eleven o'clock but did not enjoy one good night's sleep. At home he sometimes has to retreat alone to another room to stop disturbing Tina.

'If you don't have trouble sleeping,' he says, 'you don't know what a hell it can be. Sometimes I'll go downstairs and fall asleep reading. So I'll stir and go back to bed. Then I can't get back to sleep again. There's no way having a drink is worse for me than all that nonsense.'

At such times, Moore is naturally keen to keep convivial company around him but he says: 'I hope I don't influence other players, particularly younger players, to drink. I will always invite a young player into my company if he's feeling left out of things. If he doesn't want to drink that's fine by me. Every individual knows what he's capable of and what's good for him.

'It's like training. Slogging round the track all day, every day, might sound like good hard work but it can take the edge off you.

'It's a very delicate business, working out why you might be having a bad time on the pitch. At times like that I've tried anything and everything. Extra training...early nights...late nights...drinking...not drinking...eating well...living like a hermit off the bare essentials. You name it, I've tried it. And most times you just feel yourself going backwards. I've gone into extra training and strict diet but if I go below

12st 8lb I don't feel fit and strong as I should. My best playing weight is 12st. 10lb. and just those couple of pounds make all the difference. In the end, however you're living, all you need is to suddenly get one good game under your belt.

'If you're having a bad patch and people see you out in a pub or a club they start pointing the finger. But sometimes a fellow wants to forget all about it and he does himself good by going for a drink and going to the limits.'

What, one might ask, can the limits be to encompass such a philosophy?

'You can let yourself go so far and recover. Too far, and there is no going back, no sweating it out of your body and your system however hard you try.'

But how far is too far?

Moore gropes for an illustration and finds it in two well-worn words: 'George Best.'

He explains 'George should have been the best player in the world. For a time he probably *was* the best player in the world. All the skills, scored goals, courage. Complete. He was right at times when he said he *was* Manchester United. There were times I saw him dominate a whole game from start to finish. Other times he did enough in 20-minute bursts to win matches outright, even for Northern Ireland. He played teams on his own.

'What I can't understand is why he didn't enjoy doing that. He says he did, so why did he just throw it all away at the drop of a hat?

'He gave me the impression that he just didn't give a damn. That's wrong. He took liberties by just not bothering to turn up, say for training if he'd had a heavy night. He was not only abusing himself but abusing other people's respect for him.

'There's got to be something strange in a person who doesn't have feelings for his own team mates or care what they feel. These are the people you work with and spend a lot of your life with. Surely you must want them to like you and above all respect you.'

Moore's powerful sense of team identity was one of his abiding strengths. He does not like to let people down and does not appreciate such behaviour in others.

Of the somewhat tragic figure of Best, Moore adds: 'Even after the crap hit the fan at United, George was still letting people down who were putting plenty of money his way. I was in South Africa in the summer of '74 and it was reported that a Johannesburg team were paying him £1,000 a game. Three thousand people turned up to watch George's first training session there. The only person missing was George.

'In the end, of course, he let himself down as badly as he let those people down. In one game he tried a few tricks but was badly out of condition. I asked him how someone with talent like his could let himself be exposed in that level of football. He couldn't see it. So sad.'

Moore accepts that Best's problems were exaggerated to self-destructive proportions by the hangers-on who were the bewildered little Irishman's substitute for a stable domestic life.

'Those people who want to be seen out and about with the football stars are the biggest problem, bigger than smoking, drinking or anything else.

'Budgie had the same problem with them. Like George, he could never say no. He always had to go out, and go on.

'There were times when I'd start an evening with Budgie and I would love to have gone somewhere – but you've got to have the strength to say it's not possible.

'There are a million people who want to be with you because you're a name. The same people will disappear if you hit bad times. As far as I am concerned if they think the worse of you for going home, then you don't need them. If they take the point, and even encourage you to leave, they can be friends.

'It takes a bit of character to walk away from a good scene and I don't deny that being married young was a help to me. It's not a bad thing to have some responsiblities, to have somewhere to go home to, to have a family waiting. Overall I spend a lot more nights indoors. Going home to an empty house must have been hard for George. He couldn't do it. I don't know if I could have done it regularly. Sometimes I'm looking forward to getting home but Tina and the kids might be away and you arrive at an empty house. It's not the same.

'It might sound lovely being out chasing the girls every night and having a pad to take them back to. But it's not the answer. That's why I felt sorry for George.'

Girls are always mentioned in intimate connection with the social life of footballers, not least by Best himself. Moore says: 'Some players get involved, some players don't. But every time you're out late people think the worst. Take it from me, when they put two and two together they usually come up with five.'

That was how a lot of unofficial mathematics calculated the Blackpool business. Those malicious rumours annoyed Moore most of all, for the pressure they exerted on his marriage.

CHAPTER FOUR

A Boy to Take Home to Mother

If there is an approximation to the West End in eastern London, then it has to be Ilford.

The town crowds around the High Road, a main artery darting away from the milling junction of trains, buses, cars, hamburger joints and people which is collectively identified as The Broadway.

The High Road starts out full of boutiques and big stores pitching their sales at a sharp-witted community with plenty to spend if the price is less than a downright liberty. After no more than a sharp sprint, the High Road peters out into pubs and petrol pumps even before the sudden twist at Seven Kings swings you past a wasteland of used car lots and bingo halls towards Romford.

Half way down the High Road, spaced out between the old town hall and the new public baths and competing for side-street parking with the cinema, throbs the dance hall.

Without that institution, God knows how we so-called salt of the earth would propagate our species.

The chains of weekly newspapers recording the turbulent life of the East London sprawl, devote much of their space to pictures of hopeful newlyweds. In my time I wrote countless supporting captions hinged around the locally immortal phrase: 'The couple first met at a dance at Ilford Palais'. One such sentence of mine advised the worthy readers of the Walthamstow Guardian that Robert Frederick Moore and Christina Elizabeth Dean had been joined together in holy matrimony at the Church of St. Clemence, Ilford on June 30th 1962.

Since that fateful day, Ilford Palais has been renamed Tiffany's and tarted up somewhat. Yet in essence it remains the same: a cross between the cavernous Palais-de-Danse, of which a vintage specimen survives at Hammersmith, and the intimate Club-de-Smooch suggested by the fashionable new name.

There is a big band and a brash group laced with an interval disc jockey. There are several gentlemen who never look comfortable in dinner jackets designed for some previous occupant until they bounce a few locals trying to prove their manhood in a flurry of fists and bottles. There is a bar not far from the dance floor to ply the shy with Dutch courage. There are hot dogs on the balcony to supplement the first verbal sparring of the sexes and to save the cost of a meal later.

There are Teen Nights for the very young trying to look impossibly mature. There are Over-21 nights when stags run into hen parties, mostly on Fridays, the traditional East End night for extra-marital flirtation.

Most of all there is Saturday Night. Girls dress to kill but do most of the damage with withering glances at those boys who do pluck up the courage to walk away from their mates and get turned down for a dance.

Saturday Night begins full of hope, collects a bare handful of romance on the way and ends with wallflowers mincing down one side of the High Road and groups of rejected youths jeering from the other.

Tina Dean lived a brisk, well-lit walk from the meeting factory, Bobby Moore a threepenny bus ride away at Barking. Tina sat with the girls in the warmth and the dark, repelling unwanted dancers. Bobby stood with the boys, watching the fragments of light reflect from the spinning silver ball high in the ceiling and dart tantalisingly across the pretty young faces.

She was 15. He was 16. Sadly, we have to report something less breathtaking than love at first sight.

To start with, Tina played hard to get. One night Bobby made a dance, a walk home, a peck on the cheek and a mad dash for the last bus to Barking.

Tina, however, was asked by a girl friend what on earth she saw in this rather square young footballer. Her stepfather consulted record books not yet alive to the arrival of Bobby Moore and insisted there was no such footballer at West Ham. Tina was not the slightest bit interested in football anyway.

So she did not go to the Palais next Saturday. Bobby waited all evening, stood up but undeterred.

He took to spending Saturday mornings in Ilford High Road loitering at the record shops where Tina loved to listen to music, browsing absently through the racks, being rewarded by no more than a brusque nod from the pretty blonde upon whom he had fixed his affection.

That was the limit of his success until the day Tina and her mother drove by in a taxi as Bobby strolled the street. Tina jabbed at the window: 'There. That's the boy who says he plays for West Ham.' Her mother looked out at a short-haired, clean-cut good-looking young man with an open face and clear blue eyes. She said: 'He looks a nice boy. Why don't you ask him home for tea?'

Like all mothers, Tina's wanted the best for her daughter. Her instincts about Bobby were proved right. She packed Tina off to the Palais that night, saw them married four years later on that day in 1962 when the reception celebrated not only the nuptials but also young Moore's return from the World Cup in Chile with his first England caps. She lived to see them flower into the first couple of English football and is remembered with affection by both her daughter and son-in-law for her helpful influence on their early life.

First the death of Tina's mother, then the two strokes suffered by Bobby's father in the early 70's, rendering him virtually housebound, strengthened the marital bond. Those moments of private distress sharpened gratitude for their own good life.

The Moores first set up home in a classic example of the suburban semi in Gants Hill, Ilford's dormitory. They progressed to mock-Tudor splendour in stockbroker Chigwell's affluent Manor Road.

Then, in 1974, ambition to build their own prestigious residence and the urge to move their children away from fast roads took them around the corner and further up status hill to the sanctuary of 'Morlands', the new family seat.

Their mutual progress has always seemed well scripted. Tina faced the realities of earning a living in an employment agency, used her looks to advantage in sporadic modelling sessions and was ready to retire into maternity as Bobby began to reap the financial rewards of his own talent.

Roberta, Little Miss Bobby, was born on January 24th 1965. Dean arrived, to perpetuate Tina's family name, on March 24th 1968.

They are an ideal family packaged into what Bobby describes, accurately if not inventively, as 'the home of our dreams'.

Bobby and Tina looked at the cost together, took a deep breath and plunged into their £100,000 investment. By way of reward, they approach the new house through elegant white pillars, dine sumptuously behind rich velvet drapes, relax in deep sofas in a large cool lounge, dispense hospitality in Bobby's favourite room, his bar, and climb a grand curve of stairs to the pretty master suite which dominates the quiet complex of bedrooms and bathrooms.

Tina has domestic help, notably in the fully-gadgeted kitchen from which she is always promising herself to produce a Cordon Bleu meal, dabbles in charity work, takes care to look the part as Mrs. Bobby

Moore, steers the children through everything from riding lessons to the best education money can buy, lunches with friends, holidays in an assortment of sunspots and says: 'It's been a hard life.'

Anticipating the public wince at the remark, she hurries on to the qualification: 'A good life, yes, but still a hard life. There have been a lot of pressures. Not enough privacy. More time apart than we would like. Whatever Bobby's got he's earned the hard way. He's been on show almost every minute of the day. It has put us under pressure. After getting on for fifteen years of marriage the miracle is that we still *like* each other.'

The love is still there. They appear undemonstrative in public but stay close by glances, signs and personal word. The tiffs are always in private and invariably frosty rather than fiery, the flames of Tina's temper doused by Bobby's icy disdain.

The making-up is the best part. Tina dresses at her most tempting and feminine. Bobby thaws and whispers: 'Want a cuddle, Perc?' using his fond nickname for his wife.

The liking is something else altogether, and certainly no accident of passionate chemistry. Tina quickly perceived the growing gulf between so many of football's husbands and their wives and determined that she was not going to be one of the little women left behind by her husband's success.

She has never much liked football, makes no pretence about it and goes to matches only out of a sense of duty to support her husband on the big occasions.

Bobby says: 'Tina would never want to come and see a match with me. Sometimes she will come along but only because we are having dinner later with some friends.'

Yet she stayed abreast of her husband socially, developed her own personality which Bobby recognises as 'stronger than my own,' remained his closest confidante, most influential adviser and probably his only real friend.

Bobby says: 'I have never been a person to take football home to the house. I can lose a match or two and be a bit upset without regarding it as the end of the world. I can come home to Tina and escape from it all.

'But whenever there are real problems – on or off the pitch – Tina is the one I turn to. There are some things you can't disclose to acquaintances, some things you could never tell a friend. Outsiders will be nosy enough to want to know what's going on but they can't come up with the answers.

'The only person who can do that is the one who cares for you and is deeply involved in the outcome. Between us, Tina and I have always been able to talk things through. Apart from her, there is no-one I would call a really close friend.'

Moore knows that the honesty of that remark reveals a great deal about himself and will rankle with those who claim to be the closest of his social circle.

The man's latent suspicion of outsiders grew as each new success attracted a fresh crop of admirers. Even Tina admits to having felt the cold draught as Bobby has lowered the self-protective barriers. 'I know he's hard to get close to, to get through to. Very, very few people succeed.

'I can get through to him but sometimes even with me I can feel him withdraw. Do his reserved bit. Go icy quiet.'

Tina, alone, is close enough to recognise the mechanism as Bobby's way of living with external pressures. 'Everybody always says how easily he has ridden all the pressures. He does seem to cope very well. But down the years it has taken its toll deep down inside him. Most of the time he's worrying about not upsetting people, not letting them down. There always seem to be people queuing up for Bobby to do something for them.'

Moore says: 'If I've agreed to do something in good faith then I will do my damndest to be there.'

Tina is less tolerant and would be more demanding of some return for Bobby's time than he often insists on himself, despite his reputation as a commercial man. There are people who have felt more snubbed by Tina than by Bobby. She is, however, myopic and says: 'Quite often I don't recognise people because I'm shortsighted. I know they often think I'm putting them off but Bobby's better at that than I am. He can do it without being rude. If I don't like people they usually know it.'

Tina's faint irritation with Bobby's polite tolerance of hangers-on is always tempered by her personal gratitude for his generosity. 'Bobby is a high-liver but never at the expense of myself or the children. He is a very generous man. We didn't have much money until a few years ago yet he bought me a full length mink coat when I was only twenty-five. He is always buying me surprise presents for no particular reason. He always puts me before himself.

'I love the way he's always got a kind word for waiters or children, people who wouldn't dream of presuming. Have you ever seen him refuse an autograph to someone who asked politely?'

In fact, Moore's civility withstands almost any effrontery. During the summer of 1975, he had just three hours to spare in transit from a Fulham match in Gibraltar to a six-week stint as a guest player in South

Africa. Tina had been left to arrange a meeting for him at Heathrow with a group of Brazilians to discuss details of a contract for Bobby to play exhibition matches in Rio de Janeiro later that summer.

Tina also wanted to take the children to say hello and goodbye to their father. Still, it was as much as she could do to dissuade one of Moore's business partners, Freddie Harrison, from going to the airport 'just to buy Mooro a drink'.

Tina says: 'There were all sorts of things to sort out in those three hours. Above all I wanted to see Bob because we'd had a bit of a row before he went to Gibraltar and I couldn't let him go off to South Africa for six weeks with us all upset.

'But people were pestering us all the time and when the Brazil people finally went we just had a few minutes left. We went to kiss each other and say goodbye...and someone just barged up, pushed an autograph book in between us and said: 'Sign that.' I could have hit the man but Bobby signed because it was the quickest way of getting him out of the way.'

The Moores rarely move about unrecognised. Not that they would want to. Both are tanned and fair, tall and upright. A proud and handsome couple. They dress expensively: Bobby studied and immaculate, even in his preferred casual clothes; Tina varying from chic to the carefully tossed, deliberately carefree look which her generation of girls made fashionable. She is always making appointments for the hairdresser's which she never keeps.

The very fact that they look good together sharpens the speculative daggers pointed at the hearts of all public couples. While football marriages have creaked, groaned and collapsed all about them, Bobby and Tina have blithely frustrated the gossiping predictions of a crack-up.

Both travel extensively. Both mix freely. Both are aware of the dangers. Bobby, as England's World Cup winning captain, would be a prize notch on many a suspender belt, Tina a conquest to boost many a male ego.

Tina says revealingly: 'I believe in fidelity in marriage...and Bobby knows it.'

The Blackpool affair was the severest test of their trust. A rumour that girls were present to compound that indiscretion was shabbily hinted at in some sections of the media, suggested with a leer in some sniggering conversations.

Bobby says: 'There was nothing like that but I knew what some people would try to make of it. I rang Tina and told her 'You're going to read some things in the papers which may not be true but which you're

44

not going to like.'

'I told her what to expect. That didn't stop all the aggro. We had some bad moments over it. That sort of incident is going to put your marriage under strain, whatever the truth of the situation.

'If it had come early on in the relationship it might have presented a lot more problems. As it was I was able to say to Tina: 'If you don't know me by now, you never will.' Tina knows me. Some of the chaps can't stand in a bar without their eyes wandering over every bird. That's up to them and its not up to me to blow the whistle on them. But my game is a few beers with the lads.'

They now reflect on such traumas as minor interruptions of the good life. The social pace quickened most vividly after Moore led England to the World Cup in 1966.

Immediately they were invited on a goodwill visit to Malta. The itinerary was packed with ambassadorial duties. 'An engagement every hour, on the hour,' Bobby said to Tina. As the strain told they begged an afternoon off to relax on a boat but were due back in Valetta for an evening reception.

They changed aboard the motor cruiser. A launch brought them rippling back through the clear blue waters to where welcoming dignitaries clustered on the weathered jetty beneath the bleached buildings of the ancient city. It was an idyllic scene bathed in the amber sunlight of early evening.

Tina tip-toed prettily up the gangplank to take the outstretched hand of a beaming bishop, tripped, and began toppling towards the water. The bishop held on to Tina, a priest clutched at the flying skirts of the bishop's frock coat. All in vain. Mrs. Moore and her attendant clerics plopped into the harbour in full regalia.

Tina surfaced to hear Bobby coming, cursing, to the rescue. The bishop was blowing water and failing to prevent his steel-rimmed glasses sinking gently to the bottom, to join one lost shoe.

They stood dripping on the quay: Tina all streaked hair and make up, shins torn and bleeding, trying to preserve some decency with knees together and hands tugging at the hem of a skirt which had begun the evening as a typical Sixties mini and was shrinking before the company's eyes.

Bobby was spluttering, not with water but with the effort of trying not to laugh: 'Everyone seemed so upset, I didn't like to hurt their feelings by bursting out laughing.'

The Mooro and Tina laugh-in was continued next day, on Gozo, Malta's little sister island. Bobby recalls: 'We took the boat across and a

45

cavalcade of cars came down to the harbour to pick us up, all flags flying. The front one was for us, a convertible so we could wave to the people. The entire population of Gozo, just a few thousand, were out lining the streets.

'We pulled away and were just accelerating down the quayside when our driver must have thought a kiddy was going to run into the road. Whack, he sticks on his brakes. Whack, whack, whack, whack, the other cars come piling into the back of each other. Tina's legs go flying in the air. I get out and look back and every limousine's got steam coming out of the bonnet and the chauffeurs are throwing their hats on the ground and shouting and hollering.'

Bobby walked back to the second car, helped the Mayor of Gozo from his seat and begged: 'Please let us out of the banquet tonight. We've got to sleep.'

They went to bed at eight that night. At six a.m. they got up in preparation for a seven o'clock engagement and opened the curtains of their hotel room to a burst of applause from a crowd gathered beneath their window.

'They thought we'd done great to wake up in the morning,' he says.

'We could do no wrong. In a restaurant everyone else would be sitting watching us. We'd cut our steak and a roar would go up like we'd scored the winning goal or something. Kind but crazy. The day we left Malta we had two appointments before our flight, which was at nine o'clock in the morning.

'They were so courteous and kind but sometimes kindness can be a cruelty. Once when we were invited to Israel the people were desperate to show us everything, make sure we missed nothing. The trouble was they were trying to get twenty-five hours into a twenty-four-hour day. We were walking about like zombies and by the time we got the plane home we were on our knees.'

Mostly, they accept that pressure for the rewards. They still warm to the memory of the surroundings in which Bobby soothed the wound of losing the World Cup in Mexico, 1970. He and Tina flew to Acapulco and spent two healing weeks drinking in the view of the city from a hotel suite which numbered among its luxuries an individual swimming pool sweeping from a private patio into the heart of a lavish lounge.

'Holidays,' they will assure you, 'never come any better than that.'

There are times when Tina begs to be excused from the more taxing engagements. Bobby, however, is as meticulous in keeping appointments as in everything else he does.

The measured perfection of his football is mirrored in his everyday life. The scrupulous appearance is matched by an almost obsessive tidiness at home. If Bobby opens a beer can, the metal top is *always* slipped back into the empty container, which in turn is *always* placed in the waste bin. Bobby's clothes are always hung up or folded away.

After a day by the pool or on the beach, Bobby will always fold towels and neatly stack away the reclining chairs, however many staff are hurrying to relieve him of the chore.

After training or a match, the kit boys with West Ham, England or Fulham always found Bobby Moore's kit folded away and his boots cleaned.

In fact his whole game was built on his methodical nature. Knowing his left foot to be comparatively weak, he spent countless hours perfecting a curved pass with the outside of the right foot to achieve the same effect as a pass with his left.

Knowing that he lacked a sharp change of pace, he painstakingly programmed into his make-up a positional sense which made it almost impossible for opponents to exploit that flaw. Never, for a moment, does he relax those standards. 'I never understand players messing about in training routines or five-a-sides. Bad habits are too easy to catch. If you waste a ball in training, the odds are you will waste it in a match. Even in the kick-in I pass every ball as if the World Cup depends on it.'

That intense concentration, that search for perfection, was just one of the investments which matured Bobby into the best defender in world football.

Tina paid her price for the ensuing yield of creature comforts by accepting repeated separations from her husband.

Within a year of becoming Mrs. Bobby Moore, Tina was learning from first-hand experience that wives and football do not mix.

CHAPTER FIVE

The Days of Wine and Pansies

New York has been to the footballer what Las Vegas is to the businessman: a place to make an exhibition of yourself, to pick up a fast buck, to mix business with pleasure. Only of late has Soccer in the States become a phenomenon to take seriously.

In the Summer of 1963, West Ham were playing their part in educating our American cousins in the mysteries of the rolling ball game. They were competing in an international tournament against teams drawn from a representative cross-section of Europe and Latin America.

The football was more demonstrative than competitive, which was to West Ham's liking. After eight matches spread through the month of June they were top of the League. That minor achievement required them to return to New York in July to play Gornik, the winners of a second series of matches, then a grand final against Dukla Prague.

Perhaps moved by the relaxing spirit of the whole venture, West Ham's players opted to take their wives on the return trip, in lieu of a bonus.

The womenfolk had applied a certain amount of pressure to that end. Tina Moore recalls: 'While they were away the first time Ron Greenwood's wife invited us all for a coffee morning. The idea was to keep us happy while the boys were away. But we got talking about taking the trip instead of the bonus.'

Unhappily, some of the wives were scratching each other's eyes out within an hour of landing in New York. Bobby Moore: 'There was more aggro in that hour than we'd had in the whole of the first month with just the lads out there. In the end, the players were getting on at each other because of the girls.

'You couldn't even get organised to go out to dinner because one girl wouldn't go if her best friend wasn't coming. Two more wouldn't leave the hotel because a third wife was moping about homesick. They were talking behind each other's backs, dragging the lads into arguments. It was a disaster. Would you believe we lost?'

Dukla won the first match 1-0. The second leg was drawn 1-1. The Czechs went home with the trophy. West Ham returned to England with a repair job to do on team spirit without which they could not have won the F.A. Cup ten months later, or the European Cup Winners' Cup a year after that.

Moore and Johnny Byrne worked on that problem in their usual way, keeping the social wheels nicely lubricated.

For all that labour of love West Ham's form in the League was as unremarkable as ever. They eventually finished the 1963-4 season back in 14th place in the First Division. They were, however, blessed with good fortune in the draws for succeeding rounds of the F.A. Cup.

They beat Charlton, Orient after a replay with their poor East London relations, Swindon and Burnley on their way to Hillsborough and the top semi-final. That was a modest record from which to challenge the brilliance of Manchester United. Most people forgot that, on their day, West Ham could beat anybody. Moore cherishes that semi-final as West Ham's best day of all. United's all-stars were thumped 3-1. Ron Greenwood cried on the train home. West Ham laughed all the way to Wembley.

The 1964 Cup Final is remembered fondly in the environs of Upton Park as the highlight of West Ham's recent history, lent, by the distance of time, more enchantment than the 1975 Wembley victory which Moore tried so hard to deny them on Fulham's behalf.

Moore has found no reasons down the years to change an opinion formed at the time, dispassionately, amid all the hullabaloo of Wembley.

'It was an anti-climax. A lot of finals are like that anyway because you pour so much into striving to be there that winning a semi-final and setting up a trip to Wembley seems like the major achievement in itself. But it was more than that.

'We were playing against Preston North End, a Second Division side.

'We'd been magic in the semi-final against Manchester United ourselves. Wembley should have belonged to West Ham. We won and it was good to win the first major honour. Apart from that it was a wash-out.

'We simply played badly. We spluttered. We didn't fulfill anything we had promised ourselves. Most of us felt let down. We were lucky to beat Preston, and bloody lucky Preston were no better than they were. Who could explain it? That was West Ham.'

Holden gave Preston an early lead as the veteran Lawton and the very young Kendall took advantage of the space offered as usual by West Ham. Sissons equalised but the burly Dawson sent Preston in at half time leading 2-1. Greenwood negotiated a tactical switch to subdue Lawton, West Ham strained for Hurst's equaliser and Boyce scored a rare goal from midfield in the dying moments to win the Cup.

Moore: 'The game looked certain to go into extra-time until Ronnie scored. I suppose it was exciting for the fans. I was pleased to see us get it over with. But I didn't feel any great excitement.'

He remembers collecting the trophy and going through the ritual of holding the glittering silver aloft before leading a lap of honour around the milling stadium. He remembers his abortive attempt to embrace Greenwood, the manager.

The perfectionist in him would not permit enjoyment of a sub-standard triumph. He remembers almost everything better than he remembers the football, even his irritation at the banquet that night: 'We went to the London Hilton and West Ham had kept down the guest list. There were about 300 of us huddled up in one corner of the big banqueting room. It was like going to a funeral. Nobody enjoyed it as far as I could see.'

Hollow as it was, the victory over Preston opened up the playing fields of Europe to West Ham. It was in the following season, in competition with their fellow Cup-winners from all over the Continent, that the technical niceties of Greenwood's playing philosophy where to show up to best advantage.

Here in Europe they were not so likely to be bludgeoned out of their elegant stride. The European Cup Winners' Cup was more a contest of skill and science than our League football and West Ham were perfectly equipped for the challenge.

Even so, they had to overcome the insular belief of the English that Continental clubs were second rate.

West Ham went to Ghent in the first round, beat the Belgian Cup holders 1-0 and played out a 1-1 draw in the second leg at Upton Park to go through on aggregate.

Moore recalls: 'So many people were disappointed. They had never heard of La Gantoise so they thought they must be a bunch of second--raters and figured we should have thrashed them.

'In fact they were the first two of a lot of hard matches.'

West Ham slipped through by the odd goal against Spartak Prague of Czechoslovakia and were given all sorts of shocks by little Lausanne of Switzerland before winning 6-4 on aggregate to qualify for the semi final.

Just as in the F.A. Cup the year before, the semi-final proved to be the classical tie of the tournament. West Ham were pitted against Real Zaragoza of Spain and were a bare 2-1 ahead at the end of the first leg in London.

Moore: 'We put a brave face on it but none of us believed deep down that it would be enough. They called the Zaragoza forward line the Magnificent Five and we knew they would give us a real going over in Spain.

'Sure enough they wiped out the lead early on and we were left trying to contain them for most of the match. Suddenly John Sissons and Brian Dear broke away and knocked in a goal between them and we'd got a great result.'

The Magnificent Five had foundered on the Magnificent One.

Bobby Moore was as unbeatable for West Ham that day as he was to be for England so often in the future.

This time they went to Wembley and did themselves justice. By chance, the Cup Winners' Cup Final was scheduled for England in 1965 and West Ham were in irresistible form against the German Cup-holders, TSV Munich 1860.

Alan Sealey scored the two goals and Moore glows with the memory of a gala night. 'We benefited from the experience of the previous year and took part in what many people believe was one of the best matches ever played at the old Stadium. There was a lot of good football and we played really well against a good side with a lot of good players. We felt ourselves lucky to get the chance of satisfaction at Wembley so soon after the F.A. Cup Final.'

The club had also learned their lesson from 1964. This time there was no banquet. Everyone went off to celebrate in his own way. Greenwood went home to his wife. Bobby and the boys made tracks to their favourite watering holes and drank the night away, not knowing that they were celebrating the end of West Ham's brief flirtation with success.

The following season they scraped through to the semi-final of the European Cup Winners' Cup, where they were well beaten at home and in West Germany by Borussia Dortmund. West Ham were already sliding into long years of agonising self-appraisal. After 1965, they always seemed to be asking themselves: What's gone wrong?

Moore concedes that the answer was more complex than his basic belief that Greenwood bought some stumers. The great enigma of English Soccer was enmeshed in the fine strands of a complex West Ham philosophy which was straining to produce football of stunning simplicity.

Like a delicate cobweb glistening in the sunlight, West Ham were beautiful to behold but inspired no feeling of permanence.

On so many days they spun a silken web of delightful football, only to be blown into tatters by a storm of old-fashioned British sporting aggression.

'It was well known,' says Moore, 'that everyone enjoyed playing against West Ham as much as they enjoyed watching them. We had endless discussions about what went wrong but nobody seemed able to put their finger on it.'

Moore suspects they should have sought the answer in the difference between the West Ham which won the F.A. Cup and that which won the Cup Winners' Cup a year later.

All the brilliance of West Ham was distilled into that performance against TSV Munich 1860. The difference between that and their earlier Wembley performance could be traced to the emergence of one more West Ham player of sheer class.

Moore: 'It still surprises a lot of people to be told that Martin Peters was not in our 1964 F.A. Cup Final team. Martin is remembered as being as much a part of West Ham as Geoff Hurst and myself. But Eddie Bovington was the wing half in '64 and Martin didn't get the position until we went into Europe.

'That worked out well in its way. In the Cup Winners' Cup you needed more skill and Martin added an extra quality to our game. Yet whenever West Ham have been successful at home they have had a strong man, a battler at wing half.

'In the mid-Sixties we had Eddie Bovington. In the mid-Seventies they've come up with Billy Bonds. Its been loosely talked about as adding steel to the West Ham team but that's too simple.

'There was plenty of bite about the West Ham team if you knew where to look for it. Even Martin had a nasty streak in him if something made him angry.

'It was a question of emphasis in the minds of the management. Ron Greenwood and John Lyall still shy away when you mention putting some stick about. The emphasis was on skill. That was also the thought in our minds.

'I look on tackling as a skill. Any time I see a defender just whacking through the back of a forward's legs to get at a ball, that to me is ignorance. You can't win the ball if you've got a body in front of you. You don't have to go around kicking people up in the air to be a good tackler. The art is to deny a forward space and force him to knock the ball away.

'One of the problems was that sometimes West Ham didn't do this as a whole. They were so obsessed with creating space for themselves that they could not or did not recover when moves broke down.'

That failing conspired with a lot of Northern antagonism to undermine West Ham. The delicate football they played and the glamour surrounding some of their players made West Ham bear the brunt of the anti-London feeling which exists in most football centres outside the capital.

Moore noticed it even before he got into the first team. 'I was a reserve standing in the tunnel at Upton Park one day when Bolton Wanderers came down with a team of hard nuts. They were all saying: 'We're going to wipe the field with you pansies.'

'Every team seemed to feel the same. Wherever we went they seemed to want to get stuck into us; got all steamed up about giving West Ham a kicking. We were everybody's London hate team.

'Maybe we brought it on ourselves. In midwinter, we'd get to some of those tough, cold grounds in the North and we'd upset the locals by going out to play wearing gloves. They just thought we were a bunch of fairies. It was like a red rag to a bull with their players. They couldn't see the sense of it. Ron used to say 'Put the gloves on; you can't concentrate on playing football when you've got cold extremeties.'

'The teams lower down the League were as bad. All wanted to stuff West Ham. That Johnny Quigley seemed to have all his best games against me. Turned us over again when he was with Mansfield and we went up there for a cup-tie in the mud.

'In the end our own fans turned against us. In 1967 we got a home draw with Swindon in the third round of the F.A. Cup and Geoff Hurst got a hat-trick but we still only drew. Went up to Swindon for the replay and lost. Awful. When we got back they had smashed in the windows of my sports shop opposite the ground. I couldn't be angry. It was as hard for us to understand how a team with three World Cup-winning players kept getting it wrong.'

What bothered Bobby most was that when he looked through the West Ham team he, like the fans, could find no really glaring weakness, no excuse for repeated failure. 'You looked at a few of the individuals and felt there might have been room for improvement. But the eleven pieces of the jigsaw fitted when we won the cups. They'd put the ingredients in the cocktail shaker and the team had come out right.

'It's like a drink. Sometimes a cocktail is fabulous, sometimes is diabolical. But when you get it right it's a crime to let it go.

'Our successful team had the right mix even if some of the lads didn't seem too brilliant. If you wanted to be really critical you could find better goalkeepers than Jim Standen...but at £6,000 from Luton he was perfect for West Ham.

'Ken Brown was far from being everyone's ideal at centre half but he was right for us. He was powerful in the air and his priority was always to get the ball the hell out of the danger area.

'Sometimes he would whack it away when I thought we should capitalise on a situation and I'd say "Brownie, what are you doing?" He'd say: "Don't worry, it's no trouble up there." But he was always positive and it took a long while to replace him.

'He had a good understanding with Jim Standen and with John Bond. It's no surprise they went on to work together as coach and manager at Norwich. Understanding is vital at the back. Ken and Jim Standen were good together and Jackie Burkett at left back was a very limited player and shy sort of person who was happy just to do what was asked of him and balance out the rest.

'Ronnie Boyce kept things ticking in midfield. Peter Brabrook or Alan Sealey took 'em on and knocked in some goals. Johnny Sissons kept threatening to be the best left winger on earth.

'Why didn't West Ham make something more of that boy? When he came into the League side as a teenager Johnny was pure gold. Specially that fabulous left foot. Early on he played against Liverpool and went to go down the line. As he went by Chris Lawler, the full back, Tommy Smith, came hammering across and knocked him clean over the low wall at Upton Park into the crowd. I thought: 'Jesus, Poor little feller. That's the last we'll see of him.' But he picked himself up and came back to run Lawler and Smithy ragged. It was one of the sweetest sights I've ever seen.

'He scored a goal in the F.A. Cup Final and was still only nineteen when he played in our European Final. At that time he would have been in my squad for the 1966 World Cup. But he never got any better. Ron Greenwood was still calling him young John when he was twenty-five. Perhaps it was because he was still young. But he should have been demanding things of Johnny Sissons as one of our experienced players.

'I'm sure there were many times in those five or six years when Ron made up his mind to leave John out of the side. Then you would see him Monday to Friday in training, up front in the road runs, fastest in the sprints, drilling them into the net with that left foot in five-a-sides, showing you ball skills which demanded a place in the team. Come the Saturday afternoon, nothing. John Sissons was non-existent. He was a thoroughbred who never matured.

'Against that, Ron has his successes. He had a lot to do with me and he turned Geoff Hurst from a bit of a cart-horse at wing-half into a truly great forward. None of us thought Geoff was going to make the switch. It took him years of hard work and patience to become the man who scored three goals in a World Cup Final.

'For a time he got away with it because he was just a foil for Budgie Byrne. He was so willing he ran himself into the ground and we used to give him terrible stick for all the things he was doing wrong. He was so willing it was untrue. He ran and ran and ran and was always just short of everything. I don't know how he put up with the abuse but it was worth it because in the mid-Sixties he became for a few seasons a genuine world class player.

'Playing behind Budgie and then playing up alongside him must have helped. That man was magic. Real touch, real class. If it hadn't been for the drink aggravating his weight problem Budgie would have been with us in the 1966 World Cup Final as well. Always chatting us through it, joking about. He virtually finished his top-class career with horseplay. We were over in Canada in 1965, had a few drinks and Budgie jumped off a stagecoach. Did his cartilage.

'So we had all that going for us and then up popped Martin Peters. Such talent. Played in every position for West Ham and was obviously best known as a midfield player who scored goals. Yet he could be a tremendous centre-half because of great ability in the air and long legs for tackling. Not the quickest man on earth but would never leave himself in a position where he could be vulnerable. Martin was a natural sportsman from the start, good at any game he tried. We might be travelling somewhere and see people playing an unusual game and Martin would ask to try it and be good at it straight away.

'It's laughable that people don't remember who scored the other goal in the World Cup Final. Martin's subtlety was probably the very reason he was never a big hit with the fans. Yet he was virtually a complete player. In addition to all his talent he had vision and awareness and a perfect sense of timing.

'In fact he was so subtle that when he moved on to Tottenham I felt the players there did not appreciate all his gifts and did not cash in on Martin the way we used to at West Ham.'

Sometimes, when West Ham were cashing in on all their varied attributes, they were irresistible. One Bank Holiday when Budgie was really on song, they put seven goals past the invincible Leeds United. Don Revie, Leeds manager later to take charge of England's national team, went to the West Ham dressing room to offer congratulations and was disappointed to find Greenwood leaning against a water pipe, apparently unmoved by the brilliance of his own team. Revie went back to the Leeds dressing room and told his players: 'You will never lose to that man's team again.'

A few days later, in the return holiday fixture, Leeds thrashed West Ham by a similar margin. Yet the day came when West Ham hit form at Leeds to win a League Cup replay and Moore says: 'That was a real pleasure because they were the best side in the country and they had been hammering us stupid ever since we put those seven past them.'

There were other days like that, when the touch of genius was upon West Ham. But they dwindled in frequency. Other teams cloaked the increasing violence of their play with the euphemisms of the times: full blooded, competitive, professional. Other teams turned more to defence, ironically enough in the wake of what Moore, Hurst and Peters helped Alf Ramsey to achieve for a methodical England team in 1966.

Greenwood stuck to his principles. West Ham, somehow, clung to the lower reaches of the First Division. Moore: 'Often we had to play championship-class football just to get out of trouble at the end of the season. Then we would go away congratulating ourselves we had put everything right and sometimes we even started the next season the way we left off. No problems, until half a dozen games had gone by and slowly we lost the momentum.'

So what did go wrong?

Moore was unhappy with many of the signings Greenwood made to try to put matters right. 'After Jim Standen and Ken Brown went we always had trouble with goalkeepers and centre-halves.

'They never replaced Budgie up front. Even when they did find a striker who might have done the job they didn't know how to handle him.

'When Ted MacDougall came down from Manchester United it was obvious he was the sort of player who needed to be geed-up, encouraged. But when Ted had a bad time Ron just dropped him and said: 'The best gee-up any player can have is to be left out of the side. It will make you more determined to get back.' That worked with some players but it killed off Ted McDougall as a West Ham player. All Bryan Robson needed was to be told how good he was. But he was sold.'

Alternatively, there were plenty of fingers pointed at Moore himself. The man who captained England so majestically was accused of being less than interested in the fortunes of his club, of pacing his game to come to a peak for international matches.

Greenwood confessed he thought of Moore as a big-occasion player. Moore says: 'Some of my best games were played on cold days in the

North of England when we were well beaten because we were sent out with hardly any sort of team at all. No-one said a word about those games. They just listened to the other rubbish. I wanted a League Championship medal so badly I would have lifted West Ham to the top single-handed if it was possible.'

If not culpable as a player, Moore may, however, have been partly to blame off the pitch. West Ham certainly lost something by the mutual failure of Greenwood and Moore to build a secure relationship between manager and captain.

Bobby's lack of affection for Greenwood kept him firmly in the players' camp. When he did feel obliged to bridge the gap – as on the day he agitated for Greenwood to sign Maurice Setters – he was more often than not met by resistance. So West Ham had a captain unable to act either as an intermediary between the management and players or as a powerful influence on policy.

Those qualities hallmarked the captaincies of Danny Blanchflower in the Spurs League and Cup Double-winning team of the early Sixties, Frank McLintock in the Arsenal Double team of the early Seventies, Billy Bremner in the Leeds United team which spanned more than a decade of greatness. Moore has the insight to put the finger on the flaw in his own make-up. 'I would have liked more powerful, more dominating people around me at West Ham. People like that inspire me to involve myself and to enjoy life. I need to react to big personalities because I know that deep down I'm not like that myself. Not when I'm alone.'

That goes a long way towards explaining the change which came over him when he played for his country. It was with England that Bobby Moore found himself surrounded by characters big enough to help him develop into one of the most important personalities in world football.

CHAPTER SIX

Guess Who's Coming to Chile

The moment Ron Greenwood held open the door to the England team, Bobby Moore could cheerfully have relieved his mentor of a few front teeth.

The problem was that West Ham's manager amused himself by giving the bad news first. Greenwood called Moore to his office, looked stern and said: 'You won't be coming with us on the trip.'

Bobby had worked hard in that 1961-2 season and, like any inquisitive young man, was looking forward to the reward of a summer tour of Rhodesia and Nigeria. It was more a challenge than a question when he said: 'Why? What the hell have I done wrong?'

He should have asked what he had done right. Then 21, he was still the apple of his manager's eye. For some months Greenwood had been alerting England team manager Walter Winterbottom to the rapid progress of his protege.

Greenwood was doubling as manager of the England under-23 team and the then-traditional eve of Cup Final match between England and Young England gave Moore the chance to justify Greenwood's propaganda. Moore did them both proud even without realising what was at stake: 'As far as we all knew the World Cup party had been picked. The under-23s were always ready to have a go at the seniors and that year the lads in the full squad were still out to impress because places in the actual World Cup team were up for grabs.

'It was a good game. I felt I'd performed well and went home happy. For me, that was that.'

Not for Winterbottom. He and Greenwood discussed Bobby at length that Friday night. As the pre-selected squad for the 1962 World Cup in Chile gathered in London, he bounced Moore's name around with his assistants Jimmy Adamson and Harold Shepherdson.

By Tuesday morning, Winterbottom had played out the necessary charade with the members of the international selection committee, the archaic cross England managers before Alf Ramsey had to bear, and Moore was summoned to Greenwood's office at Upton Park.

Greenwood smiled at Bobby's flash of anger and came on with the good news: 'Walter wants you to go with him to Chile.'

Despite the subsequent clash of their personalities, Moore acknowledges his debt to Greenwood: 'I don't doubt that Ron worked on that chance for me with everyone at the F.A. He and Walter were particularly close.'

Winterbottom relieved the publicity pressure on his recruit by doing nothing to dispel the public impression that young Moore was merely gathering experience by training with his elders and betters in the England party.

It was not in Bobby's nature to trumpet his own arrival. He joined in the training, studied everything and everyone, said little or nothing. The deception grew as the rest of the party kept returning to their hotel while Bobby stayed at home to deal with injections, suit fittings, and the collection of playing gear, and to finalise personal arrangements for an unexpectedly long absence from England.

The rest of the players were too preoccupied with their own prospects, some dreaming of victory, others just hoping for a game, to realise that the greatest career in the history of English football was beginning in their midst.

Not until the Friday, Moore's third day with the squad, did captain Johnny Haynes realise Winterbottom was talking to Bobby as well as the rest of them about the travelling arrangements. Haynes at once went to Moore and said: 'Look, I'm so sorry. I didn't know you were coming with us. I thought you were here just to make up the numbers in training. But welcome.'

That was the fumbling start of a mutual admiration society which is still going strong.

Even after that, many of the players remained unaware that Bobby had been added to the playing party. For the members of the squad were allowed to go home for the last weekend before their flights to South America.

At that time the Munich air crash which wiped out the bulk of Manchester United's great team was a vivid scar on every footballer's mind. It was the practice of most teams, England included, to divide their party between two flights in the belief that half a disaster was better than losing every player in a single crash.

Winterbottom had told Moore to be ready for the first plane out, then realised how that move might give away his private intentions. Moore reflects: 'When that late call-up came I thought it would be an experience to train with these players and see them play against some of the best teams in the world, just be with them preparing for a tournament like that.

'Then Walter sorted out who was going on which flight and it seemed logical to me that the team for the warm up match in Peru would be chosen from those on the first plane. It arrived 24 hours earlier and gave people a day longer to acclimatise.

'When he put me on the first plane it just stirred in the back of my mind that I might have an outside chance of being a surprise selection. But when we got together again on the Monday I was switched to the second flight a day later. I accepted he'd made a mistake and I was going for the ride, I was a player for the future.'

Winterbottom had everyone fooled. Moore stepped off the late flight to Lima and into the right half position in the England team. Jimmy Greaves provided what Moore describes as 'his usual three goals', Ron Flowers scored a penalty. And Bobby Moore was a fixture in the England team by the end of his full international debut.

Moore has a disarming knack of using understatement to emphasise the measure of his achievements without appearing a braggart. He says of his first effort in the white shirt of England: 'Walter was also pleased with the defensive performance and kept virtually the same team for all four matches in that World Cup.'

That team comprised Ron Springett, Jimmy Armfield, Moore, Maurice Norman who also made his debut in Peru, Flowers, Bryan Douglas, Greaves, either Gerry Hitchens or Alan Peacock at centre forward, Haynes and Bobby Charlton.

Together they travelled high into the Chilean mountains for ten days acclimatisation to South American altitude and were promptly beaten by another European nation, Hungary.

Winterbottom, however, saw nothing in that 2-1 defeat to shake his faith in Moore. He simply replaced Hitchens with Peacock and let the rest of them get on with it against Argentina.

Flowers converted his customary penalty, Greaves and Charlton both scored and England were 3-1 winners of a match Moore expected to be the hardest in their group.

Moore was adjusting more readily than he had dared hope to the rarefied atmosphere of the World Cup, helped by an instant rapport with Haynes who 'always wanted the ball, just like me' and Greaves 'who showed where he wanted it and usually stuck it away'.

60

His instant education programme continued from a successful debut in Peru, defeat by the technicians of Hungary and satisfying triumph over the brooding Argentines into a purely political match against Bulgaria.

The experience saddened him far more than losing an attractive match to Hungary. 'Right to the end of my England career that game has stuck in my mind as the worst international I ever played in. Bulgaria had lost both their other group matches and we only had to draw to qualify for the quarter finals. They wanted to salvage something to go home with, a point at least. So they played with nine men in their own half.

'We started off trying to play the game but as soon as we realised what they were up to we knew we would go through if we didn't take any chances. So we kept nine men in our half. It made me feel terrible. We would have a dozen passes at our end and then try to hit the ball up to our one forward. He was bound to lose it. So they had fourteen passes at their end and tried to hit their one forward in our half. It was one of the worst internationals of all time.'

Nevertheless Moore, an optimist by nature, felt England were ready for Brazil. He could be forgiven that mistaken judgement. Until that quarter final day in Vina del Mar, he had never seen the Brazilians play.

Moore had slipped so comfortably into the England routine, had seemed so exactly talented for international football that he was already regarded as a well-integrated cog of the machine. Brazil provided a timely reminder that he would never stop learning about the game: 'Thank goodness there was no Pele. But they had the Santos boys, Garrincha, Didi, Vava, Amarildo, Zagalo...most of the team that had won the World Cup in Sweden four years before.

'I really felt we were doing quite well against them. Garrincha got a goal in the first half but Gerry Hitchens got us back on level terms and I felt we could hold them. But when we came back out Garrincha suddenly produced one of his famous free kicks. It bent all over the place. I'd never seen anything like it. The ball hit Ron Springett in the chest and Vava was in like a flash to make it 2-1. We felt we had to push forward for the equaliser and Garrincha used the space to take another goal off us. Like candy. Goodnight.

'We came home. Didn't stop to see them win it. I knew they'd win it easy. Stuck four past Chile in the semi and three more past Czechoslovakia in the Final, always having plenty in hand to turn on the magic when they went for the kill in the second half.'

Moore came home enriched by an experience which ironically put the skids under Winterbottom.

Bobby was putting his life in order that summer. The rookie who boarded the plane to Peru returned a World Cup veteran, a five-cap international, to marry his girl and set up house. By the time England played France that October, Moore's existence was neatly packaged to the liking of his tidy mind. That mind was already coming to the conclusion that England were a bad side.

In every player who settles down to a long international career, the initial exhilaration at being picked for his country sooner or later gives way to a realistic appraisal of the quality of the team. With Moore, it was sooner.

Bobby's natural acceptance of his own success and his calculating nature set his mind to assessing England's shortcomings even as he lazed on his honeymoon beach. In theory he was the new boy. In practice his thoughts were coincidentally grooved into the same channels as those of the England manager.

Winterbottom had been pondering his own and England's future for many weeks when France came to Sheffield Wednesday's Hillsborough ground on October 3rd 1962. The occasion was the first match in the Nations Cup, the Championship of Europe which was also to become a blight on Alf Ramsey's record.

The one great team in the history of French football – hinged around Kopa and Fontaine and good enough to reach a World Cup semi final against Brazil in 1958 – was past its physical prime but still rich in class. England were spared home defeat only by a Flowers penalty and Moore says: 'Even though we drew 1-1 we were played off the park. An awful performance. No organisation. No nothing. It was clear to me I'd come in on the end of an era.

'A little earlier England had a tremendous run after adopting a 4-2-4 formation using Haynes and Robson in midfield. I'd seen them beat Spain 4-2 at Wembley a couple of years earlier and thought they were a helluva side. I'd understood why when I first spoke to Walter. He was a warm, outgoing man who loved talking about techniques, tactics, skills, attitudes. You could bet your life he knew every good player in every country by his Christian name, knew every individual's strengths and weaknesses.

'The man was a walking education on football. But he was at the end of his reign. Walter had impressed me because he knew so much about the game, every aspect of it. I had been with him on youth and coaching courses and he was responsible for getting coaching organised in this country. He made people think about football. He did such a great deal for English football that I couldn't understand how he allowed himself to be messed about by the amateurs on the F.A. selection committee.

'I felt he'd lost the will to fight the system. Some of the lads were already asking how much he had to nod to the F.A. It was obvious to me he had to answer to the selection committee, which made it hard for him to retain his respect. His time was up.'

Winterbottom knew himself it was time to move over. The fire was going out in his team. Loyally, he stirred the embers sufficiently to achieve formal, predictable wins over Northern Ireland and Wales in the next two months while his employers opened negotiations which brought Ramsey from astonishing success at Ipswich Town to the far more profound challenge at Lancaster Gate.

Ramsey had seen how Winterbottom had been undermined by the interference of the selection committee and took the England managership on condition that he had the sole right to pick the team.

By February 27th 1965 the word 'selection' had been dropped from the title of the F.A.'s senior international selection committee and Ramsey was exercising his perogative in Paris, against France, in the return match in the European Championship.

Bobby Smith and Ron Henry were brought into the side from Ramsey's old club, Tottenham Hotspur, and all England waited for the kind of tactical miracle which had spirited Ipswich Town from nowhere to the First Division Championship.

Moore recalls all the players being wary of Ramsey, a much quieter, more introvert character than Winterbottom, when the squad gathered. Within a few minutes of the kick-off Moore had his suspicions confirmed that he was still part of a bad team. By half time England were 3-1 down and Ramsey faced his first real test. Moore: 'France were still going strong and we were diabolical. Everyone waited to see how Alf reacted. He stayed very calm, told us we could still win the game if we went out and started to play a bit and believed we could do it.

'There was none of the ranting and raving you might have got from some managers in the middle of a bad defeat.'

For a few minutes, at least, it worked. Bobby Tambling, Chelsea's all-time record scorer, added an England goal to the one scored by Smith in the first half. But the organisation was weaker than the belief in recovery and France swept gracefully to a 5-2 triumph.

Superficially, it was anything but an auspicious start to Ramsey's stewardship. But while the world mocked the result, Alf began seeking the answers. He was already in no doubt of whom to ask the questions.

Moore had no sooner settled into his seat in the coach taking them sadly from the Stadium in Paris than he looked up to see England's new manager sitting alongside. Bobby recalls: 'Alf started asking a million things about the way things had been done under Walter. I was playing a sort of old fashioned right half at the time, neither playing properly in midfield nor in defence. I was falling between two stools and he was obviously going to sort that out. Ron Springett had a bad night in Paris and he played in goal for England only occasionally after that. Gordon Banks was one of the new faces introduced to the side.'

Ramsey had already settled on Moore as his lieutenant, partly because he knew he had not been involved with England long enough to store up tight-lipped loyalties to Winterbottom. The foundations were set down of a long relationship which never once became blurred by emotion.

The icily resolved ambition of both men to conquer the football world had to survive one blistering test, six weeks later. Scotland came to Wembley full of literal and metaphorical spirit – the fans with fumes on their breath, the players breathing fire – to give Ramsey his first bitter reason for hating the Auld Enemy. A goal from Douglas was not enough to stop Scotland winning 2-1, and inevitably making a great deal of noise about it.

A month later the tide of results turned. Douglas scored again at Wembley, and this time his effort sufficed to hold Brazil to a draw. There was method and morale, organisation and optimism about the new England as they embarked for Ramsey's first summer tour.

The vital cornerstone was laid on May 20th, 1963, without ceremony, in grey and distant Bratislava. Jimmy Armfield was injured. Ramsey leapt at the chance to give the England captaincy to his young lieutenant, Bobby Moore.

Those closest to Moore advised the world and his wife to put their mortgage on England beating Czechoslovakia. Those who thought they knew better compared records, studied the teams and deferred judgement.

Moore recalls: 'I loved that first experience of leading England out. The atmosphere was magic. The crowd are fanatical in Bratislava. I decided we'd only get beat over my dead body. The Czechs were still a great side. It had taken Brazil to beat them in the World Cup Final the previous summer and the stars were all there, Popluhar, Novak, that magical man Masopust.'

Jimmy Greaves, two, Bobby Smith and Bobby Charlton shared the goals in a 4-2 win. The way Moore presided over the match had the accompanying jostle of journalists writing about Englishmen again

Home
and
Family

Robert Moore, O.B.E.

D. J. STEPHENS

REVEILLE

Moores at home. *Inset* Less affluent days.

Above With children Dean and Roberta. *Below* Roberta with real and waxwork Daddies at Madame Tussaud's.

appy family scene — except for the detective in the background: this was shortly after a kidnap threat to the
lren.

TERRY O'N

Above and opposite Mrs Bobby Moore.

TERRY O'NEILL

The Moores' home in Chigwell.

holding their heads high on foreign fields.

Chauvinism was reinforced as England went on to Leipzig and 2-1 victory over the East Germans. The testing Iron Curtain stretch of the tour was over and Ramsey was able to leave out Moore, among others, to give loyal reserves a game in Switzerland, which was duly won 8-1.

Moore returned for a string of autumn wins over Wales, the Rest of the World and Northern Ireland. The latter 8-3 romp, on November 20th, 1963, celebrated Wembley's first floodlit football match.

Already the milestones were piling up. So was Moore's confidence in Ramsey's administration. 'For the first time since I'd come on the scene, England were really getting organised. I don't mean that to be disrespectful to Walter but I'd come in at the end of his reign, when he'd done it all. Alf was fresh and full of ambition.'

Scotland popped up in the spring of '64 to dent a few mushrooming egos, beating England 1-0 at Hampden Park. Yet even defeat seemed to serve Moore's purpose.

That was Jimmy Armfield's last international and there was no longer a valid rival for the captaincy.

Other faces in other places changed as the games ticked through Ramsey's meticulous preparations for the World Cup itself. Pickering, Wignall, Bailey, Hinton, Baker...all came and went as the caps piled up for Bobby Moore.

Only once did Ramsey detect in Moore's attitude to England the subtle drift from convincing arrogance to worrying complacency which sometimes afflicted his football for West Ham. Corrective treatment was at once forthcoming.

By June 1966 Ramsey had crystallised his eddying pool of talent into a final squad of 22 players who left for a warm-up tour of Europe. Moore recalls: 'Alf numbered everyone from 1-22 and the feeling was that those who were numbered from 1-11 were going to be the World Cup team. I was number six and full of myself. And Alf left me out of the first game of the tour.

'From being Jack the Lad I was now on the run. A lot of people had been punting to get Norman Hunter into the team in my place. A lot of the Press were saying I wasn't good enough and Norman should be in. When they won 3-0 in Finland everyone thought the writing was on the wall for R. Moore.

'It made me sit up. From that day on I never *expected* to be in an England squad until the letter from the F.A. dropped through the letterbox, never took it for granted I would be in the team until I saw my name on the sheet or heard Alf call it out.

'Alf was driving it home to me that there are always enough players for any team to get by without any one player. I was disappointed. So sick. I'd gone through all those games. The preparation had become really intense during ten days in the training camp at Lilleshall.

'No-one was more relieved when he brought me back in Oslo. No-one was more on his toes.'

Moore led England to wins over Norway and Denmark, then on to Katowice. Gornik were doing well in European club competition and most of the critics thought Poland were too tough a choice for the last test of Ramsey's World Cup team.

Roger Hunt's goal gave 1-0 victory to Banks, Cohen, Wilson, Stiles, Charlton, Moore, Ball, Greaves, Charlton, Hunt and Peters. Yet it was Moore who made it possible. A performance of chilling, almost brutal, authority declared the skills and the studs of England's captain well and truly sharpened for the conflict ahead.

There was just one problem. Secretly, not even Alf Ramsey was sure if Bobby Moore was eligible to play for England in the 1966 World Cup Finals.

CHAPTER SEVEN

Arsenal and Old Lace

The Hendon Hall Hotel is secreted in the outer fringe of north west London, a short, nervous and invariably silent drive in England's team coach along the North Circular Road to the turreted portals of Wembley.

It would have provided apt headquarters for the English footballers in 1966, had the footballers been typical Englishmen.

Normally, there is a sort of hushed reverence about the dark brown rooms, the modicum of noise generated by the regular inmates being absorbed as much by the cloistered atmosphere as by the Regency carpets. It is the kind of hotel you imagine creaking, even if the doors are well-oiled and the floorboards firm.

Periodically, Hendon Hall used to be shaken out of its metaphorical mothballs by the glamorous and muscular presence of the cream of England's footballers. This was Alf Ramsey's handy hideaway for his beloved team, vine-clad security from public eyes prying into private little dramas, like that which clouded the dawn of England's World Cup. On the morning of July 7, 1966, with the nation waiting for England to set the jamboree in motion, Bobby Moore was football's equivalent of a stateless person.

West Ham and their most famous son had been playing brinkmanship with each other for months, right through Moore's preparations for captaining England in their finest hour.

Other, bigger, wealthier clubs had sensed Moore's dismay as defeat in the semi final of the European Cup Winners' Cup had turfed West Ham out of the honours for the first time in three years.

The season at Upton Park had ended on a flat, sour note. The pressure on Moore to seek a move to a grander club had been intensified by his deep involvement with the England squad, whose meetings are a notorious tapping ground for unsettled players.

Moore was not only ripe for tapping – a clandestine approach from another club, in this case via one of its own players – but also concerned that Norman Hunter's success with Leeds United might edge him out of the England team.

He went to see West Ham manager Ron Greenwood, but recalls: 'There was no way we could negotiate. West Ham said they would not let me go in any circumstances. Ron and I had it out for hours. Finally we agreed to let it ride until after the World Cup.

'Our differences were supposed to be our secret. But then a big story broke in the newspapers. I stormed in to see Ron and he admitted he'd let it out because he was so sick of the whole business and all the talk and rumours that he wanted to get it off his chest. So I dug my heels in and refused to sign a new contract.'

With a dramatic sense of timing, Moore's contract with West Ham expired on June 30. For the first seven days of July he was working with Alf Ramsey towards the pinnacle of their mutual ambitions, yet he was not officially contracted to any club in the Football League. So, legally, he did not exist as a player in the eyes of the Football Association, whose team he was about to lead into the World Cup Finals.

Ramsey's whispered and frantic consultations with F.A. officials ended with him urging Moore to regularise his position by signing a contract for one month; long enough to get their hands on the Jules Rimet Trophy.

All of a lather, Greenwood was summoned to hurry the appropriate forms to Hendon Hall. He found England's manager and captain waiting in the foyer. Ramsey pointed to a dark, panelled door and told Greenwood: 'You can have him in that room for just one minute. Then I want you out.'

Moore signed the form in seconds, barely exchanging a word with Greenwood before returning to the business of the moment, the struggle with Uruguay.

West Ham's manager escaped, the reason for his visit undetected, silently cursing the tapping which had inveigled him into that embarrassment.

Moore admits: 'I knew perfectly well which club I was going to join if I could twist Ron's arm to let me go…Tottenham Hotspur. I'd had a good run in the cups with West Ham, got the England captaincy. And everyone knew Spurs were interested.

'The Hammers looked like they might be going on the blink. A lot of people were suggesting that Norman's form made me a bit iffy in the England team. Tottenham caught me on the rebound from our Cup

Winners' Cup defeat. I'd heard a lot of rumours that they would like me. It was easy for Spurs because I used to see a lot of Terry Venables. After talking to Terry a lot and to other Tottenham players it was obvious there was a genuine interest.'

Venables' stay at Spurs, en route from Chelsea to Queens Park Rangers and eventually to assistant managership at Crystal Palace under Malcolm Allison, was far from popular with the White Hart Lane crowd. Yet he was already a deep thinker about the game and became a confidant of manager Bill Nicholson.

Venables lived near Moore's Chigwell home and the pair were warm acquaintances, moving in similar social circles. Moore says: 'Spurs are supposed to be above these things, but the fact remains that they wanted me and I was itching to go there. Tottenham would have suited me down to the ground. They were *the* team of Sixties. No trouble.'

Tapping, of course, infringes the laws of the Football League, who try to insist that players are the last to know about transfer negotiations supposedly conducted in seemly fashion between the gentlemen in charge of their clubs.

Moore's sympathy for West Ham's chagrin at the trouble caused by Tottenham's interest would have been more acute, had he not had solid grounds for suspecting that Greenwood was himself a skilled player of the transfer game.

The first evidence for that had come in 1960 when Greenwood was assistant manager at Arsenal and vitally interested in relieving West Ham of their future England captain.

Moore was then making headway in an England under-23 team managed by Greenwood. He says: 'Ron used to talk to me a lot at that time. He never actually said anything I could put my finger on but I kept going home from those under-23 sessions with the distinct impression that he wanted me to go to Arsenal. Then one of the Highbury lads in the squad gave me a pull one day and said: 'You know they'd like you at our place.' Finally one of Ron's pet journalists came on my ear about getting away from West Ham to Arsenal.

'If the chance had come I would have loved to have gone to Arsenal for the same reason that Spurs appealed...a big club. But I suppose when they made the official approaches West Ham knocked them back.

'The funny thing was that Ron came to West Ham instead. He told me that the chance to work with me in club football was a big reason for him moving from Highbury to Upton Park. That was a twist.'

That was in the Spring of 1961. Within a year Greenwood was using Moore to help him sign another player who was to have a profound influence on West Ham's cup fortunes in the mid-Sixties: Johnny Byrne.

Moore and Byrne were combining well in England's under-23 team and Moore recalls: 'We were even rooming together on the trips so it was easy for me to establish that Budgie was as interested as West Ham in a move of this kind.'

Even so, West Ham still had to pay a then-record fee between British clubs of £65,000 to secure Byrne from Third Division Crystal Palace.

Moore, like most people in football, has been involved in clandestine negotiations and feels no remorse whatsoever for his part in breaches of football's vaguely ludicrous laws.

He says: 'Is it wrong? Maybe it would be if clubs had the decency to keep you informed of everything that might affect your career. It is a player's life yet often he is not even told when another club has made an offer which could change his whole life.

'They probably feel they are playing it straight because they are the guvnors. Yet managers move, like Ron did from Arsenal to West Ham. How infuriated a manager would be if a big club went after him and he did not find out until six months after the approach was made to his board of directors.

'The facts of the matter are that football has been just about the only business which denies a craftsman the freedom and liberty to work for whoever he wants. Whatever opportunities came my way, if West Ham said No, that was the end of that.'

Much as Moore wanted to join Arsenal and Spurs early in his career, he felt the keenest frustration when, much later, West Ham denied him a transfer to Derby County.

On that occasion Brian Clough a gentleman with about as much reverence for officialdom as Al Capone, did not so much tap Bobby Moore as beat him about the head with a sledgehammer.

Clough's latent interest in adding the England captain to his championship team at Derby was fanned to life by Moore's performance in West Ham's 1-1 draw at County's Baseball Ground towards the end of the 1972-3 season. Moore says of his efforts that day: 'I played more than well. Derby paralysed us but they only got a draw with a penalty in the 84th minute. Even Ron Greenwood came up to me and said well done.'

The image of Moore's majestic performance then was still alive in Clough's mind that summer as he strolled the tea lawns at Wimbledon as a paying spectator at the 1973 Lawn Tennis Championships.

By chance he fell into conversation with Nigel Clarke, a Soccer reporter and occasional tennis writer for the Daily Mirror, Moore's closest friend from the media.

Clough expressed his interest, Clarke telephoned Moore with that juicy piece of intelligence, then relayed his friend's eager response to the Derby manager, complete with Bobby's ex-directory telephone number.

One morning that July, Moore picked up his home 'phone to hear: 'Hello Bobby. This is Brian Clough. If you want to play for Derby will you pop up to London and meet me.'

Moore: 'I'd love to. Where?'

'Churchills.'

Churchills is about as quiet as any American-orientated hotel can be. It is plush and velvet and a trifle garish, yet kissed with a touch of aristocratic class and comfortably expensive. Clough could have made no better choice of venue to sell his deal to a working class boy who had grown accustomed to doing things in style.

Clough has a habit of coming to the point. The men shook hands in the bar and this is Moore's recollection of their conversation. Clough said at once: 'I hear you're interested in winning a League Championship medal.'

Moore, touched on the sensitive spot of his one unfulfilled ambition: 'Who wouldn't be?'

Clough: 'Would you play for Derby County?'

'Why not?'

'That'll do me.'

The pair headed for lunch in the restaurant and were at first turned back by the maitre d'hotel because Moore was dressed in a casual shirt and sweater.

Clough brushed the protest aside: 'My team will never stay here again if *my* player can't sit in this restaurant.'

Moore protested: 'I don't play for you yet.'

Clough: 'Shut up. You're my player. That's no trouble. I'll ring Ron up now.'

Moore recalls: 'I'd only been with the man five minutes and I shouldn't have been with him at all. Yet he phoned the West Ham ground and asked for Mr. Greenwood. He was on holiday. Cloughie asked where but they didn't know. He left a message for Ron to ring him the minute he returned.'

Clough's larger than life behaviour and burning passion for the game were already exciting Moore. He was then deeply flattered when he asked why Derby wanted another central defender when they already had the future England pair, Roy McFarland and Colin Todd.

Clough said: 'I'll play Toddy alongside you at full back and tell him to

71

watch, listen and learn from the Master.'

Bobby was hooked. 'All I could see was a white shirt with a ram on the chest. I felt at the time that I needed lifting, a gee-up, needed a boost. I felt that all through my career my own pride had carried me on. It had been self-motivation. Now I needed help to maintain my position in the game. Cloughie was generating that enthusiasm within a few minutes. I was impressed by the man. I loved him for wanting me. The pen was as good as in my hand.'

West Ham did not quite see it that way. The next Moore heard was that the directors had agreed in principle to a Derby bid in excess of £400,000 for himself and Trevor Brooking.

Then he heard that Ron Greenwood had blocked the deal and once again he was knocking on his manager's door. 'They were huffing and puffing through another season and Ron said he felt they couldn't let me go.'

Greenwood, echoing the public suspicion of the time that Moore would not relish a move away from his favourite watering holes in London, asked: 'Why do you want to go to Derby?'

Moore: 'Because it would be good for me.'

'Is it money? Has someone spoken to you?'

'No,' Moore lied. 'But if it's true I'd like to know and I'd like to go. It's more than money. I want to speak to Brian Clough. Can I go if the deal's right?

Again the answer came in the negative. Moore: 'I had to accept a sort of compromise that if I stayed to help them through that season that they would let me go on a free transfer at the end, so I could negotiate a good deal for myself.

'Transfers are often about luck and timing. It wasn't long before Cloughie left Derby and Ron was telling me what a favour he'd done me by stopping me from going up there. Who knows? As time went on and I was at Fulham I just know I felt sorry that Cloughie had gone on to put his head on the block at Leeds United and wasn't making immediate headway at Nottingham Forest.'

The mutual respect between two men who hardly knew each other was brought back into focus when Fulham were drawn against Nottingham Forest in the 1974-5 F.A. Cup. Clough, in his capacity as Forest manager, went to study Fulham's replay against Hull City, Moore was warmed to see an evening newspaper interview in which Clough was asked what he thought of Fulham and replied: 'Bobby Moore plays for them, doesn't he?'

Fulham came through that round of the Cup into a four-match saga with Forest. After one drawn match, on 3 February 1975 in Nottingham, Clough walked into the Fulham dressing room and quickly pressed a packet into Moore's hands, saying: 'Just a little present for Tina.'

Moore unwrapped a tablecloth of finest Nottingham lace and wondered if it was some sort of a joke, until he read the attached note.

Dear Bobby,

Just a little bit of Nottingham lace for your wife. I didn't have time to have a word with you the last two times we were at Fulham but judging by your performance you are in excellent condition. It was a tragedy we could never get together as a team but that's just one of the barmy parts of football.

Brian.

It was a barmier part of football that Moore had gone into the 1966 World Cup Finals knowing that the better he played for England, the less his chances of the transfer to Spurs on which he had set his heart.

'At the moment I was signing that one-month contract in that room at Hendon Hall, I felt convinced that Ron Greenwood was so sick of the whole business that he would let me go. If England had done badly I would have been on my way to Tottenham the minute the World Cup was over'

No-one watching Bobby Moore at Wembley could have guessed at his dilemma.

CHAPTER EIGHT

Home Sweet Home

Bobby Moore's capacity for playing great matches to the background of personal drama was matched only by his unfailing sense of occasion.

The vulturous critics of this most successful young man were about to be confounded at the one place which Moore knew mattered most in English football: Wembley.

The lushest turf, the twin towers, the 100,000 admirers filling cavernous terraces; never mind the cracks of obsolesence, feel the atmosphere. Here was the grassy Shangri-La of all our boyhood dreams.

Moore had grown up with those dreams, and with them the ability to have realised already the ambition of playing to full houses at the famous stadium.

By the Summer of '66 he was ready to unfurl the full standard of his greatness and make the place his own. Many splendid talents were to grace the World Cup stage that July, but by the time the drama was done, Wembley belonged to Bobby Moore just as surely as the Old Vic to Sir Laurence Olivier.

Don Revie, then manager of Leeds United, was among those campaigning at the time for Moore's replacement in the England team by his own awesome defender, Norman Hunter.

Later, much later, after Moore had finished amassing international caps and Revie had succeeded Sir Alf Ramsey as England manager, owning-up time came over drinks in a London penthouse.

Revie admitted the impact of Moore's World Cup: 'Had I been England manager earlier, I would have picked you in front of Norman. Because you could produce it for the big one. Week in, week out for Leeds I would have gone for Norman. But it would have been you at Wembley.'

Moore: 'If I'd been at Leeds instead of West Ham there would have been no ordinary matches. Every game would have been a big game,

74

every game might have meant a championship medal. I'd have given you a Wembley, every game.'

Either by accident of the draw, or devious design of the Football Association, every England game of the 1966 World Cup was at Wembley.

The world put tongue in cheek and said: 'Lucky England.' Moore relished the experience, yet recognised the demands Wembley made on the limbs of England players straining to satisfy the expectations of the home nation.

'There had been talk of the semi-final going to Everton's ground if the groups worked out that way. As it happened we did eventually play all our games at Wembley. I'm not saying that didn't help in some ways. But at the same time it was an exhausting achievement to play six games in eighteen days on such a tiring pitch with all the tension and atmosphere surrounding the World Cup.

'It was nice not to have to uproot ourselves from the hotel and travel to another centre. Yet at a club ground we would have felt closer to the crowd and sensed their support far more. Wembley is wearying and the tension was heightened because London was the focal point of all the interest and pressure.'

Pressure? Moore's computerised resilience under fire supplied priceless support for the man under the most savage strain of all...Alf Ramsey.

Ramsey had turned the screw on himself two years earlier with the uncharacteristically rash prediction that England would win the World Cup. 'That was one of the few times he let his pride show through,' says Moore. 'He had also spent two years getting together the players he wanted and felt in his heart that we would not be beaten too often in the next few years.

'We weren't beaten on many occasions and Alf knew the way it went in players' minds. If you don't lose you start believing you are unbeatable, especially if you are playing a big tournament in front of your home supporters. Then the other teams start worrying about you, think you're the big obstacle, the team to beat.

'Alf had it all mapped out. The players and the matches he needed to win the Cup. So he went and blurted out that we would win. That was bad enough. Then he took stick from the critics all through the build-up because it didn't look as if he was getting the right team together.'

Oddly, the hounding Ramsey was receiving from the Press – whom most star footballers the world over tend to generalise as the enemy – helped cement the corporate will to win and community spirit of mutual

75

aid which became the trade marks of Ramsey's team. Moore recalls: 'The spirit in the camp had been good from way back, but with every new blast at Alf the spirit grew. We believed we had a great chance. Alf believed in us. We would show 'em.'

Not at first, they didn't. England got the show on the road to a great roar of anticipation which fizzled into a 0-0 draw with Uruguay – 'We just didn't function at all.' Then came a 2-0 win over Mexico – 'We were struggling until Bobby Charlton got a goal out of the blue.' Then they beat France 2-0 to qualify for the quarter finals in a blaze of anxiety – 'France hadn't won a game and were not a good side at all by 1966, yet we weren't very convincing against them.'

Ramsey was convinced of only one thing: that his wingers were not good enough. Moore: 'Everyone refers back to the 1966 team as the wingless wonders, yet Alf played wingers in all those first three games.'

Ramsey had first picked a team without a semblence of a good old-fashioned winger for the last preparatory match in Poland. Prophetically Alan Ball had worn No.7 and Martin Peters had won his first cap at No.11, both functioning as wide midfield players coming late to support attacks. It had worked well, creating unusual spaces in a packed Continental defence which could be exploited by intelligent players. Yet it deprived the Press and the public of the drama of ball-playing wingers plying the penalty area with crosses and incidents.

So against Uruguay, Ramsey, who paid more heed to the critics than he ever cared to admit, replaced Peters with John Connelly. Peters came back against Mexico but Ball was dropped to make way for Southampton winger Terry Paine, Ramsey confiding in Moore: 'I'm going to have to leave out Ballie. I know he'll be sick but I need a winger.'

Against France, Paine was replaced by Liverpool's Ian Callaghan. Still everyone knew the blend was far from perfect. Moore: 'The sad part for Alf, looking back, is that he wanted to play wingers but he's been crucified for doing away with them.

'Paine, Connelly, Callaghan. Peter Thompson was also in the party. They all had their opportunities but Alf got no success with any of them. He wanted wingers because they give you a way to get round behind defences, create chances and win games. But the ones who were available didn't have the right attitude, the right temperament...the right something.

'What do you do if the people you play aren't good enough and aren't doing the job for you and you've got other people you can utilise better in a different way? I tell you. You use Ballie and Martin Peters.'

That was Ramsey's solution for the quarter final match which had the entire country in an advanced state of jitters. One other decisive alteration was made for Ramsey by injury. Jimmy Greaves, whose genius never quite compensated in Ramsey's mind for his unwillingness to run as far or tackle as hard as the others, was injured against France.

Greaves was Moore's room-mate at Hendon Hall and Bobby had to console him as well as congratulate his West Ham team-mate, Geoff Hurst, on being selected for his first appearance in the World Cup.

'Greavesey was sick at being out,' says Moore. 'He was to be a lot sicker by the end of the tournament.'

Yet before the match against Argentina, the betting shops were conspicuously empty of people rushing to put their mortgage on Hurst ending England's goal famine.

Argentina were the menace crouched in the undergrowth. A dark, brooding, panther of a team, spitting, snarling and waiting to devour the unwary with an explosion of lithe and powerful movement.

England had watched with grim fascination as Argentina and West Germany had kicked a goalless draw out of each other in their group.

Ramsey's team talk amounted to one sentence which was something of a parody of the British war-time spirit against the odds. Like a Blimpish colonel at a briefing, he said only: 'Well, gentlemen, you know the sort of game you have on your hands this afternoon.'

'That was enough,' says Moore, whose recollection of his own doubts sums up all England's anxiety. 'The players didn't say anything or admit anything publicly or even among ourselves, but deep down we all had secret fears about Argentina.

'We accepted in our guts it was going to be hard. Maybe brutal. We hadn't conceded a goal in the tournament so we didn't feel that they ought to beat us on overall quality. The problem was that this was a sudden death, knock-out quarter-final and that in going for the win they might upset us, frustrate us, and catch us unawares. We even knew the public doubted we could do it, because we hadn't looked like scoring goals.'

The Argentinians were nursing similar neuroses about England and set about their problem in a way which was to draw an atypical outburst from Ramsey. After the match, England's manager lost his head and called the Argentinians: 'Animals.'

Even during the heat of the battle, Moore retained his composure and held the rhythm and the temper of his team together. Moore's splendid form had done much to get England that far without conceding a goal, and the captain was not about to let his men throw it all away because of

Argentinian intimidation.

'Animals? I don't know. The South Americans play the game by a different code. They were sure as hell not very pleasant to play against. They did do nasty things. They did tug your hair, spit at you, poke you in the eyes, and kick you when the ball was miles away and no-one was looking.

'It wasn't nice, but it wasn't worth losing the game over. I managed not to get involved. Around and about me I could see lads like Ballie and Nobby Stiles and big Jack Charlton getting steamed up and finding it difficult to get on with the game.

'I just said that the only way to deal with them was to beat the bastards. That was what would hurt them, because their attitude was simply not to lose. Not at any cost. Off the pitch they were supposed to be charmers. I just said that off the pitch we didn't even have to look at them. Just beat them out here.'

Even under such steadying leadership, even with the latent understanding Hurst had built up at club level with Moore and Peters, England might still have been playing Argentina today but for the intervention of a short and balding referee.

In the midst of all the mayhem, Rudolf Kreitlin of West Germany sent off Antonio Rattin, millionaire aristocrat, midfield thoroughbred, captain of Argentina almost by birthright.

For what? 'Who knows?' says Moore. 'Swearing? Taking the mickey? Anyway the little bald fellow gave him his marching orders. They argued, they strutted about. It seemed to take for ever. It was probably four or five minutes. I looked around and saw Ray Wilson sitting calmly on the ball. Liked that. Someone else was asking if I thought we'd start again. They had FIFA officials down out of the stand. Ken Aston, chairman of the referees' committee, was on the touchline putting in his two pennyworth.

'I watched Rattin go. Alf had great admiration for Rattin as a player. During the game he'd lived up to it all. An upstanding, strong man; powerful, fine skill, good appreciation of what was happening around him, knew the game inside out.

'As he went down the tunnel he left the door open for us. Just a crack. Even with ten men they still put up a hell of a struggle, but then the understanding between Geoff and Martin got us through.

'They knew each other's play by instinct and they found a chink of space they'd used a million times for West Ham. Martin laid in a near post cross and Geoff got that priceless goal. The game was as good as over, the hard part done. It taught a lot of people the value of having the

78

understanding of good club units in the England team.'

Moore, Peters and Hurst represented West Ham's strong thread of understanding through the team. Bobby Charlton and Nobby Stiles elevated their midfield partnership with Manchester United into a vibrant international force.

That was why Ramsey fought so hard to resist the political chicanery designed to force Stiles out of the team. That, and the small matter of Stiles' murderous tackling scaring the living daylights out of Eusebio, the one man Portugal prayed could fire them to the Championship.

'Nobby has this thing with a lot of Continental forwards,' says Moore. 'He was a tough little nut and they didn't have the heart to try to go past him because they knew it would be a battle.

'They felt it was easier to get him banned than to take him on out there in a match. So there was a lot of pressure from the world Press and a lot of talking in the corridors of power.'

The waves of trouble barely washed against the shores of the England camp. To the players it had become unthinkable that they should go into a major match without their Nobby, and footballers by and large pay little attention to football politics until it affects them directly.

Stiles had become a sort of playing mascot. A comical little ferret of a man with no front teeth on the pitch and owlish spectacles off it, he was also the first out-and-out ball winner, a destructive, abrasive species which blossomed under Ramsey in the face of withering criticism from the rest of the world.

Ramsey was the man left to conduct Stiles' defence.

He did so by having no truck with the charges that the little man was too robust. He said simply: 'If Nobby Stiles doesn't play, then England don't play.'

The team loved their manager for that and Moore says: 'Everyone felt that was great. All right, we were biased, all right Nobby was there first and foremost to spoil, to mark people, to niggle and upset people. But he could still play the game. Like Peter Storey later on when he was playing well, Nobby did a great job for Alf.

'Nobby was there to get the ball and give it to Bobby Charlton to go and do something constructive for us. And on top of all that he had the Indian sign on Eusebio.'

Portugal had themselves hacked Brazil, and more particularly the great Pele, out of the tournament. Eusebio was challenging to become the new Black Prince. In the early games he looked full of muscular grace, lithe athleticism, fluent skills and explosive finishing.

England were so sure that the unlikely-looking Stiles would cut him down to size that Moore was convinced they would survive their semi final. 'For the first time that Wednesday we felt the country was getting behind us. The morning papers at last looked as if they thought we could win the thing.

'I had no doubts by then. I never felt that Portugal could beat any England team. They were the sort of side I would think about playing against with England the way many League clubs thought about playing West Ham. . . that it would be a good game but not a hard fight and we would probably win in the end.

'They had a lot of good players: Torres, Coluna, Auguso, that terrific winger Simoes. Their top club side, Benfica, were having a great run and this was probably their best side ever. Yet they had needed Eusebio to pull them out of trouble against North Korea, of all people. And Eusebio didn't have the stomach for Nobby Stiles.

'For the first time we felt the crowd were really in there with us, sensing we were all on the verge of a World Cup Final. Thank God we finally thrilled them, gave them something to cheer. Portugal were a good team who wanted to come forward, not physical at all. It was a good, open game and we were the only winners.'

Bobby Charlton converted England's expectations into giddy reality with two goals. Eusebio was left with the dubious consolation of scoring the first goal of the tournament against Moore's immaculate defence. That penalty, ten minutes from time, helped establish Eusebio as the leading scorer of the championship but was too late and too little to keep England from the Final.

That Wednesday night, as secretively as they had done after most of the earlier matches, Tina Moore and several of the players' wives joined the restrained celebrations at the Hendon Hall Hotel.

As usual, Ramsey bought the drinks, just sufficient to reward and relax his gladiators, never enough to erode their fitness. The manager's gesture ended by midnight with the wives slipping quietly away in the darkness.

They were not allowed near the bedrooms. 'There was,' says Moore, 'no fun and games. We'd been with the squad for the best part of eight weeks and not a soul had stepped out of line. Now there were only three days to wait...and that one game to play.'

CHAPTER NINE

1966 And All That

The happenings at Wembley on June 30th 1966, have already been copiously treated with purple prose, dissected by expert analysis and replayed into the memory banks of the English people on any and every screen big enough to take pictures of the World Cup Final.

You had to be devoid of all the senses and incarcerated on a forgotten island to be alive in England and yet avoid contact with football's finest hour. It was not enough to be dismissive of the working man's game. For in its way, that afternoon's sport changed the society in which we live.

The emotional magnitude of the occasion broke through the barriers of class and culture to harvest thousands of wealthy and influential converts to the muddied arts of the round ball game; people who would help Soccer survive a later depression.

Jut one of the many economic spin-offs was the beginning of the boom in colour television. England awoke that day to the rattle of the tumbrils, the flutter of Union Jacks in tens of millions of patriotic stomachs...and countless early morning deliveries from rent-a-set.

It is less public knowledge that the man who was about to be acclaimed as the world's paramount footballer started his day of coronation trying to console a friend.

Bobby Moore woke that Saturday morning to find his room-mate, Jimmy Greaves, packing his bags. Greaves was fretting for the place he had lost to injury and Geoff Hurst. Moore, the ice man himself, suffered with his friend. 'Jimmy was hurt. I don't care what people say about Jimmy, about how he didn't work and didn't care and how his attitude was all wrong. I know the man and I knew what he was going through. All he wanted was to play in the World Cup Final. He believed he could get the goals to win it for England. He believed he was something special and it broke his heart not to have the chance to prove it.

'That moment began Jimmy's disenchantment with football. I knew that if he'd stayed fit or got his place back the Germans would have been frightened of him. I believed Jimmy Greaves could have won us the Cup. But I also knew Alf Ramsey couldn't change the team.

'Geoff had come in and done too well. It was helpful to have someone else in the team who knew me and Martin Peters as players. From the start he had a good understanding with Roger Hunt and their running had opened the way for Bobby Charlton to start scoring vital goals.

'Alf had been given that bonus out of nothing. He couldn't turn it down now. Not for this match.'

Just as Nobby Stiles had a psychological advantage over Eusebio in the semi-final, so Bobby Charlton held the key against West Germany.

Moore knew it. 'The preparations virtually took care of themselves. There wasn't much for Alf to say by now. He just reminded us that Franz Beckenbauer was more worried about Bobby Charlton than we were about Beckenbauer. That was their mistake. Franz was the man who made it all happen for the Germans but he was weighed down by the responsibility of playing against Bobby, with all his fantastic reputation abroad.

'We all felt keyed up and confident going to the stadium. Alf seemed all right. Everyone seemed more or less in control of themselves. And when the coach got through the people and up to the dressing rooms you had no chance to notice how any of the lads were being affected, because it was complete and utter chaos.

'The old favourite dressing room was jam packed with photographers, arc lights, TV cameras. Okay, you accept it at first. But come 2.15 I couldn't believe Alf hadn't thrown them all out. I think I'd have stood for it until then. Co-operated. Perhaps even hoped it would give us something to occupy our minds. But most players like half an hour or more peace and quiet to get changed and prepare themselves to go out.

'At half past two there were still one hundred people in the dessing room. Terrible panic. At twenty-five to three I said to Jack Charlton: "This is the most important game of my life and look at this lot. I can't even start getting changed yet."

'Big Jack grinned and said: "That's why it is the most important game of your life, isn't it?" It was half an answer but not good enough. Everything was a rush. It was bothering me so much that even now I don't remember going up the tunnel. The hand-shaking. Tossing up. Nothing. A blank until I woke up to the fact that we were kicking off, somehow still confident of winning.'

Moore was relieved to find his brain functioning again, ticking over the endless permutations of covering positions, attacking ploys, sweaty tackles, switches of play.

The game hurried by as quickly as the words come spilling out to paint the images of the drama from the inside. 'We believe this is our destiny and all that. Yet we get off to a bad start. Helmut Haller gets a goal for the Germans from a bad headed clearance by Ray Wilson. Pride stung because its the first time we've conceded a goal in open play. Not the best day to go behind for the first time in the tournament. Yet all I thought was that Haller shouldn't be the sort of player to score against us and certainly isn't the class of player to win a World Cup Final.

'It wasn't right. So I still feel confident and Hursty proves me right by getting on the end of my free kick and heading us back on terms. That's better. Going nicely. No fuss at half time. Keep working to break the stalemate and get in front midway through the second half.

'Again it's not a good goal. Not nicely worked. But it will do. Geoff tries a shot from the edge of the box which is blocked and spins into the air. It falls perfect for us in oceans of space in the goalmouth. Martin Peters and Jack Charlton are tanking on to it and Martin wins the race to blast it past two full backs and a goalkeeper, all marooned on the line.

'At that moment I felt we'd won the World Cup and felt proud. Time was running out nicely. For the first time I noticed the crowd. A hundred thousand singers. Happy voices. Makes you realise there's only minutes to go.

'Out of the blue they get a free kick. Out of nothing, danger. You know the decision should have gone in favour of Big Jack because the other fellow's backed into him. But there's no percentage in arguing. Only a minute left. Get lined up right. Only a minute left. Deal with this and we're home. Crowded back here. Keep our heads. Here comes the free kick. Make it ours. Someone's trying to clear. Too frantic and the ball hits a body. Schnellinger handles. Come on, ref, bloody handball. No whistle. It spins across the goal. Like running too slow in a nightmare. Everyone heaving and scrambling to get there. Weber scores.

'I'm looking round and I'm asking: "Christ, how did that happen?" Then comes the whistle and time to think.'

Ramsey's most serious words of warning about West Germany were haunting the players as their manager came stonefaced and steady of pace on to the pitch. Moore: 'He'd reminded us how many times we'd been outplaying the Germans but they had come back at us simply by believing in the things they were doing and by staying patient.

'By the end of ninety minutes I was sure we were the better side. Yet they were so methodical and composed that even at 2-1 down with a minute to go they took their time over a free kick. Most teams in the world would have been panicking and rushing all over the place. They had done exactly what Alf admired them for. He always used to say: "You're better than them. You can beat them. But never forget they're not beaten until the final whistle goes and you're one goal in front."

'If he'd gone on about that right then, he could have killed half our team stone dead. They were gutted enough as it was. I didn't know what he would do. You never know absolutely and for certain how people are going to react until the really big moment comes. Alf was unbelievably good. He could have come on screaming and shouting, hollering and hooting, saying "I thought you'd know better. I thought you'd have learned after all these years as professionals." Instead he said: "All right. You've won the World Cup once. Now go and win it again. Look at the Germans. They're flat out. Down on the grass. Having massages. Flat on their backs. Just have a look at them. They can't live with you. Not for another half an hour. Not through extra time." '

So Ramsey pushed England on from what should have been a simply satisfying triumph towards great drama and heavy controversy.

Wembley had gone limp in those interval moments. The players could afford no such luxury. 'I believe it was worse for the spectators,' says Moore. 'Watching would have been worse for me. We were all pig sick but the people in the stands had time to think. . . and get sicker and sicker. Even when extra time got under way and the ball went out of play they had a few seconds to sit and wonder how the Germans got the ball into our net.

'Being involved was just a matter of getting on with it. Alf was right. We did overpower them. Still there was that debate over Geoff's goal, the third goal, the one that mattered.'

Moore's usual understatement refers to disagreement which at the time seemed violent enough to cause yet another breakdown in international relations between the United Kingdom and the Federal Republic.

Geoff Hurst shot against West Germany's crossbar. The ball bounced down and out of the goal. Roger Hunt turned away to celebrate his belief that the ball had crossed the line. And one Tofik Bahkramov, a grey haired, long-shorted Russian who many Germans suspected of harbouring grudges from the Eastern Front, raised his linesman's flag to declare England the World Cup winners.

West Germany protested. Referee and linesmen conferred. The goal stood and Bobby Moore risks re-igniting the entire controversy by admitting: 'We won the World Cup on the best appeal of all time.

'I believe Roger Hunt got us the verdict. I was fifty yards away on the halfway line and in no position to offer an honest opinion at the time. But in my eyes it had to be a goal from Roger's reaction. He was right there, a yard from the line, and the ball came out his way. Yet he made no attempt to knock it back in. Just turned round with arms in the air.

'If the goal hadn't been given that would have been the biggest ricket of Roger's life. As it happened, I believe old Bahkramov was convinced by that reaction.

'I've watched the film a million times. At normal speed it looks as if it might be a goal. In slow motion it's much more debatable. I don't know how the linesman could decide. At the time I was in no doubt but now I've got to say I wouldn't have liked a goal like that to be given against England.

'We went to West Germany the following year and all the time their people were coming up and clapping me on the shoulder and saying: "Look at this picture. It didn't cross the line. You never won the World Cup." What could I say a year later? Only that we deserved to win. I believe that. And remind them that we got a fourth goal.

'I'm glad we got that goal. It takes the pressure off that linesman's decision. It came with the last kick. A lot of people have said it didn't matter and that it was a bad goal anyway. But to me it was a great goal.

'It was another West Ham job. I couldn't count how many times I knocked that same pass into that same space for Geoff to make that same run. They were shattered and it split them wide open. Geoff was exhausted but he was stronger than them. He set off for goal but said he knew it was near the end. He intended to put everything in the shot and not care if it missed as long as it went a long way back up the terraces, out of harm's way.

'It ended up a diamond of a goal.'

The positively final whistle sent Hurst towards immortality as the first and perhaps the only man ever to score a hat trick in a World Cup Final. It sent Moore towards the Royal Box steps through a chaos of extravagant emotion: 'The scenes right at the end were very vague. I dunno. Sort of misty and unreal. I saw Jack Charlton dropping to his knees and putting his head in his hands. I saw Bobby crying. I remember seeing Ray Wilson's face but not what he was doing. I could see myself running round to all the lads and saying: 'All right. It's okay. We've done it.'

By the time he was climbing the steps to lay claim to England's golden, glittering prize, Bobby Moore was being elected supreme player of the tournament, by a landslide. And Bobby Moore was worrying that his hands were dirty.

'It had been a wet afternoon and when I got about two yards from the Queen I saw her lilywhite gloves. I thought: 'My God. My hands are filthy.' All the front of the Royal Box was decked out in velvet and there am I more worried about scraping the mud off my hands on the velvet than getting hold of the World Cup.

'Once I did, nothing else mattered. We were down the steps giving Alf a look at the trophy and hugging and bursting inside and trembling. Everyone elated but most of us trying to be correct. Not get carried away by it all. Typically English. Perhaps that was me and Alf. Don't show people too much. But even seeing the film now gives me the shivers. It's the be-all and end-all of football.'

That night, the Royal Garden Hotel seemed like an enchanted palace, seen through starry eyes. Limousines nosed through crowds choking the streets of Kensington and spilled their celebrities into a laughing throng of guests illuminated by sparkling chandeliers, flashing cameras and the sheer dazzle of success.

The official banquet was stag. The wives dined sumptuously but separately in an ante-room while the players basked in the back-slapping acclaim and strove to keep their beaming smiles within modest proportions.

'It was,' says Moore, 'just fabulous. We all felt, well, expansive. The memories of the Royal Garden are sharper. That was when you realised what you'd done. When it first started to sink in. Only one thing was wrong. No Greavesy.'

Jimmy Greaves had finished packing on that morning, disappeared from Wembley as soon as the Final was over, fleeing to lick his wounds of personal disappointment on some distant holiday with his wife, his brother and his sister-in-law, shying away from questions, inquisitive eyes, even from sympathy.

Ramsey took Moore's elbow and quietly expressed concern for Greaves and about the little man's motives.

Moore said: 'Don't take it wrong, Alf. He's not doing anything malicious. It's not a protest. He's not walking out on you. He's not even angry. Just disappointed. Jimmy's hurt and doesn't think he can take all this. Accept it, Alf. He's better off away from all the fuss.'

Moore felt better about Greaves for having the chance to put his friend's case. He led the rest of the players on to the balcony to wave to the cheering crowds packed solidly round the hotel.

As in most good fairy stories, the best moment came at midnight. Bobby had found Tina and they came out of the hotel entrance to find thousands of people still waiting for a glimpse of their heroes. 'I couldn't believe they were still there, still standing in the street after all those hours. It made me realise how much it meant to them. It really touched me. Moved me. I'd never felt, what can I say, such a bond with the fans. It was a real lump in the throat moment. Never forget it.'

The players went several different ways through the early hours, mostly, like Moore, drinking in smaller groups at quieter West End places.

'Next day,' he says, 'We all went to the TV studios. Then, suddenly it was over. All breaking up. We tried to drag it out. A few strained jokes and silly laughs and handshakes. But that was that. One went to this plane, one to that train. This one gave a lift to that one in his car. All gone.

'Apart from the odd weekend at home we'd been together for the best part of eight weeks. The spirit had been fantastic, I can't remember one moment of bad feeling. We'd all become part of each other. It left a funny, empty feeling.'

Where do you go from the top of the mountain? Bobby drove home to Chigwell with Tina that Sunday evening. He wrestled with the growing depression and sense of anti-climax; poured a lager; fidgeted with the television switch; sat thinking about the men whose personalities had become extensions of his, names which the events of the day had linked with his own forever.

'I remembered Alf saying some time during the interviews that he was lucky to have three world class players in key positions in the team. He meant Gordon Banks in goal. He meant Bobby Charlton in midfield. And I figured he meant me. There were others on the verge of world class yet you could look at the team man by man and say oh yeah, there were better players than this one or that one. But we fitted together like the best jigsaw you ever saw.

'I remembered Walter Winterbottom saying that if you got eight world class players and stuck them in a team then they would take care of themselves. But was that the case? Some world class players need a bit of guidance. They can be irresponsible. Put eight irresponsible people together and then what have you got? Even if they've got the right attitude it might not work. Denis Law and Jimmy Greaves were both great players, great goalscorers, world class. Would they have worked together? Alf got eleven to work together.

'Gordon Banks? The complete goalkeeper. Best ever. Easy going but brave. A quiet character but a dry sense of humour.

'George Cohen? Old Oddjob. Could find plenty better right backs for

87

going forward on the overlap. More often than not George hit his cross on to the terraces. It was a bad ball for George if he got it across the face of the goal. But how many wingers went past him? He was there to stop them. And he stopped them.

'Ray Wilson? For my money, Ray was also a world class player. It was a comfort to have him at left back. A quick little tackler and tremendously fiery little fellow who was so much better going forward than he was ever given credit for. You knew his character would stand up to all the pressure. Always looked good. Meticulous. I saw him years later, after he became an undertaker. He gave me his card and said: 'You don't look so good. Better put that in your top pocket.' Nothing could shake him.

'Nobby Stiles? Not a bad passer of the ball in his own right but prepared to do the marking and the ball-winning job we needed...and take all the stick without complaining. We needed him to feed Bobby like he needed contact lenses on the pitch. It's been argued that his bad eyesight made him look a dirtier player than he was; made him mistime tackles. But he would keep going in, full of heart, honest, competent. Definitely a better man to have with you than against you.

'Jack Charlton? A big man and a big character. Some days we'd be going out and I'd look at him and wonder how the hell this giraffe played football, but he was tremendously effective. We used to argue black and blue because I wanted to get the ball down and play the game and he wanted to hoof it away to safety. But we made a pair. They talk about Don Revie being a great manager but if my grandmother had Giles, Bremner and Jack Charlton in her team she'd be half way to being a great manager.

'We all knew Jack had the personality to end up as a manager himself but in 1966 some of his ideas about facing up to free kicks were hilarious. Alf was petrified about the way Continentals and the Latin Americans could bend free kicks round or over our defensive wall to the half of the goal Banksie wasn't covering. So Big Jack suggested he should stand on the line behind the wall and head the ball away. Then he wanted two walls of three players each to block both ends of the goal, leaving a gap a yard wide in the middle for Gordon to peer through. We were falling about laughing, even more so because Jack was perfectly serious. But what a pillar in your team.

'Alan Ball? Ballie had been showing us tremendous promise and potential and even as the lad he was then he was full of bounce. A firework character under that red hair. Just the busy little man you needed to ginger up the squad when we were together so long. The Final was the making of him. Ballie was marked by Karl Schnellinger and there was no way that was your birthday. But he ran that good player ragged. Turned him inside out. Really captured the crowd. Never stopped running but still chased a long ball from Nobby down to the corner flag in extra time to lay on that third goal.

'Bobby Charlton? Had a tremendous tournament including the goal that broke the ice for us against Mexico and both goals against Portugal to put us in the final, where West Germany were terrified of him. A lot of pros have their arguments against Bobby, but he's world class all right. Sometimes he would lose possession by attempting the impossible or doing naive things instead of playing the simple ball. But he had all the lovely skill and talent and that awful habit of suddenly getting a ball in a nothing position on the half way line, dropping one shoulder, then the other, drifting past two people and plonking it in the back of the net from thirty-five yards. You'd find yourself still screaming at him to give the simple pass. So you'd break off in mid-sentence and go pat him on the cheek. Bobby had two tremendous feet, could run all day, was better in the air than people thought and scored magical goals.

'I'd seen him play his first game for Manchester United. He scored three goals against Charlton from outside left. At times he looked like the best winger in the world. But his irresponsibility was worse out there. Playing midfield for Alf, he used to run the game. I don't know how he achieved all he did in the game after being carried out of the horror of United's air crash in Munich. No wonder he was the quieter brother.

'Martin Peters? The emergence of Martin was the factor which settled us down to a very efficient formation. When Alf said he was ten years ahead of his time he was on about his perception. Martin was never afraid to play the killer ball. He would look for the decisive pass and even if it was dodgy he would still try a curly little ball or a dinky little chip to try to create a vital goalscoring chance. They used to call him the ghost even though he was always involved in the game. People didn't notice him because he played so many perfect first time balls. We'd lose count of the time he made great runs into ideal positions and just kissed the ball off to present another forward with a great chance. A player with the same skill but who didn't see things so quickly would pull the ball down, roll it under the sole of his boot and have the crowd in raptures before playing it into the same spot, a few seconds too late. Martin was a really clever finisher. He would never be panicked into hammering a shot. He always hit the ball sweetly and invariably at the right spot. It seems crazy that people forgot he scored the goal which put us in front in the World Cup Final.

89

'Roger Hunt? The goals fell to Geoff but it could just as easily have been Roger scoring off Geoff's running. They came together through the circumstances of Greavesy's injury, not through planning. Yet it was the final touch to the team. Roger worked himself into the ground for the players around him. He didn't score a goal in the tournament but all the lads knew the value of his contribution. You couldn't keep us away from his testimonial match up at Liverpool a few years later. It was teeming with rain at 5.30, sleeting when the game kicked off at 7.30 but we were all out there. Anfield was packed and there were 10,000 people locked outside. Everyone loved Roger Hunt.

'Geoff Hurst? The Final changed Geoff's life. On that day a wonderfully honest trier became a truly great striker. From that day on, Geoff drew confidence from his achievements and went out to live up to his reputation as the man who got a hat trick in the World Cup Final.'

All of which leaves one man, the leader who even made a virtue of his economy of words on the pitch. Against teams whipped on by voluble captains, England rallied to the blond, imperious defender whose very presence injected essential arrogance into the team, whose superior attitude pervaded Wembley with an aura of invincibility and whose football breeding blessed the team with a special intellect.

To lead successfully from such an aloof position, he just had to be the most accomplished footballer in the tournament. Bobby Moore was the only rational choice as the outstanding player in the World Cup. Deep down he knew it.

'I felt the award must go to an Englishman. Perhaps to Gordon or Bobby. I can't honestly say I was surprised it went to me. I'd enjoyed the World Cup so much and you only enjoy things if you know you're doing well. Sometimes your team can win a trophy but you feel you could have done better personally. Perhaps some people who were watching in 1966 could point out some slight errors on my part. Yet a player knows best of all when he's on top of his job. At the time, I didn't regret a single thing I did. Looking back, I can't recall putting a foot wrong. What more can I say?'

The world was getting ready to say it for him. The East End kid was about to rub shoulders with princes, politicians and the tin-gods of his jet-set age.

CHAPTER TEN

Room At The Top

Overnight, footballers were in fashion.

There always had been an upper crust patronage of soccer, visible at big matches in the patriarchal shape of a smattering of aristocrats looking down benignly on these gladiators of our time.

Below them, cavorted the fringe element of *nouveau riche,* social climbers and showbiz risers fussing round the edge of the game for their own various purposes, like carrion after the feast.

Footballers could always rely on being entertained by those who believed their own appearance to be enhanced by reflected glory.

Now, however, the *right* doors were opening. With the help of television's intensifying focus on their deeds, the cream of England's footballers were becoming international celebrities.

Just as pop groups had surged above film stars on the social ladder, so footballers were on their way to ousting vocal guitarists as the cult figures of their generation. Their glamour was enhanced, most of all for the faintly bored majority of society ladies, by their robust athleticism. It was quite the thing to have a pet footballer.

Rough diamonds were in demand for adding sparkle to a host of swank functions and putting a kick in many of the best parties.

Most mornings, the Bobby Moores found their doormat ankle deep in gold-encrusted invitations. They were *persona* most *grata* at the best clubs. Annabels at first, Tramp later.

The late Sixties were English football's golden age. The abhorrence of the maximum wage was long gone, the austere struggle for economic survival was in the unforseeable future.

The world had been conquered at Wembley. Commerce queued up to put the smiling faces of our heroes on the breakfast table, the beer mats, the billboards and the bottles of after-shave. The money poured in, the drink flowed and no-one stopped to wonder where the next extravagance was coming from.

There were invitations to the Palace and Number Ten.

Moore remembers: 'Some of the parties at Downing Street were riotous affairs. There was one at Number Ten to honour the American astronauts who were the first men on the moon. To start with the political people were thinking about their image. Harold Wilson had asked Kenny Lynch, Harry Fowler, Sean Connery. All the chaps.

'The bigwigs stood together while the chaps started telling jokes and doing impressions. Once the Prime Minister started laughing they were all falling about, the drink was flowing and everyone ended up nicely oiled.

'There were a couple of invites to the Palace but once Tina was pregnant and another time she was ill. I suppose you can turn them down once and get away with it but not twice. Never been asked again.'

Some footballers plunged so deeply into the social whirl that they never regained their feet, not noticing the erosion of will and muscle, not realising how quickly the society which plied them with drinks would turn its back when they slipped from the pinnacle of their form. Bobby Moore had seen the opportunities ahead and worked too hard getting there to be that foolish. Early on, Ron Greenwood had described his protege as 'a very ambitious young man.' Moore's career had flourished from the roots of several calculated decisions in his youth.

Not the least important came in November 1960, when Bobby was nineteen, a few days after he was sent off for the only time in his career.

'We played at Manchester City that November 4. Never forget that day. David Wagstaffe was playing on the wing for City then, before he went to play for Wolves. He was at it from the first minute, shirt pulling, niggling. I kept my head until the last minute. Then Joe Kirkup took the ball off him and pushed me a pass down the touchline. I played the ball forward and some seconds later, as he was running back past me, Waggy kicked me across the back of the legs.

'That was me gone mad. I turned and gave him exactly the same treatment. Of course Waggy went down in a heap, putting on the agony. I got my marching orders. He didn't. I got suspended for a week. He didn't.

'I detest that in a player. The niggling, the aggravating, the feigning injury. So-called professionalism. I was due to join an England under-23 party the next day and it was a great consolation to me when one or two of the lads who were a bit older than me said they had the same trouble with Wagstaffe. But it was a lesson in itself.'

Still it was a lesson which needed translating into Moore's benefit.

When he returned to West Ham a few days later, he was buttonholed by Jack Turner, then a sort of counsellor and advisor at the club who was eventually to become Moore's business partner and financial aide.

'Jack had been biding his time and waiting his chance. At the time I was in what I now call my blue period. I'd been dropped from the side once by Ted Fenton, the old manager, and when I came back I was so keen I was getting stuck in, kicking everything.

'West Ham didn't have any players who did that, and the other, older lads in the team were delighted to have someone doing it for them. I was quite an aggressive player at the time and the rest of the team kept congratulating me. The wilder I got the more they encouraged me and I got carried away with it all.

'Jack had the Press cuttings ready when I got back from the under-23s. They were asking if I was the right sort of man to be playing for England. Jack asked me if the kicking was really necessary. He pointed out how it could damage my career. I sat down, thought about it and made a conscious effort to steady down my game.'

Turner had made Moore realise just how far his career could go. It was the start of a deliberate climb towards the England captaincy – and all the social advantages that go with the title.

Moore drank his public rewards to the full. Unlike many others, he slaved away in private to stay at the top. All the beautiful people were still sleeping in some of the smartest holiday resorts in the world as his lone figure pounded across the sands and pumped along the water's edge.

'England would come back from an overseas tour towards the end of June and people would be expecting us to join them on holiday somewhere exotic and West Ham would let me start late on summer training because I was still match fit. But I'd know when the rest of the lads were starting. Say July 12. And that date would be burning a hole in my head. We'd have some spectacularly late nights but from July 12 I'd be up at six every morning, running round the bay, stomach exercises in the surf, sprints on the sand.

'When I finished they'd all still be asleep and I'd shuffle into the room like a sand dancer. If Tina woke up she'd start mumbling about was it worth it, that hour's training that day. I couldn't answer. Maybe not. But it seemed important not to miss it.'

There are no stories told at West Ham or Fulham of Bobby Moore missing a single morning's training, however profound the ravages of the night before.

So, ten years on, when others had fallen by the wayside, Moore was still walking in high places. He does not delude himself that he is sought after socially for his stunning wit or towering intellect, admitting: 'In truth, I've no real interests outside football. I'd like to play golf well but that's a game at which most men have a fancy for looking the part. I can't read a book which isn't light and easy and gets hold of your interest quickly. I read Robbins, Fleming, Wheatley. Books you can pick up and put down with no problem. But I know if I'd made an effort to read more widely it would have broadened me as a person.'

Nevertheless, Moore's single-mindedness preserved him for another Cup Final, in 1975, and more celebrated encounters. The social pre-amble to his Wembley appearance for Fulham against West Ham again threw him into conversation with the Prime Minister: 'All Harold Wilson wanted to talk about was football. He made a joke about knowing he was a bad politician but how he was a good forecaster. So I asked him who was going to win the Final and he said he'd have to see the state of the pitch first. I said I could tell him that already.'

That touch of irreverence – 'I'm not politically minded, in case you hadn't guessed' – is withheld only from the handful of men Moore has idolised. They are a small but revealing collection.

South African golfer Gary Player epitomises all that Moore appreciates in a sporting professional. 'I admire success and I've found the common theme to success is putting in some private sweat, and actually enjoying what you are doing. Look at Gary Player. Practice, practice, practice. Working hard at what he loves. He said the other day he wants to go on at the top for another fifteen years, well beyond fifty.

'It must mean the world to Gary to give up so many pleasures in life to keep himself so fit. The man's dedication is fantastic. How can you have anything but admiration for a man who has kept himself at a peak for so long?'

Muhammad Ali, the greatest sporting showman of all time, excites Moore's esteem. 'It's impossible for us to agree with everything he says and does, but he's all talent. Great for boxing and great for his people. The man's electrifying. I went to a dinner in his honour in London and was talking to one of his henchmen about his training. The fellow said that Muhammad has four trainers but no-one trains him. If he feels like training one day he will drive himself for hours. If not, all the shouting and pleading in the world won't get him off his backside. He'll pretend he's listening but he knows what's right for himself.

'Whenever he needs to be driven through something special he goes to his old masseur who no-one ever hears about and sweats it out behind locked doors. Before he fought George Foreman the masseur gave him hours of abdominal exercises every day. Come the fight all he was worried about was stopping George hitting him in the head. He let the big man punch himself out on his stomach and then put him away. Muhammad's in a class of his own.'

It was not a sportsman, however, whose presence turned Moore's legs to jelly. 'I'd idolised Frank Sinatra all my life and then got a chance to meet him in Los Angeles when I was over in the States with West Ham. It was nothing really. I was doing a regular column at the time for the Daily Mirror. Their photographer Kent Gavin managed to fix up with one of Sinatra's entourage for us to have our picture taken together.

'We didn't say much more than hello but it was the most nerve-wracking moment of my life. Worse than any big match. Worse than going into the World Cup Final. Sinatra oozes professionalism and he loves his business so much that he can't bring himself to give it up.

'We were lucky that while we were in L.A. he was doing what was supposed to be his farewell concert. Geoff Hurst and I bought 100-dollar tickets as soon as we got the chance. Later in the day the West Ham team were offered tickets at half price and I couldn't believe that some of them wouldn't pay fifty dollars for a unique experience. I couldn't understand them having no sense of occasion. How often do you live?

'It delighted me when he decided to make a comeback. I saw the T.V. show of *Old Blue Eyes is Back* from Madison Square Garden. He got a terrible Press. They were on about him slipping from his pedestal. What rubbish. The man was knocking on sixty but he was still all class. Still that aura about him. All right, so he's past his best. All right, so he's been a bastard in his time. So who else is there?'

Apart from the almost childish trauma of meeting Sinatra, Moore was as much at home in opulent surroundings and celebrated company as on a footballers' binge. He became the prime example of a social phenomenon spawned by the frivolous ideals of the inflationary Sixties.

Soccer was no longer just the opium of the masses. It was the creator of gods. Moore wore the mantle with the greatest conviction. He dressed with more panache than most footballers, a little less flash than others. The manners were more studied, the carriage erect, the demeanour quiet. He looked and lived out the part of England's captain. 'In public I never forgot who I was.'

Bobby Moore was pleasant to have around, even if it was impossible to put your finger on the real man behind the watchful blue eyes.

To the world, he appeared self-possessed and unapproachable. Yet it bothered him that he was not loved. 'Henry Cooper's a pal of mine and look at him, lovely feller and everyone loves him. Yet people seem so nervous of me, so on the defensive when they approach me that they have to hide behind snide remarks. Later, when they get to know me, they admit I'm different from what they expected.

'It's like my relationship with football crowds. I enjoy the adoration, same as every player, but I know I mustn't let it affect me. Adoration can make players want to do too much with the ball. At times I have to shut them out just to get on with the job the way it should be done.

'I used to love playing at Manchester United and Liverpool, 52,000 people and not one of them on my side, every one a challenge to overcome. Success is about overcoming challenges. That's why I was delighted Norman Hunter and Colin Todd were elected as the first two Professional Footballers' Association Players of the Year. That's the biggest compliment I could be paid. I kept those two fine players out of the England side. The only positions for which there were several real challenges were goalkeeper and my No.6.

'That was the satisfaction of the England job. It would have meant nothing to me to be picked only because there was no-one else. I wanted to be picked because I was the best.'

Moore's unconscious air of superiority and his unshakeable belief in his own ability were a powerful combination. He needed only the occasional jolt to keep his ego in check.

The Scots, who resented Bobby Moore's golden boy image as passionately as they hated the England team, were falling over themselves to oblige.

Winning
and
Losing

Above England win the World Cup: Bobby Moore rejoices and Bobby Charlton weeps. *Below* The Captain meets the fans.

Bobby Moore

Mrs. Moore

by and Tina beneath a giant replica of the World Cup at the celebration banquet.

Above Bringing the F.A. Cup home to West Ham. *Below* Winning the European Cup-Winners' Cup a year later.

OWEN BARNES

en by Jimmy Greaves

Beating George Best and *opposite* Charlie Cooke.

Moment of failure: Bobby and Sir Alf Ramsey after being knocked out of the World Cup competition by West Germany in Mexico in 1970.

CHAPTER ELEVEN

Bloody Foreigners

It is a much-loved part of football's folklore that Denis Law, Manchester United's undiluted Scot, was at pains to spend the afternoon of the 1966 World Cup Final playing golf in his homeland.

Sanity insisted West Germany were unlikely to prevail at Wembley; chauvinism therefore decreed that Law put himself beyond reach of any television, radio, newspaper, or even passing stranger likely to broadcast the details of England's triumph.

The stark result was itself enough to stick in Scotland's gullet through the ten months they had to wait before flinging themselves upon the new world champions.

To their perverse satisfaction, England remained undefeated through that time, beating the Irish and the Welsh but being held to a home draw by Czechoslovakia.

By April 15, 1967, the Wembley stage was perfectly set for the Scots to play like dervishes, Law himself to score their first goal and Scotland to win 3-2. Bobby Moore's memories are acute 'They went absolutely mad over it. The eyes of some of the players were wild. Their supporters came pouring off the terraces to cut up the pitch, waving lumps of earth at us and saying this was the turf on which they destroyed the world champions. Some of them were seriously suggesting we ought to hand over the World Cup.

'Playing the Scots was a thing apart. For so long their football was retarded by the belief that beating England was all that mattered. They used to drop numerous daft results against foreign teams because they never charged themselves up to play with the same heart as they did against England. In a way it was tremendous. The atmosphere was unique, it built up a magnificent tension and it took each new lot of England players a while to come to terms with the experience.'

For a long time the Scots had relished puncturing what they regarded as the arrogance of Moore and the supercilliousness of Alf Ramsey. Moore's first game against Scotland, at Wembley in the spring of '63 was England's first Home International under Ramsey's managership.

'We lost 2-1,' recalls Moore, 'to what I believe was the best side Scotland ever had. Jim Baxter was in his keep-the-ball-up heyday and scored both goals. They also had Dave Mackay, John White, Denis Law, Ian St. John. What better players to build your side round? Alf was sick about losing to the Scots from that day on but most of the players appreciated the way Scotland played and my worst memory of that match was the collision which broke Eric Caldow's leg and quite seriously injured Bobby Smith.

'It was the next game against Scotland, a year later, which got under the skin of the players. We went up to Glasgow the following April and the irritation started as soon as we were walking to the coach at the airport. There was a lot of abuse. Chants about Bobby Moore's handbag. Bloody foreigners. All that rubbish. You couldn't be sure it was all meant in fun.

'You had to admire their supporters for their fanatacism, up to a point. But they carried things too far. Everyone admires Liverpool's support because it's fanatical for Liverpool, not abusive to others. If another team goes up to Anfield and plays well the crowd show their appreciation. Not the Scots. Their support spills over into hatred for the opposition.

'It was the first time several of the side had been up to Scotland for a full international and it was quite an experience. For the next couple of days their papers were full of a dozen pages of jibberish about how great the Scots were and what a joke we were. Then we lost the game 1-0 and of course they made the most of it. In the end it rebounded on them.

'There was a start, there and then, of a changing attitude in the England team towards playing the Scots. Me and one or two others slowly became more and more determined to ram it back down their throats, shoot them down, silence them.'

Ramsey, determined to pull the Scottish thorn from his side, promoted that attitude. One of his diplomatic gems came at the time of another landing at Glasgow airport when a Scottish journalist began the interview procedure with the pleasantry: 'Welcome to Scotland.' Ramsey replied: 'You must be joking.'

'It took a time for us to get the upper hand,' says Moore. 'But by the time I finished with England we were not only in the habit of beating the Scots, but of thrashing them by big scores. It was all the more satisfying because while it was very important for England to beat Scotland, it was just one of many important matches. For Scotland it was the end of the world to lose to England.

'In a way we did them a favour. When they realised they couldn't beat us every year they started to appreciate the importance of little things like World Cups, building experience against countries who play the game differently, learning what it takes to beat Latin teams as opposed to Iron Curtain countries, pitting your wits against obstruction and finding the concentration to break down a deep defence, understanding what it takes to become a world class team.

'Tommy Docherty really made the breakthrough for them when he was Scotland's manager, making them concentrate just as hard on games against Continental opposition as against England.'

The first really instructive lesson in the niceties of international football had been applied by England in Glasgow in February 1968. Then a 1-1 draw – 'We were never in danger of losing but at first they couldn't work out why we were happy not to win' – put England into the quarter finals of the European Championship of Nations.

Scotland's emotional win at Wembley in '67 already counted for nothing beyond its own sake. Yet, ironically, England were to find the European Championship as bitterly frustrating as so many of their previous encounters with the Scots. Each succeeding failure ended with Moore in an unfamiliar and uncomfortable role...in the dock at the inquest.

In '68 England safely negotiated a two-match quarter-final with narrow wins over Spain at Wembley and in Madrid. The closing stages were compressed into a summer week in Italy and England were camped at Florence for their semi-final against Yugoslavia. Ramsey warned his team that the Slavs were a dangerous mixture of fine skills and uncompromising strength but England's reputation as World Cup holders had gone farther ahead of them. Moore: 'They were so wary of us that they chose to play the game much the same way Argentina played against so many teams, clinging to the ball at the back, frustrating us and putting the emphasis very much on the physical.

'For all our territorial advantage we had too few chances and late in the game they got a breakaway goal which was down to me. They floated a long ball out of the ruck in midfield. It came in above me, the last man at the back. I knew someone was making a run behind me. I could have reached up and pulled the ball down with my arm. But I wasn't sure if I might be just inside the penalty area. And anyway that's not my way. I still felt I could get up to the ball with my head. Strained. Didn't make it.'

Moore turned to see Dragan Djazic, Yugoslavia's world class left winger, finish the job. 'Djazic was a very talented player. No way he would miss a chance like that. Cracked it perfectly past Banksie.'

England had grown unaccustomed to losing games that mattered. The goal inflamed their already aggravated feelings. Alan Mullery lost his head with one of the Yugoslav hatchet men in midfield and the shame of having a player sent off further soured the taste of defeat.

The failure was compounded when Yugoslavia went on to lose a replayed final to Italy, the host nation. Moore was one of many trying to pin down an explanation. 'We had been beaten so few times since two years prior to the World Cup that we felt we must have a great chance of winning the European Championship. Alf had every confidence in the team and we had every confidence in each other. We all believed in the way we were playing, the things we were doing.

'The problem was that the system of football in England didn't give us time to put the same care and thought into this competition as into the World Cup. The old club *v.* country problem. The Continentals cancelled their League programmes, moved heaven and earth to give their national teams time to prepare. We got caught a bit cold. It kept happening but Don Revie ran into the same problem in the same competition as soon as he took over from Alf as England manager. It became an obsession with Alf.'

The spring of 1972 deepened Ramsey's neurosis about the European championship into something approaching a persecution complex. A quirk of the draw paired England and West Germany, the old rivals, in the quarter final. Roy McFarland, his exciting new centre half from Derby County, was declared unfit at the last moment and he took the calamitous gamble of pairing the similar talents of Moore and Norman Hunter at the heart of his defence. Worse still, Ramsey was under mounting pressure to adopt a more adventurous style of play and he made the concession of dispensing with a midfield ball winner on a day when the team needed a Nobby Stiles or a Peter Storey to put the clamps on one Gunther Netzer.

'On reflection, both decisions were mistakes,' says Moore. 'Instead of calling up any tall, dominating, orthodox centre half you care to name, Alf went for experience with me and Norman. I think he always felt he owed Norman a game whenever he could give him one, for being so loyal and patient even though I had his position in the team. There was a lot of rubbish talked about a tactical mix-up between me and Norman but the simple truth was that we couldn't play together because we were too similar.

100

'Then it was one of those rare occasions when he picked three attacking players in midfield. We had Alan Ball, Martin Peters and Colin Bell. And we hadn't been told a thing about Netzer.'

Ramsey's suspicion of strolling ball players had apparently led him into the trap of overlooking the potential impact at Wembley of the blond, languid problem boy of West German football. Unexpected and unmarked, Netzer ran riot. Moore: 'The way we were playing gave Gunther the freedom of the park. He hates being marked tight, but in the circumstances he found at Wembley his skill and brain could take any team in the world to the cleaners. He was just allowed to carry the ball from his own half, at our defence.

'I'll put my hands up and admit it was one of the worst games I ever played for England. But we were set up all wrong and any defender struggles if midfield players are allowed to come through at him and strand him between two opponents.

'It was a whole day of mistakes. Franny Lee got a goal but we were stuffed 3-1. Even their goals came from mistakes. I was responsible for the first. There was a bad penalty and Emlyn Hughes made a ricket on the third.'

Ramsey plotted a warped revenge. He decided recovery was beyond England in the return match and went to Berlin with a negative, bruising team which made it impossible for the Germans to please their own supporters and goaded Netzer into saying: 'Every Englishman except the goalkeeper has autographed my legs with his studs.'

To the men who had cost him goals and prestige at Wembley, Ramsey said very little. 'You don't expect to win matches if you make mistakes which give away bad goals,' says Moore. 'But Alf would never criticise you for making errors. He knew the players didn't need to be told they had made mistakes.

'The only ones worth pointing out are when a man doesn't know he's doing wrong. Like getting caught in false positions.'

That is an ironic phrase. No-one doubted that Bobby Moore would personally survive England's crisis. In many ways he had built his football game and his life style around a capacity to extricate himself from just such difficulties.

The experience had already proved invaluable when a careless visit to a Latin American jewellery shop had trapped him in the tightest corner of his life.

CHAPTER TWELVE

Whodunit?

Bobby Moore loses his temper as often as Brazil lose World Cups. Maybe once every eight years.

For those accustomed to marvelling at his Aryan self-discipline, that stiff-jawed control of his emotions, one spring night in 1975 is memorable for an eruption of anger.

Moore was in Bournemouth with Fulham, sheltering on the golf course from the pressures of their F.A. Cup run to Wembley. Footballers, however, are lost without football and they spent one night off watching Bournemouth and Boscombe Athletic play a Third Division fixture. Then Moore went on to a bar with Harry Redknapp, once a team mate at West Ham, among a handful of Fulham and Bournemouth players.

Inevitably, the more pushing members of the local drinking fraternity attached themselves to Moore's company of sportsmen. Predictably, one man was emboldened by the night's consumption.

A somewhat reddened face pushed itself at Moore from the fringe of the group and said: 'I know it was a long time ago, but I believe you've still got that bracelet.'

Moore's struggle with his more primitive reflexes was revealed by a clenching of fists and a strained, stilted, almost formal reply. 'If you're going to speak like that then please leave the company because I'm not interested in talking with you.'

The man recognised the danger signs but his continued presence and bumbling apologies compounded the insult. Moore reacted by using the appropriate and explicit, two-syllable sentence. The gentleman duly obliged.

It had taken almost five years to fracture Moore's restraint; five years of forcing a smile at bad jokes, walking past jibes in the street, closing ears to the taunts of the crowd, living with the knowledge that tens of millions of people believe he stole a trinket he could have bought with the end figures of his bank balance.

The England plane spiralled into the mountain city of Bogota. Bobby Moore sat half listening to advice on avoiding the plague of street corner salesmen, those black marketeers whose stolen goods might deposit an unsuspecting buyer in a Latin American jail.

The players were warned to fight shy of the fly boys and look for presents only in reputable shops; establishments with polished showcases behind plate glass facades; like the one which caught the eye of Bobby Moore and Bobby Charlton as they checked into the hotel Tequendama, the best the capital of Colombia has to offer.

English football's two most famous players settled into their rooms, changed, and were back down in the lobby with an hour to spare before dinner. They drifted casually to the window of the shop, the very name of which hinted at intrigue as much as at specialised dealing in emeralds: Green Fire.

It was 6.25p.m. Monday, 18 May 1970. Moore preserves a precise image of the scene in a compartment of his tidy mind. 'Bobby was quite interested in getting a present for Norma, his wife. So we went into the shop, looked in a glass showcase or two, made a few inquiries about prices from the girl behind the counter. She was like any assistant in any good class shop. Dark-haired, quite nice-looking, smartly turned out. Miss Average for a decent jewellers.

'Some of the other lads looked in from the outside window. Peter Thompson strolled in briefly. Only for a second or two. There wasn't even any of the larking about you sometimes get in shops when footballers are out together.

'I admit players sometimes do get boisterous and joke about. But not this time. It was late afternoon and we'd had a tiring journey. We were just browsing the way you do to kill time in any hotel with its own shops. The way I've done dozens of times in the jewellery shop in the foyer of the London Hilton. We didn't even ask the girl to get a single piece out of a cabinet. There was nothing that excited Bobby. We ambled out and sat down in armchairs, no more than twenty feet across the foyer from the shop window.

'We were just chatting idly. I watched an elderly woman go into the shop, come out again and walk towards us. She asked Bobby and me to step into the shop. We said yes, thinking they had found something to interest Bobby for his wife. As we stood up the woman fumbled with the cushions where we'd been sitting. Still nothing registered. But as we got back inside the shop she said: "There's some jewellery missing."

Moore was the advocate from the start, instinctively turning defence into attack. 'Well, what do you want to do? Search us? Call the police? We'll co-operate: whatever you do makes no difference to us because we don't know what you're talking about.'

The shop proprietor had materialised. 'There is a bracelet missing.'

Moore: 'We haven't touched anything.'

Sir Alf Ramsey came on the scene rather like Neville Chamberlain down the aeroplane steps, outwardly reassuring but inwardly in a turmoil of anxiety for his England.

Those who find the analogy a little extreme might reflect for a moment on a saying of Bill Shankly, Liverpool's remarkable and obsessive manager: 'It's ridiculous to say football's a matter of life and death. It's much more important than that.'

There is a grain of truth as well as a great deal of wit in that observation. It is safe to assume that had a third great war been declared in Europe in that Summer of 1970, it would have troubled Ramsey less, personally, than the fear that England's defence of the World Cup was being undermined by some Central American chicanery.

Moore stood back and watched Ramsey go to work on the owner of the shop, the hotel manager and the police in his stern, acquired, English-gentlemanly way. Yet Moore knew his manager and was not completely deceived by Ramsey's unruffled exterior: 'Alf handled it like an expert and everyone thought it was done and forgotten the minute Bobby and I finished making our formal statements to the police. But there was something about Alf that made me feel he was upset. He already sensed that something was up, that it was a take-on. Felt it there and then.

'No doubt Alf was the first to react. At first Bobby and I were just dumbfounded. Then it started to get to me that perhaps somebody had done something we could be blamed for. We were spending another three days there and we had a match to play and it was on my mind that one of us might get back to our room and find a bracelet had been planted. Bobby was openly worried. Very edgy. I told him to try to put it out of his mind because it was finished. But I wasn't sure I believed that.'

Those of the England party in the know maintained tight-lipped security to keep word of the incident from the ears of the accompanying party of sports journalists, who, two days later, blithely reported that England's footballers began tuning up for the Mexico World Cup with a 4-0 win over Colombia, Martin Peters scoring twice, Bobby Charlton and Alan Ball once each.

Had they had any reason to listen more closely, they might have heard sighs of relief escaping Messrs. Moore, Charlton and Ramsey next morning as their plane climbed away from Bogota's 8,560 feet and lifted them still higher into the mountains, to Quito.

The capital of Equador is the eagle's nest of Central America, perched at 9,350 feet, but worth the climb for those wishing to plunder its eggs. In England's case the rewards could be counted in the number of red corpuscles pumped into the bloodstream of every player.

The World Cup was to be played at around 6,000 feet and 100 degrees heat in Mexico. England were mountain-hopping in Colombia and Equador to combat the physical disadvantages which would otherwise cripple sea-level Europeans used to temperate climes.

Under the direction of Dr. Neil Phillips, who practised medicine in Redcar and fussed over the fine tuning of footballers for Middlesborough and England, Ramsey's men were busy acclimatising to rarefied atmostphere. In much simiplified terms, England were playing games and spending days at extreme altitude to increase the percentage of red corpuscles in the blood. That adjustment would help their bodies make the most of every last drop of oxygen available in Mexico. It would reduce the likelihood of the England footballers collapsing with knotted leg muscles and burning lungs.

That change in metabolism established, Dr. Phillips planned to bring them down from Quito to Mexico in time to adjust to the higher temperatures. There, with the help of salt preparations and special fluids, they would combat a sweat loss of up to half a stone a player during a 90-minute football match.

That layman's diversion into sports medicine explains how England were so pre-occupied in Quito that the Bogota bracelet was pushed to the back of a few notable minds.

On May 24, four days after their win in Bogota, England found themselves sufficiently at home in the mountains to beat Ecuador 2-0. Amid all the delight over two impressive results, it hardly seemed important that in order to fly from Quito to Mexico next day, Bobby Moore and company would have to change planes at Bogota.

By the time England had snatched every last hour of altitude acclimatisation in Quito, Ramsey was so untroubled by the affair of the bracelet that he arranged to fill a five hour gap between connecting flights at Bogota with a showing of one of his inevitable Westerns, back at the very Hotel Tequendama. Like many an accused man, Bobby Moore was returning to the scene of the crime.

The thin air was soured by the whiff of conspiracy as soon as the

England party strolled into the airport building. The arrivals area was alive with plain clothes police armed with a warrant and Keith Morris, the British Charge d'Affaires and head of the welcoming delegation, had only narrowly averted an arrest in full view of waiting newsmen and photographers.

Morris spoke quickly and quietly to Ramsey as the team's baggage was checked through transit. England's manager took Moore to one side and said: 'Mr. Morris will be coming along to the hotel just before three o'clock to take you to the police station. It is only to confirm your statement and you will meet up with us again at the airport at four.'

No one was surprised as Bobby loitered in the hotel lobby instead of taking a seat for the screening of Shenandoah. He had long since tired of Ramsey's penchant for horse operas. No one noticed as Moore slipped into the embassy car. The plot was thickening inside as well as outside the curtained room.

Still Bobby was fairly unconcerned. Alf had seemed calm enough. Mr. Morris talked mostly about football. The alarm bells did not start ringing until it dawned on Moore that he was walking into a court-house instead of a police station.

The traditional nervous wait ended in a small bare room. White walls, dark wooden desk, Spanish-speaking judge, French speaking lawyer commissioned for Moore by the embassy, a student translating into pidgin English. The cross-talk darted bewilderingly about Moore's ears. The watch raced on his wrist.

4p.m.: 'I should be at the airport now.'

4.30: 'Please, I'm late.'

5.00: 'My plane is due to leave.'

5.30:'What on earth's happening?'

Always just a few more minutes. Unintelligible arguments. No sensible answers.

England's plane was in the air before the whisper hurried around that one of our players was missing. Most of the journalists would have given their writing arm for the pilot to turn back. Others, mostly those closest to Ramsey, began claiming they had known all along. If they did, it is hard to understand what they were doing on the aeroplane at all. Collectively, they would hit the panic button when the plane stopped to refuel at Panama City, racing through a downpour to commandeer telephones, Telex machines, telegraph operators.

The departure time long gone, Moore felt isolated and abandoned. He had no way of knowing that Dr. Andrew Stephen and Denis Follows, respectively chairman and secretary of the Football Association, had stayed in Bogota. The room, no more than 15ft. by 12ft. began to take on the aspect of a prison. As yet, he did not know that a cell was his intended destination.

At last, late in the evening, it was spelled out that he had been arrested because the shop girl, the dark-haired and highly-strung Clara Padilla, claimed to have seen Bobby Moore, not Bobby Charlton, toying with a glass wall cabinet, the supposed resting place of a gold bracelet studded in emeralds, worth £625.

'I knew right then it was a frame-up,' says Moore. 'I knew the cabinet they were talking about. A main display case. It was one of those to show off just a few nice pieces of jewellery. Not a clutter. I had looked at it and I could easily remember the four pieces inside. Just four. They would stick in your mind. I knew the truth then but I thought, how the hell am I going to prove it?

'There never was a bracelet.'

A little over six thousand miles away across six hours of time zones it was two o'clock in the morning of May 26 as the insistent ring of the telephone disturbed the peace of a mock-Tudor household in Chigwell, Essex. The call had been placed by a late duty reporter from the news desk of the *Daily Mail*. Tina Moore fumbled in the dark to answer the bedside phone.

'Mrs. Moore?'

'Yes.'

'It's the *Daily Mail* here. Sorry to wake you, but something dreadful has happened to Bobby.'

'Oh God. He's been in a car accident?'

'No, no. He's been accused of stealing a bracelet.'

'Don't be stupid. I don't need bad jokes at this time of night.'

The central characters in the headline dramas of our time are very often cut off from normal contact with the outside world, so enmeshed in their own extraordinary predicament that even if they are used to bathing in publicity they cannot imagine the torrent of interest they are generating.

By 10 p.m. in Bogota, after seven hours of judicial waffling unrelieved by so much as a glass of water, Bobby Moore felt very alone and very forgotten. That sense of depression was deepened as his ear deciphered the single word which Judge Pedro Dorado was now repeating with an exasperated wave of his hand: 'Detention, detention.'

In a sudden flurry of activity, Bobby was hustled through a side door, into a police car, through the darkness and up the dimly-lit steps of another, altogether more sinister building. 'I know there's problems but the subtleties have been lost by the student interpreter and I don't know how bad it is. I'm in a reception area, which is like a madhouse. I'm having to fill in a form with personal details and all around me they are jabbering away in foreign languages. The embassy man's sticking close to me but there's not much he can say because it suddenly dawns on me where we are. Like coming out of a daze. Sort of into focus. There are cells in this place. They're chucking me in jail.

'For how long? For how long?'

Unbeknown to Moore, Morris' aides at the embassy as well as Stephen and Follows had spent the night urgently negotiating a compromise which was clinched as the cell door was swinging open. Under discreet pressure from the Colombian government, Judge Dorado permitted Moore the unusual privilege of house arrest.

Senor Alfonso Senior, Director of the Colombian Football Federation, arrived breathless to sign for his country's most celebrated prisoner, an imperative step if Moore was to retain any semblance of fitness for the World Cup matches ahead. In addition to Senor Senior's personal guarantee, Moore was to be under surveillance at all times by two armed guards. Again he was driven through the darkness, this time to coffee, a snack and the hope of some sleep.

As he was shown to his room in Senior's cool and welcoming hacienda, he had company. 'The guards were watching me like I was going to pull a pistol out of thin air. One of them just came on into the room with me and when I got into bed he got under the cover of the single bed next to me. Fully dressed. Boots on. Hat over the bedpost. One hand on his holster. Watching me. I heard the other guard jam a chair under the knob outside the door and flop into it. I felt like the captured hero out of one of Alf's westerns. It didn't make sleep any easier but it did make me laugh for the first time that night.'

As Bobby Moore lay wrestling with his insomnia, it was 5.00 a.m. in Chigwell and Tina was woken again, this time by a hubbub from beneath her bedroom window which was out of character with the expensive calm of their tree-lined avenue.

She peeped through the curtains and was astonished to see television cameramen and their equipment, reporters and photographers crowding the driveway.

Tina checked the time in mild disbelief, went downstairs, opened the front door and inquired in general: 'Is it right, then? Bobby's been charged with stealing a bracelet?' She heard the answer and closed the door before they could come hammering across the porch with their questions.

Fleet Street is not so easily deterred. As if on cue, the telephone resumed its ringing.

At 6.00 a.m. Bogota time, Bobby gave up the struggle to sleep, pulled on his dark blue leisure suit – a somewhat flattering description of the misshapen cross between a lounge suit and a track suit which the F.A. required England players to wear in transit – walked past one snoring guard and tapped firmly on his bedroom door to send another jumping out of his chair.

In English words and universal sign language he told his startled captors: 'I'd like to go for a walk. Walk. I need fresh air.'

They went out together through the walled garden of Senior's delightful home into a beautiful blue morning smiling on the richest residential district of Colombia's capital; the captain of England's football team, and half a pace behind each shoulder, a policeman with dark, wary eyes and a hand on his gun.

With each step the vision of the prison cell was receding and Moore's self-assurance returning. They passed a milkman on his rounds. Bobby sought out some coins in his pocket, bought a litre of milk and the incongruous threesome went on their way, taking turns to drink from the cooling bottle. The state penitentiary was never like this.

On their return to the house, Moore's Colombian host loaned a clean shirt, socks and underwear to supplement the clothes he stood up in. The rest of Moore's belongings had been loaded aboard the England flight with the rest of the team's baggage.

He set about placing a call to his wife in England. It came after the usual delay.

'Hello? Tina? Can you hear me?'

'Yes, yes. Are you all right?'

'All is well. How are you and the kids?'

'We're okay, but how are you? What are they doing to you? What's happening?'

'Look, its all right. There's no need to worry. Don't worry because – '

At that critical moment the line was interrupted by the voice of the international operator: 'Mr. Moore? One moment please. Long distance for you.'

'What the hell...?'

'Hello? Bobby? Its the London *Evening Standard* here. We just wanted...'

This time Moore terminated the call by slamming down the receiver. 'I had to do that. I wasn't sure what the score was with the Bogota legal system but I knew I couldn't afford to upset anybody by being quoted in the newspapers.'

Whitehall would have been proud of Moore's diplomacy. The Foreign Office were already applying pressure for the release of England's captain. Tom Rogers, who had taken over as Britain's ambassador in Bogota on May 22, in between the alleged theft and Moore's arrest, was at once facing a major test. The Prime Minister, Harold Wilson, intervened personally and was accused by Conservative MPs of trying to attract votes by taking up diplomatic cudgels on behalf of such a *cause celebre.*

Moore was isolated from the negotiations and kicked his heels through the first day of his confinement. By now, however, it was apparent that he was under the loosest form of arrest and Stephen and Follows took what steps they could to break the monotony and thereby nourish Bobby's morale. Arrangements were made for their party to dine with the family of a friend of Follows, a former airline pilot domiciled in Bogota. Moore's guards were now thoroughly enjoying their work. 'They changed a couple of times a day but I called each pair Pedro and Jose and they came to dinner and got stoned and loved every minute of it. They were like friends.'

When the household retired that night, Senior offered the guards a bottle of scotch. When Moore rose at 6.00 a.m. walked downstairs and shook them by the shoulder, the guards groaningly declined an invitation to join him on his morning constitutional. They went back to sleep soundly convinced that their prisoner would report back from his walk. For May 27 was scheduled as the Day of Confrontation.

When the line went dead, Tina Moore pumped frantically at the receiver for long minutes before accepting that Bobby's call was lost for good. She telephoned the Football Association who advised her to call the Home Office who re-routed her to the Foreign Office. She was then told that Bobby could be released at any hour, a message which was to be repeated to her, Ramsey, Stephen and Follows many times in their various parts of the globe in the ensuing days.

Morris Keston, a wealthy supporter of Tottenham Hotspur and social acquaintance and admirer of Moore, called with an offer to pay for Tina to fly to Bogota. She recalls: 'I felt helpless sitting at home. I wanted to be as near to Bobby as I could but they kept saying he might be released and if I went to Colombia I could miss him altogether.'

For the sake of the children, or more specifically the older and more aware Roberta, Tina attempted to keep the day on a normal course. 'Dean was only a baby but Roberta had just started school and I was worried about the effect on her and what the other children might say to her. Kids can be cruel without thinking.'

Tina visited the headmistress of the private Braeside School for reassurance that Roberta would be treated as if the newspapers were not trying to find type big enough to express her husband's plight. In the event, the only mild tremor was when Roberta came home from school that afternoon and mentioned: 'One little girl says Daddy has found a necklace.'

Nevertheless, the close attention of the media was making it impossible for life to continue unaffected. 'Everywhere I went,' says Tina, 'crowds of reporters followed. I felt I had to get away and I felt I ought to visit Bobby's mother, because she was very distressed.'

That family visit proved anything but a simple procedure. It needed the help of the police to arrange and required Mrs. Moore to become a mistress of disguise. A plain-clothes policeman arrived at the house with a dark wig and left minutes later in Tina's car accompanied by the au pair girl wearing Tina's hat and large sunglasses.

As the majority of the reporters and cameramen set off in pursuit of the decoy, Tina was hiding her distinctive blonde hair beneath the wig. 'I had to slip out of the side door, crawl across the grass on my hands, clamber over the fence and make a run for the neighbour's garage.'

Another plain-clothes man was waiting with a plain saloon car. Tina was hidden beneath a blanket in the back and driven to Moore's family home in Barking.

'Looking back, it seems funny,' she says. 'At the time it was a nightmare. The doctor put me on tranquilisers and for the first couple of days I just read the newspapers and it seemed unreal. I was in a daze.'

Finally, the activity in Chigwell's Manor Road became too much and Tina effected another clandestine getaway, this time decamping with the children to the home of Judith Hurst, her closest friend and wife of Geoff Hurst. 'Until then I'd more or less had to have control of myself. But round at Judith's I watched the news on television and it was all about Bobby and for the first time I started crying and I couldn't stop.'

The Confrontation is one of the more entertaining twists in the long course of justice in Bogota. It brings together accuser and accused at the scene of the incident in question and attempts to reconstruct the happening.

In theory it should take place *in camera*. In practice, in a major case, the time and the date leak out and The Confrontation takes place for the cameras. So it was that everyone from the head of Colombian television news to the head porter of the Tequendama Hotel knew that the re-match of Bobby Moore versus Clara Padilla was scheduled for the Green Fire shop at 10.00 a.m. on the morning of May 27.

The only person they forgot to tell was Bobby Moore.

'I was pacing up and down the house,' he recalls, 'wondering when on earth somebody was going to do something to get me back to the England team when the phone rang. It was Denis Follows asking where I was. They were down at the hotel after being told there would be a meeting with the prosecution and I would probably be released to fly to Mexico. I couldn't get down there fast enough.'

It took Bobby several minutes to fight his way through the crowd in the hotel foyer and into the jewellery shop. There he was well and truly confronted by the Padilla girl, shop owner Danilo Rojas and a supplementary witness, one Alvaro Suarez who had been rounded up during England's sojourn in Quito. Once again, Judge Dorado was the referee. Painstakingly he traced the events of May 18.

Padilla claimed she saw Moore open the glass wall cabinet, remove the bracelet from a display stand of white coral and slip it quickly into his pocket. Suarez, who was dubiously described as a dealer in native Indian craftwork but was subsequently discovered to be known to the police as a trafficker in black market emeralds, swore he saw the whole thing from outside the shop window. Rojas insisted one of his bracelets was missing.

Moore was invited to cross question his accusers. A career in top football had taught him to pressurise the weak link in the opposition. He concentrated on the fidgeting, chain-smoking Senorita Padilla. 'It was like a hot-house in the little shop and scores of people were pressed up against the door and window. I knew she was jumpy and she had told so many conflicting stories that I couldn't understand anybody taking her seriously. I gave her the old Muhammad Ali stare for a few seconds and broke her story down.'

After hours of waiting, Moore relished a chance to indulge his competitive instinct. The nature of her job in an international hotel demanded that Padilla spoke fluent, if somewhat accented, English. Bobby's rush of questions paved the way to the key point in his interrogation, a glaring flaw in her initial statement.

'Can you show us which way I was facing when I was standing by the showcase?'

112

'This way.'

'And what do you say I did with the bracelet?'

'You put it in your pocket.'

'With which hand?'

'This hand. Your left hand.'

'In which pocket?'

'The one away from me. The left pocket.'

Moore was again wearing the England leisure suit. He raised his arms from his sides to show the judge a suit with only one pocket. On the right hand side. And he burst out laughing, confident that that would be the end of it. Whatever Judge Dorado thought of the evidence, he was not impressed with Bobby's sense of humour. He described the England captain's attitude as 'unhelpful' and adjourned the charade from the limelight of the shop to the relative calm of his chambers in the court house.

The Confrontation had lasted ninety minutes. The legal arguments raged on for another seven hours. Again Moore was driven through the night to Senior's house. Still the judge could not decide if there was sufficient evidence to warrant a trial.

Bobby's next, unguarded early morning stroll was coloured by the knowledge that he was still under formal arrest and that England's first match of the 1970 World Cup was only five days away. A vague concern about his fitness became a determination to begin repairing his physical condition. 'I'd hardly had any sleep at all thinking about this thing until my head hurt. In fact the hardest part was being alone in my room, but for the first couple of days I'd simply been delighted that I wasn't locked in a cell. That would have been a hell of a physical and pyschological problem. I never felt at any point that they would keep me beyond the start of the World Cup but I began to worry that if they let me go at the last minute I would be badly out of shape. I knew I had to have some sort of work-out.'

Senior secured permission and equipment for Bobby to train on a local open football pitch that morning. As usual, the Bogota bush telegraph was in good working order. By the time he turned away from a punishing and self-inflicted session of sprints and exercises, he found his smiling guards and a gaggle of wide-eyed boys waiting with a football. The police left their hats behind a goal but kept on the guns. The boys padded hopefully across on bare feet. So began a kickabout friendly match which had very little in common with World Cups but which was, unwittingly, a magnificent exercise in public relations by England's captain.

113

Cameramen and reporters arrived in time to record a smiling moment. It confirmed the suspicions of the majority of Colombian people that Moore was the latest victim of several notorious attempts to frame visiting celebrities into paying the costs of alleged thefts.

Public opinion added its weight to diplomatic pressure. Colombian newspapers denounced the charge against Moore as a national scandal. Later that day Judge Dorado offered conditional release, subject to Moore signing a declaration that he would make himself available for future questioning at Colombia's consulates in Mexico or London and return to Bogota if requested.

Moore signed – 'I have nothing to hide and no reason to fear returning to Colombia' – and was booked on a flight to Mexico next day.

May 29 is the only day in Moore's memory when Bogota's international airport lived up to its name: Eldorado. The airport precincts were packed with thousands of Colombian well-wishers. Women struggled to get their children within touching distance of the departing footballer. 'Overnight,' he says, 'I was transformed from a jailbird into a national hero.' He passed through them like a cross between a messiah and a prospective Member of Parliament, kissing babies on the forehead, shaking warm, brown hands and waving to the throng.

Word of Moore's release was brought to Sir Alf Ramsey as England emerged dripping from one of several training sessions conducted in the heat of the day in Guadalajara, Mexico's second city. Since the arrest of his captain, England's manager had kept his team moving steadfastly through their scientific preparations for the World Cup.

The initial, shocked disbelief of the players had quickly been replaced by a sense of anger. At first, some of those in the know had been reluctant to board the plane from Bogota without Moore, a protest which might have precipitated Bobby's release but which Ramsey feared was more likely to disrupt their schedule.

Once in Mexico, the anger of the players became an ally, Ramsey did nothing to discourage the feeling in his camp that Moore was the victim of a Latin plot to unsettle England and thereby make it easier to relieve them of the world championship. The players were damned if they would let them get away with it, whoever they were supposed to be.

There was some mild speculation that Norman Hunter might have to deputise for Moore in the defence and some debate about whether or not Alan Mullery could assume the captaincy after being sent off in England's colours. But by and large the other England players shared

Moore's belief that he would be returned to them in time for the first match of their qualifying group, against Rumania, on June 2.

Nevertheless, the Colombians had cut it fine enough to intensify Ramsey's anxiety and when they told him Moore was on his way Sir Alf replied: 'I will not smile until I see Bobby walking towards me.' He had another twenty four hours to wait for that pleasure.

Bobby would cheerfully have travelled in the hold of any flight to Mexico but as it happened there were only first class seats available that morning. So he left Bogota in style and, by chance, in the company of an ideal fellow traveller.

Omar Sivori, a splendid veteran of Argentina's midfield, was also bound for the World Cup. He was the first reassuring voice from Moore's own fraternity of footballers.

'Hello, Bobby. We all knew you would be out today or tomorrow.'

'I wish I'd known, Omar.'

'Ah, it is normal out here. they always try these tricks for the money. Some people are so worried for their reputation they pay a few thousand dollars for the jewellery they are supposed to have stolen. It is good you fought them. Now, do you think you can stop Brazil in our part of the world...?'

The illusion of a return to normality at 30,000 feet was shattered on touch down at Mexico City. Moore was required to make a night stop. Again the airport was seething with journalists and sightseers and the authorities had contingency plans to spirit him away to a British embassy safe house with the minimum of fuss and exposure. Of the waiting journalists only the delightfully eccentric Geoffrey Green of *The Times*, a doyen of Soccer correspondents, got close enough to exchange a few words. Forever nourished by his favourite beverage, Green would not have been panicked out of his benign stride by the end of the world. He called out:

'Roberto. Nice to see you back, baby.'

'Thank you, Geoffrey. Where have you been while I've been away?'

'Over the rainbow, baby.'

'That's lovely, Geoffrey. See you in Guadalaraja.'

With that Bobby hurdled two barriers, sprinted across the tarmac to his designated car and sped away, leaving Green to weave a long, lyrical and absolutely captivating piece of prose from that shred of an interview.

Moore was driven briskly to the home of Eric Vines, Information Officer at the British Embassy. As safe houses went it was about as secure as a piggy bank in prohibition Chicago. It's whereabouts were such a secret that anybody who wanted to find Bobby Moore in Mexico City had only to read the newspapers. And Lou Wade certainly wanted to find Bobby Moore.

Bobby was standing in the lounge of the Vines home with Stephen and Follows, discussing arrangements for flying to Guadalaraja next morning, when he was confronted by a bespectacled gentleman of some six feet, seven inches wearing patent shoes, rust trousers, green check jacket, pleated yellow shirt and wide, multi-coloured tie. The guards had been so dazzled by Lou Wade's appearance that they had forgotten to arrest his progress through a back door of the house.

Wade's mode of attire belied his enriching involvement in the rag trade. He, too, lived in Chigwell and spent a small fortune literally following the career of his friend and neighbour round the world. Moore was still dressed in England's leisure suit, nylon shirt and slim tie. Wade straightened Bobby's collar and proclaimed: 'My boy, you're all over the front pages and look at the way you're dressed.'

The tension broken, Moore collapsed into laughter. Stephen and Follows, amazed by the apparition before them, were confounded to hear Wade advise them: 'Don't worry, gentlemen, I'm Mooro's insurance broker.'

Wade had tracked down the embassy house in company with Jimmy Greaves, who had arrived in Mexico City twenty four hours earlier as a driver in the World Cup saloon car rally. Greaves strolled through the same rear entrance and said: 'Come on, Mooro, you've got your release. Let's go out for a drink for an hour.'

Wade plus Greaves was more than the embassy staff could bear. The housekeeper said: 'What are you doing in here? It's supposed to be a complete secret where Mr. Moore is staying. I've been told not to let anyone in. Who are you?'

Moore interceded: 'Please. Mr. Greaves is a great friend of mine and we've played together for many years and there's no one I'd like to see more than him.'

'No. No one's allowed in. Worst of all he just walked in the back door. Where does he think he is?'

'I don't know about it being a secret,' said Greaves, 'but I couldn't get in the front door because of all the TV cameras.'

'Out. Out.'

Greaves on the front doorstep, under the arc lights. Rings the doorbell.

Housekeeper: 'Yes? What is it?'

'My name's Jimmy Greaves and I'm a friend of Bobby Moore's and is

116

it possible to see him?'

'Please come in, he'll be delighted to see you.'

More laughter helped Moore's repatriation, the last phase of which was completed the next day. The morning flight from Mexico City to Guadalajara was greeted by Ramsey and his assistant, Harold Shepherson. It was a brisk reunion. England's manager said to his captain: 'Nice to have you back. Delighted to see you, Bobby. How's it been? The lads can't wait to see you again. Let's get off and see them.'

The scene was witnessed by a mere handful of the journalists attached to the England team. Moore: 'I can only remember the two *Daily Express* men, Desmond Hackett and Alan Thompson, being at the airport.' The rest were waiting at the team hotel for a high-powered Press conference which was to provide another test of Moore's diplomacy. He had been advised that the case was legally *sub judice* so the details could not be discussed. However, he and Ramsey were aware they would have to give the media something to get their teeth into if they were to be left in comparative peace to prepare for the tournament. Bobby trod the tightrope of questions carefully enough to win a whole new crowd of admirers. One senior reporter, Laurie Pignon, of the *Daily Sketch*, declared: 'I used to have my doubts about Bobby as England captain but the way he handled that conference was marvellous. He must be the best football ambassador we've ever had.'

Ramsey himself was moved to pronounce his first glimpse of Moore as the most welcome sight in all his years in football. Coming from the man who sat impassively on the touchline bench the moment England won the 1966 World Cup, that was quite an admission.

The vagaries of the time zones and the complexities of airline timetables conspired to usher Tina Moore through Mexico City a few hours behind the final lap of Bobby's ballyhooed flight from captivity.

It had long been planned for her to travel in a foursome of players' wives – herself, Judith Hurst, Kathy Peters and Frances Bonetti. The news of her husband's release had sent Tina tripping gaily up the aeroplane steps in London onto a flight also conveying Ramsey's wife, Lady Vicky, to the World Cup.

The journey was uneventful until touchdown. Then a member of the flight crew came down the aisle and said: 'Mrs. Moore? Come with me please.'

'Can't my friends come with me?'

'I'm afraid not.'

'Why. What's happened? What's gone wrong now?'

117

In fact the authorities were simply spiriting Tina past another gathering of excitable Latin cameramen on to her connecting flight for Guadalajara and the unexpected bonus of a reunion with Bobby.

It was an unwritten law of major England tours abroad that even if players' wives travelled to see the matches, they would rarely, if ever, see their husbands. Ramsey was far from happy at having the womenfolk at all – 'We are here to do a job.' – and they were billetted in another hotel across the city.

That evening he made an exception, calling Moore to one side and saying: 'Go over and see your wife and reassure her, Bobby. The rest of the lads understand.' The Moores are not overtly emotional but they embraced unashamedly at the end of Bobby's ten-minute taxi ride.

It was also the end of their separate traumas and they were not to know then how much more of the Bogota Affair they would have to face together in the coming years. They were no sooner home from Mexico than the telephone was being rung by newsmen seeking reaction to all kinds of improbable developments. Clara Padilla was sacked from her post at the shop and fled for a time to her father's home in the United States. The Green Fire shop itself closed after a total of only six months' trading, much to the shame and chagrin of its owner, Danilo Rojas, for whom very few people felt very much sympathy at all. All of that happened during thirty days of deliberations by a tribunal of three judges as to whether Moore should be brought back for trial under an extradition agreement between Britain and Colombia.

That worrying possibility did not recede until the August of 1970 when Captain Jaime Ramirez, Chief of F.2, the special branch of the Colombian police, published evidence of a plot to frame Moore. The intervention of the secret police gave vent to a whole spate of wild stories in the world's Press. There was talk of an unidentified double of Bobby Moore snatching the gems, of the bracelet itself being seen on the Bogota black market, of intervention by Interpol, the FBI and even the CIA.

Moore carefully refrained from commenting on successive rumours as the Colombians tried to find some way of extricating themselves from the case with a minimum of national embarrassment. Instead of extraditing Moore, the judicial triumvirate under Judge Jorge Cardenas Ramirez insisted on Moore and Bobby Charlton reiterating their statements under oath at a British Court. That was duly done at Bow Street Magistrates' Court, London, on December 18th, 1970.

Still the case remained under review for two more years. Then, on November 17th, 1972, Judge Ramirez declared that the charges had been shelved. Moore says: 'The same old voices came on the phone and the same old faces were back on the doorstep in the early hours of the morning wanting to know what I thought.'

'Well, what I thought was that it wasn't good enough because it left a question mark against me that I knew didn't deserve to be there. It wasn't conclusive and I guessed we hadn't heard the last of it. So I more or less kept quiet.'

Sure enough, Judge Ramirez re-opened the case in October 1973 and it was another two years before Moore was let off the hook. On December 2nd, 1975, the Foreign Office sent a letter to Bobby expressing their delight at notification from Colombia that, at last, 'the case could be considered closed for all practical purposes.'

By then Moore had incurred legal expenses approaching £1,000 for a specialist solicitor in international law to handle the London end of the argument. The Foreign Office insistence that the case had come to an end persuaded him the time had come to pass on a bill for the final reckoning to the Football Association.

Yet the conclusion leaves a sour taste in Moore's mouth. 'It's all very well getting a letter saying the case is being dropped for lack of evidence but that's not good enough. It's not what I'm looking for. I want my name cleared. People keep advising me I should let it drop but I don't like the feeling that whenever I walk into a jeweller's to buy a present for Tina I have to keep my hands behind my back and point to the goods with my nose. I don't like being told it would be dodgy for me to go to a certain part of the world in case they arrest me all over again.

'I'm innocent and I want the world to know I'm innocent. It makes me sick to my stomach that some people think I've still got that damn bracelet.'

Oddly, that belief is more powerful in Moore's own country than in Latin America, where they know about such matters. When Bobby resumed training with England that morning after his reunion with Tina, he was approached by Joao Saldanha, immediate past manager of Brazil, who said: 'We all know exactly what happened. It happened to me recently in a different shop in the same hotel. So I locked the door, threw away the key, called in the police and made them try to find what they said was missing. They wanted money but they were not getting any from me. That is what you must do in future.'

'Thanks,' said Moore, 'but I hope it never happens again.' And he resumed training in a manner which amazed and delighted Ramsey.

England's opening match was only two days away. Moore had lost 7lbs, the only visible sign of his acute anxiety under arrest, and would sweat away as much again in the heat of the first match. Ramsey had said little but was privately and deeply concerned about Moore's loss of weight, loss of sleep and loss of five days' acclimatisation to heat and preparation with the team.

The automated perfection of Moore's football was under its heaviest stress. His singlemindedness prevailed. 'Even the training was a relief, an escape from all the pressures and emotion. When you're indoors at home or in a hotel people can reach you with phone calls. When you're in the street people can shout at you about the bracelet. It was marvellous to get back to work. I knew it would be even more of a release to get into an important match.'

By the afternoon of June 1, by the end of what was only Moore's second spell of activity in soaring temperatures, Ramsey was no longer in any doubt about who should captain England against Rumania the following afternoon.

CHAPTER THIRTEEN

Montezuma's Revenge

Modesty, never the most conspicous quality in England's footballers, was virtually a forgotten word among the strutting young peacocks who were defending the World Cup in 1970. The close-cropped champions of '66 had become the *nouveau* aristocracy, preening themselves in their wide ties, flared trousers and belief in their own invincibility. As if that conviction needed reinforcing, Bobby Moore, the prime example of their species, had come unscathed through the green fires of Bogota.

Bring on the world.

'We all knew,' says Bobby, "that we were at least as well prepared, no, probably better prepared for the tournament than any other nation. The acclimatisation had been perfect. It was hot, it was high and it was supposed to be the easiest place in the world to pick up stomach bugs, yet everyone felt in great shape. Even though I'd missed five days with the squad I had no physical problems coping with the heat, so I knew the other lads must be okay.

'I looked around the squad and felt convinced we were stronger than in '66. We had most of the best players from Wembley, with all that experience. We had learned from our mistakes in the European Championship. Now players like Terry Cooper, Alan Mullery, Colin Bell, Allan Clarke and Franny Lee had emerged.

'We all believed we had the best squad in England's history. We all believed we were going to win it again.'

The way they started the tournament convinced a growing number of outsiders. The first test was provided by the hatchet men from Rumania. Moore, as usual, led by example, aloof and disdainful of some wicked tackling. Geoff Hurst, reliably, came up with the only goal. It was a performance of chilling English efficiency which gnawed at the confidence of even the Brazilians.

The Mexicans, who knew in their hearts that even as the host nation their own team's involvement was unlikely to last beyond the quarter-finals, shared the universal affection for Brazil's lyrical football. They took steps to support the cause of their favourite visitors. Or, rather, they took a drive in their motor cars. The Brazilians had come among the Mexicans dispensing smiles, compliments and souvenirs. Sir Alf Ramsey, who as a public relations man would have made a splendid secret agent, presented the face of England resenting the intrusion of the Mexican Press and scowling with suspicion at their food, their weather, even their modes of transport. Brazil v. England on June 7 was to be the showpiece of the Guadalajara group. So, on the night of June 6, hundreds of offended Mexicans took their cars into the streets, encircled the England team's hotel and kept their hands firmly on their hooters. It was, in its way, a modern parallel of one of Ramsey's beloved wagon train scenes. Stoically, the players huddled into back rooms on the top floor, snatched what sleep they could and came out to face the favourites as if nothing had happened.

In most considered opinions, England have never played better than they did that day. By common consent, Bobby Moore produced the paramount performance of his own career. To world-wide acclaim, Gordon Banks defied a header from the imcomparable Pele with a reflex save which has its own place in history. Yet England lost; lost by the only goal on a day when the tall, gangling Jeff Astle might have secured for himself a niche in the folklore of the game by despatching the simplest of scoring chances in first moments on the pitch as a second half substitute.

Nevertheless, there seemed no need for despair. Both teams could still qualify for the quarter-finals and the scenes at the end expressed with warmth and dignity the respect between the greatest footballer of all time and the best defender in the world. Pele and Moore stood bare-chested, exchanging shirts, streaming with the sweat and strain of their classic duel, unable to speak each other's language yet declaring mutual admiration with a hand on each other's shoulder and a slow, shared smile. Such moments restore the faith of the people in a game forever threatened by cynicism and brutality.

Later, Pele said simply: 'Bobby Moore is the best defender I have every played against.'

To Moore, Pele was the ultimate challenge. 'I used to love playing against him because there is no greater satisfaction than impressing against the best in the world. His mere presence on the pitch had to bring out the best in you because only your best could ever be good enough. Pele was the most complete player I've ever seen. Had everything. Two good feet. Magic in the air. Quick. Powerful. Could beat people with skill. Could outrun people. Only 5ft 8in tall yet he seemed a giant of an athlete on the pitch. Perfect balance and impossible vision.

'When you play against people of that ability, at the highest level, for those stakes, you don't have to speak the language to come to know each other. At that time Pele hardly spoke a word of English yet, without thinking, I knew him as a nice, quiet, sincere man; a gentleman and a sportsman. Later I had the privilege of going across to Brazil to see his two retirement games. To me, it was a compliment to be asked to be there, to see what he meant in his own environment, to sit in his home town of Sao Paulo among tens of thousands of people all with tears in their eyes.

'He was the greatest because he could do anything and everything on a football pitch. I remember Saldanha being asked by a Brazilian journalist who was the best goalkeeper in his squad. He said Pele. The man could play in any position. And when he had to, he could take care of himself. England played a mini-World Cup in Brazil in 1964 and we went to watch them play Argentina. they tried to do terrible things to Pele. Had some of the tackles caught him properly they might have crippled him for life. After twenty minutes he waited for one Argentinian to go for him, miles off the ball, and he just laid him out on his back, nose splattered, on the edge of their penalty area. I didn't like the incident but he had to protect himself. He hated having to do it because his concentration was gone from that moment and he did very little more in the game. He looked sad. Yet he remained the greatest of all players, even though he was the most marked man.

'Portugal were not really a violent side but they were so scared of Pele that they kicked him out of the World Cup in England in 1966. He said that if that was what World Soccer was coming to he did not want to know. He would retire. He was a millionaire but· thank goodness he loved the game so much he had to come back. Brazil were always trying to find a replacement. Edu, the Little Bird. Paulo Cesar. There were great players like Gerson, Rivellino and Jairzinho. But there was only ever one Pele.

'I like to think our admiration was mutual because I never resorted to foul tactics against him. It would have been an insult to myself. The way I was brought up to play the game was as a contest of skill and ability and thought...unless someone takes too many liberties. Then you've got to do something like Pele did that day against Argentina. But at the highest level it should be a test of ability, not who is the biggest and strongest and kicks the hardest. It was the right way with me and Pele. The best man wins.'

When they left the pitch that day in Guadalajara, both men believed that one of football's most noble contests would be rejoined in the Final. That was the way of the draw if they finished first and second in their qualifying group.

England duly finished runners up to Brazil. In the last match of the group they had only to draw with Czechoslovakia, who had been beaten by both Brazil and Rumania. In the event they eked out a cautious victory by virtue of Allan Clarke's clinical penalty. In the sudden-death quarter-finals, fate pitched them once more against West Germany.

Any worthwhile attempt to chart the decline of England's football under Ramsey must begin that day, 14 June 1970. It was a day which began in a mood of arrogant optimism. The memory of the '66 victory sustained England on the long and dusty road from Guadalajara to Leon, where the Germans had won their group. Helmut Schoen, West Germany's gentle St. Bernard of a manager, appeared to have only his team's limited familiarity with the Leon surroundings in his favour.

Schoen had no way of knowing that morning that Montezuma's revenge for England's disdainful attitude towards Mexican cooking was entirely concentrated on the stomach of Gordon Banks, the most daunting of goalkeepers. Even the England players ignored the first warning sign when Banks first complained of gasto-enteritis the night before.

Moore recalls: 'In all that time away there had been only one other hint of sickness. Peter Osgood missed a morning's training with a mild tummy upset. Like the rest of the lads I was sure Banksie would be all right on the day. Sure enough, he said he felt better next morning. I forgot all about it until we were getting on the coach to drive to the stadium, no more than an hour and a half before the kick off. Suddenly Gordon had felt bad again over lunch. Suddenly we were on the coach and no Banksie.

'Even then it didn't seem that important. We all felt sorriest for Gordon at missing a World Cup quarter-final but we knew we were in good shape and everyone was still bubbling with confidence. We'd put on the best performance of our lives against Brazil and the Germans weren't quite in their class.'

Peter Bonetti, Chelsea's cat of a goalkeeper, deputised for Banks, as he had done several times in the previous four years. After the first hour of the scheduled ninety minutes there was still no reason to doubt that England could live up to their own expectations. Mullery and Peters scored the goals which had been missing against Brazil and Moore was as certain as any man has ever been that he was in a World Cup semi-final. 'We'd done everything right. The performance was almost as good as against Brazil, and this time we'd got the goals. That had been the only question mark against us until then. The game was won. Done with. Over. England 2-0 up with twenty minutes to go could not be beaten.

'We'd been proving for years that our defence was unbreakable. No one had put two or three goals past us since 1967.'

In the stands, where the fans at such matches rake up the old political emnities far more bitterly than the players, the forest of German flags hung limp before the jubilant, taunting Union Jacks.

Ramsey, too, believed the field was won, believed it so firmly that again he let his suspect instinct for a substitution run away with him. Bobby Charlton had, as usual, exercised his restrictive influence on Franz Beckenbauer. Martin Peters had once more asserted himself as a ghostly goalscoring threat to be forgotten at Germany's peril. Yet Ramsey warmed-up Colin Bell and Norman Hunter, strong men and true, to take their places. Sir Alf was in the act of bringing the World Cup crashing about his ears. The Germans, for the first time, were able to get close enough to Bonetti to expose a remarkable fissure in his concentration.

Even Moore's powers of calculation were defeated as it all went wrong. 'We were two up. We might have been three up because one cross went a foot past a post with Franny Lee standing watching because he thought it was going in.

'Alf has taken stick for those substitutions but at the moment he was putting on Norman and Colin it seemed right. You figured he was thinking it worth sparing Bobby Charlton the latest twenty minutes because the semi-final was only three days away. Bobby was no youngster and it would have looked bad if such a key player had seemed jaded after an unnecessary twenty minutes in that heat. Norman seemed ideal for making sure we locked them out. Bellie was strong, powerful, just the man to run a beaten team into the ground.

'But when you thought about it, Bobby was one of the fittest men in the squad. Always had been. Loved to play and could play all day in an oven if you asked him. You could tell Bobby didn't want to go off and as soon as he walked away it was like a ton weight had been lifted off Beckenbauer. They hadn't had a kick at the ball for seventy minutes but suddenly Franz starts coming at us for the first time. They also made a substitution of their own, bringing on Grabowski. And right off he was turning Terry Cooper at left back. From home and dry one minute, we're in all sorts of trouble the next.'

Grabowski, of course, was torturing a tired man. Ramsey had still not found any wingers and his 4-4-2 formation demanded a commitment from Cooper and right back Keith Newton to make run upon murderous run through the heat into space on the flanks. Cooper was still labouring back as Beckenbauer, on one of his first forward runs, was forced out to that side of the penalty area by Mullery. Beckenbauer's shot made the first moderate demand on Bonetti to do justice to his hours of personal dedication and preparation.

When all the debates about substitutions are over and you ask Bobby Moore to answer the mystery of this defeat, he does not relish pointing the finger at the likeable and highly talented Bonetti. But point the finger, he does. 'As Mullers pushed Franz out to the corner of the 18-yard box there was no cover from the left. But I still felt happy about the position. It's not a good angle to shoot from and when Franz hit the shot it was nothing special. Peter has gone on record as saying that the goal was not his fault, that it was a good shot, that he couldn't do much about it. Now I'm not a specialist goalkeeper but I do know a good shot from an ordinary shot and that wasn't anything like one of Beckenbauer's better shots. The ball went under Peter into the middle of the net. If Peter's going to be honest with himself he must be disappointed. I know how bad the rest of us felt. Psychologically it was a desperate goal to concede. If Franz had gone past a couple of people and smashed it into the roof of the net you'd have put up your hands and said what a great goal and got on with the game.

'But it wasn't like that. It was the sort of goal which cut into your confidence from the back. It became a big psychological barrier for us to overcome and it gave the Germans hope. From that moment it was one way traffic towards our goal. A total turnabout.'

Tactically as well as psychologically England were in trouble. The various substitutions all seemed to be conspiring against Ramsey. Grabowski's instant mastery of Cooper caught Hunter between two crises. The problem at left back was serious enough to stop him pushing forward and defying Beckenbauer with physique where Charlton had stifled him with skill and reputation. Yet he could not drop too deep. So he was trapped doing little more than fill space on the left hand side just in front of the defence.

Again the Germans scored a late, late goal to take England to extra time in a major World Cup match. This time Germany's beloved Uwe Seeler was the scorer. Again it was a goal full of blame in Moore's dismayed eyes. 'There was an iffy clearance and not everybody got out quickly enough and Seeler was left deep at the back but still onside. So they lobbed the ball back in. Only hopefully. Really it was too far. On any ordinary day any player in the world would have given it up. But not in a match like that. Uwe did a feat, straining to get his head to the ball. He admitted he had no intention of scoring. He was just trying to keep the ball in play. Yet it flopped over Bonetti into the net. Peter's concentration might have been adrift. '

That suspicion stemmed from the team's appreciation of Bonetti's personal qualities as a genuine family man. Tina Moore, like the Hurst and Peters women, was already a seasoned traveller, having supported her husband in various corners of the globe. Bobby knew Tina had quickly put the Bogota business behind her and would readily cope with any of the myriad problems that can present themselves during a long stay in a foreign continent. Mexico, however, was Frances Bonetti's first travelling adventure of its kind without the constant companionship of her husband and Bonetti may well have been distracted by concern for his wife's well being. If so, it was the very problem Ramsey had feared might arise from the presence of the players' wives in the wings of the World Cup arena.

Ninety minutes earlier it would have been hard to find a more confident group of people anywhere on earth than the England football team. At the start of extra time, all those permutations of doubt were whirling through their minds. There was never the slightest chance that they would go back out to win the match a second time, the way they had at Wembley four years earlier.

Moore's memories of the killer blow are no happier. 'We were doing all we could to stop it but somehow you knew it would come. Peter and Brian Labone were beaten by a ball going backwards and forwards over their heads in the goalmouth. Gerd Müller poked it in. The old story with Müller. He hadn't done a thing all game but he got the winner. Kept on doing it after that until they won the World Cup in 1974.

'I don't remember walking to the dressing room. Just being there. Nobody said anything. Certainly not Bonetti. No point. It was his last cap. Just silence. Looking at each other. Little Ballie stood there with tears in his eyes.'

Outside it was the turn of the English supporters to suffer the jibes. Yet West Germany proved to have defeated themselves as well as England. The physical demands of extra time cost them dearly three days later. In an astonishing semi-final against Italy, another team who seldom gave away goals, they were again required to play an extra half hour and this time lost 4-3.

Moore stayed to see the tournament through. He went to watch the final in Mexico City's monumental Aztec Stadium convinced that Italy would, in their turn, be physically spent. 'I felt Brazil only had to turn up to win the cup. Yet after an hour it was one goal each and I thought Christ, they might get beaten. But I'd also gone there thinking it should be England playing Brazil and believing England would have won. I was sure they would have been worried about us because we'd come so close in Guadalajara. Every game against them I felt we might beat them and I couldn't understand how we'd failed to do it in half a dozen attempts.'

As a spectator, he found the reason during the last half hour of the 1970 World Cup Final 'It looked like Brazil would get caught out but suddenly they found that little bit extra. Just as they had against us down the years. Boom, boom, boom. They rifled in three more goals.

'That was the trouble with them. Always something special in reserve. Pele was a lot to do with that. Most people have teir own special memory of him. In that match. There was the first goal when he curled himself up around a difficult cross and made scoring look easy. Earlier in the tournament there had been the dummy to let the ball run one side of the goalkeeper while he went round the other. That was brilliant even though he screwed the final shot across the face of the goal. Against Uruguay he had picked up a loose clearance on the half way line, turned and shot just over the bar – with their goalkeeper stranded around the penalty spot. Even as a pro with a vantage point in the stand you wondered at first what he was doing. Then you were lost in admiration for the man's vision and appreciation of a situation.'

Moore took those memories and his wife with him to a soothing sunshine holiday in Acapulco. There, with a delicious sense of irony, Tina presented him with a gold identity bracelet as a loving reminder of their headline affair. As he toyed with that memento, Bobby began asking himself for the first time: 'How could Alf have left me in Bogota?'

Friends
and
Superstars

Above Bobby and Tina toast the great Eusebio of Portugal. *Below* A soccer christening: *from left* Geoff Hurst, Noel Cantwell and son, Bobby and Tina.

ve With Jimmy Greaves, Sean Connery and Yul Brynner. *Below* Grand Masters of soccer: Bobby and Franz
xenbauer.

With Ronnie Corbett . . .

TORS
OWED
GE AREA
PERFORM
MIO

and Perry Como.

Above Bobby and Ann Jones — Sportsman and Sportswoman of the Year in 1966. *Below* With Pele — friend and rival ding West Ham out of the Wembley tunnel: Moore and Ron Greenwood.

'Now, let's not start talking about who is the greatest . . .'

CHAPTER FOURTEEN

The Doctrine According to Sir Alf

It was no more than a wisp of disappointment which drifted across the shimmering skyline of Bobby Moore's holiday. It did nothing to impede the sun's healing progress through the heavenly days in Acapulco. It never once clouded the waters of the personal pool in which England's beaten champion periodically cooled his scorched limbs.

Yet it nagged his consciousness about the manager who had been knighted by his Queen for success built upon unquestioned loyalty to his men.

Loyalty was Sir Alf Ramsey's byword. The fierce devotion of manager to players and players to manager had proved to be England's most enduring quality. The lads believed good old Alf would always support them. So they might be off form, so they might be beaten, but the lads would never knowingly give good old Alf anything less than their best on the pitch.

Loyalty was Ramsey's most powerful weapon and he had used it to greatest effect in charging Bobby Moore with the captaincy. The world of football at once identified certain similarities of nature as solid reasons for the choice. Both men confronted responsibility with an impeccable, impenetrable image. Both appeared cold. Both seemed calculating. Both certainly wanted to win.

Ramsey said of Moore: 'Bobby is an extension of myself on the field.' Moore says of Ramsey: 'Alf chose me because I projected on the field the qualities he impressed on the players off the pitch. We were both calm, methodical, deliberate and kept our cool. We both ached for success.'

The destiny of both men had been linked from the day of Ramsey's first match as England manager, in Paris in '63, when he had turned his back on defeat to take the seat next to Moore on the team coach. They were interdependent and it was more than coincidence that their international careers both ended some ten years later, after Ramsey chose to break their link for the first time in an important match.

So how had Ramsey found it in his heart to leave Moore to his fate in Bogota?

The availability of Dr. Andrew Stephen and Denis Follows, the need to be with the squad, the irrational attempt to stave off publicity were all reasons. Yet the more Bobby weighed them against his own predicament, the less he could accept them as an answer.

'If there was a man I believed was as important to me as Alf said I was to him, then there's no way I could get on the plane without him. I can only think that, at the time, he did not appreciate how complicated it was going to become.'

The thought jarred on Bobby's image of Alf, an image which had been hardening ever since that bus ride in Paris. 'He started asking me questions then about the way things were done with England. And he didn't stop even though there was a man on the plane home who I thought should have been playing for England, could still have been captain and would have answered all the questions.

'Johnny Haynes had gone over to watch the match in Paris with a group of fans and they were on our plane coming home. We'd lost 5-2 and the punters were shouting down the plane "Can't leave him out now, Alf," and "All right, John, must be back for the next one." It was as embarrassing for John as it was for Alf but it seemed to make sense.'

Moore's potential, however, excited Ramsey more than even Haynes' reputation. He continued their dialogue through successive meetings, tried him as captain in Czechoslovakia and had him established in the job within a year. Even the drinking escapade prior to the 1964 visit to Portugal was turned to advantage.

The Press did not begin to suspect a showdown until after Moore and his friends had redeemed themselves with a 4-3 win in Lisbon and the summer tour had moved on to New York. When the captain was left out of the England side which beat the U.S.A. 10-0, questions were asked, whispers of a drinking spree overheard and some newspapers published the mistaken conclusion that an indiscretion in America had forced a rift between Ramsey and Moore.

In reality, Ramsey had promised the supporting members of the England cast at least one appearance as reward for backing up the stars on tour, and the easy game in New York was the obvious consolation for the reserves. Moore returned for Little World Cup games against Brazil, Portugal and Argentina. After a close-season for due consideration. Ramsey was ready to offer Moore a permanent partnership. The deal was cemented in an hotel in Belfast in October 1964, on the eve of a 4-3 victory over Northern Ireland.

'Alf just asked me to join him for a few minutes,' says Bobby, 'and we talked about being ready to commit ourselves to the objective of winning the World Cup in 1966. We sorted out our priorities on and off the pitch and agreed we would back each other up. Alf made it clear he expected the captain as well as the manager to conduct himself in a responsible manner and that was that. No problem as far as I was concerned. On we go.

'All the lads felt already that he was a players' man. We were attracted to his loyalty. He shared our desire for success. Really, that's all any players ever want. Success. If you win things and get your rewards for them, you're happy. Alf's first thought was for his players so there was never any problem about getting the players to do what was asked of them.

'What more can you want from a manager than being successful? What more can a manager want from a player? We both had the same incentives so we had a deal.'

Almost unconsciously, Moore was forging the very relationship with Ramsey which he had resisted so resolutely with his club manager, Ron Greenwood. It was less obtrusive, yet closely akin to the liaison between Greenwood and Johnny Byrne. Even now, Moore is not sure to what extent he influenced team selection, but he does know that his counsel was sought and frequently acted upon. It is a tribute to the discretion of both men that the rest of the players never once suspected, let alone resented, their captain's often unwitting part in deciding their places in the team. Careless talk could easily have cost games.

'Looking back,' says Moore, 'Alf started drawing me into it that day in Paris. From then on he asked as many questions about players as about anything else.'

Sometimes, the questions were about Bobby's friends and the answers measured the strength of Moore's ruthless control over his emotions. Although it was not his final word, there is no doubt that Moore was aware of the decisions to omit Alan Ball from two early matches in the 1966 World Cup Finals and then, harder still, not to recall Jimmy Greaves, the closest of all his footballing friends, for the Final itself.

If he needed an excuse for hardening his heart. it was provided by the philosphy he shares with many successful men in Soccer: 'When did a team of nice guys ever win anything?'

Ramsey was of a similar persuasion; partly, no doubt, because he hailed from a similar background. Both were born and bred on the working-class borders of Essex and East London and after the World

Cup had been won in '66 Moore, Ramsey and Martin Peters, all sons of the borough of Barking, were called to the town hall to be honoured by the Mayor.

Moore recalls: 'Alf was no better or worse than Martin and myself because he was born just next door in Dagenham. That's why he was always at his happiest in the company of his players, his own people. Left alone with us he could relax, share in the jokes. He always bought the drinks. When he was at Ipswich that was the be-all and end-all for him. Then it was England. The trouble with being England team manager is that you spend so long away from your team, planning to get them together, that when you are with them you have to use and savour every second of it. When he was knighted nothing changed. The players were delighted for him but some of them felt a bit strange when they met him again for the first time after he became Sir Alf. Someone said: "What do we call you now?" and he said: "I'm still Alf, aren't I?"'.

So England played on to 1970, in proletarian harmony. Even in the hours after their impossible defeat by West Germany, Ramsey still appeared to be putting players before even himself. Moore says: 'He never said a great deal about what went wrong. He just went round trying to console this player and that player. He was more worried about consoling people than finding reasons.'

So it was left until poolside in Acapulco for Moore to define his own vague sense of disillusionment. Whatever the reason, Alf *had* left him in Bogota and Bobby decided: 'Despite what the outside world thought, I would never regard myself as being the same as Alf. Not at all alike. The only Alf I knew was the football manager. We were together maybe a total of a month or two out of every year, in different spells of a few days here, a week in this country or that country. That didn't mean I knew the person.

'Alf never drew Tina and me into his social company with his wife. Tina had flown out to Mexico on the same plane as Lady Vicky and said she seemed very nice but had her own friend with her and stayed reasonably detached.

'It became quite clear to me that Alf and I were different personalities outside our working relationship. Apart from football, Alf would never talk in depth about anything at all. In company the conversation might flit across the usual small talk about cars and holidays but would invariably settle on football. Socially, I like people who are interested in what you do but can also relax you and take your mind off your own line of business once in a while.

'Alf had just two worlds, his players and his home. And they were kept strictly apart.'

Nevertheless, Moore was close enough to Ramsey often enough to study the manager the Press dubbed Old Stoneface. His conclusions are remarkable and their simplicity suggests they touch on the truth of a man who remained an enigma throughout his lengthy period in the full glare of publicity.

'For years everyone's been busy trying to pin down the real Alf Ramsey. They look at that great photograph of everyone else on the bench leaping up into the air when England scored in the World Cup Final and there's Alf stopping Harold Shepherdson from running onto the pitch to congratulate us. Just sitting there. And they say that's Alf behind his mask, being conscious of his position. Behaving correctly. Suppressing his emotion. They say he wasn't like that when he used to go to the greyhound racing with the lads in the old days and they say they wonder what he's really like now.

'Well, I say that the serious, responsible Alf is the real Alf. Without trying to or meaning to, he's fooled everyone. It was in the old days that he wasn't being himself. I've talked to some of the old players he used to knock about with and they'll tell you that although he used to go to the dogs or in the pub, it wasn't really his scene. He went because his one or two pals were going but he stood back a bit. They remember him changing, drifting away from them. Well I'd bet my mortgage that one day he was on the train home and he thought: "I don't need all that, it's not me." He took elocution lessons and out came the real Alf who everyone finds so baffling.'

One memorable television interview, conducted for the BBC by Ian Wooldridge, articulate sports columnist of the *Daily Mail*, provides supporting evidence.

Sir Alf and Lady Vicky revealed that in the event of a marital tiff they would always, in the end, 'shake hands and make up'.

Yes – shake hands.

Not that Ramsey was devoid of feeling. If Moore is right in his judgment, then I am one of the many journalists who, in ignorance of his sensitivity, must have cut Sir Alf to the quick.

'Unless you knew him closely,' says Moore, 'you would not have noticed when he was hurt. He had great control of his emotions and never showed it outwardly when he was under stress. He would just carry on. Yet you knew he was hurt. Alf would be deeply upset if a member of the Press expressed a damaging opinion, especially if the writer had no way of knowing the full story. He took all criticism of England very personally and very deeply.'

Many of the attendant Press corps felt that if Ramsey suffered through their ignorance of detail, it was Ramsey's own fault for withholding information. Moore says: 'I'm sure he felt he was co-operating as fully as possible. His priority was for England to win matches. He felt the English Press should want England to win and should understand if sometimes he couldn't organise the day to suit them, or release certain information which might have created problems for him.'

As Moore was sitting by his Mexican swimming pool and beginning to question Ramsey in his own mind, so the Press criticism of England's manager was intensifying. They pinned the blame for losing the World Cup on his substitutions against West Germany. They jumped down his throat when he arrived home saying England had nothing to learn from the 1970 Brazilians.

Even Moore was startled by Ramsey's exaggerated chauvinism: 'Alf explained later that he meant to say there was nothing new about the Brazilians that we didn't know already. But even that was strange. You've always got something to learn in this game. From anyone. Maybe even from the waiters kicking about on the beach if you're sitting watching them. You've got to be open-minded enough to benefit from the changes in the game.

'Alf also had plenty to learn from the Brazilians about public relations. The truth is that Alf doesn't particularly like foreigners and he was very wary of Mexico. So we went in with our own meat and other foodstuffs and even shipped over our own team coach to drive about in. The locals wanted to know what was wrong with Mexican food and what was wrong with the coaches they were supplying for all the teams in the Finals. So they hated us from the start. The Brazilians did it the other way round. Arrived early and sat on hotel balconies waving to the crowds, signing autographs, singing and smiling. *Then* they moved into hiding and smuggled in all their own foodstuffs.

'Alf was more honest and straightforward than that and did not forsee how things would backfire on him. One of his strengths, really, was his overwhelming belief in England. He honestly believed we had the best players in the world and all we had to do was go out and prove it. In many ways there was nothing wrong with that. In Mexico, Bobby Charlton and myself went to visit the Brazilian camp. There was a pool surrounded by rooms and it was siesta time when we arrived. Quiet and empty. One of their players saw we were there and suddenly they all came chattering out of their doors. We'd gone there to ask them about the marvellous techniques in their football and we ended up bombarded with questions about our physical preparations. They were the people everyone looks upon as the best players in the world. Yet they wanted to learn from us.

'Alf's strength was his organisation. He performed that remarkable feat at Ipswich of going from the Third Division to the First Division Championship in successive seasons simply by getting the best out of the players at his disposal. That was the way he carried on with England.'

Malcolm Allison, standard bearer for the thrusting young technocrats of Soccer coaching, was among Ramsey's critics and said: 'Alf is a good manager of a bad team, but a bad manager of a good team.'

Moore said: 'I understand what Malcolm meant but I only agree with the first part of it. Alf could set up a team of players to be difficult to beat. But I don't ever remember him discouraging players from expressing their skill.'

Nevertheless, Allison's criticism represented one of the many furies at Ramsey's heels as England inched into decline. In the end, not even his knighthood, nor the record of his golden years could spare him the sack by the Football Association for failing to qualify for the 1974 World Cup Finals.

Ramsey had already discarded Moore in his doomed attempt to overcome Poland in the qualifying group. Bobby greeted his manager's consequent demise as inevitable: 'Football has a habit of running in ten-year cycles and when you come to the end of that period it takes a very flexible and adaptable man to move out of the pattern which has been successful for him. The cycle turned against Alf. Everyone in the world knew what he and his teams were doing. It was predictable, but Alf still believed it was right. But there comes a time for reviving spirit and interest by doing things a little differently.

'Alf was inflexible and I knew there would have to be a change of manager. The problem seemed to me to be finding the right way of doing it. That was where the F.A. let Alf down. Maybe they should have done it as soon as he failed to qualify for the World Cup. Not let it dwindle on for a couple more matches.

'Maybe they were a bit in awe of Alf and never really got on with the job. They let him pick a squad to go on a summer tour in Europe, which was a funny thing to do if they didn't want him to be the manager any longer.

'It was right for both parties, for Alf and for England, to make a change. But neither party seemed to see the position clearly. I understand they finally gave Alf the chance to resign but he refused. He said he wanted to go on to the World Cup in Argentina in 1978. That would have been one enormous challenge for him because they still hate him there for calling them animals in '66 and they still believe the only reason they ever lost to England was because Rattin was sent off.

'Alf had taken stick for saying that, been hurt by the criticism, and even by '74 he still couldn't see what he'd done wrong. The pressures on him would have been greater than ever. He couldn't see how very difficult it would be for him in Argentina. So they had to give him his cards. It was a messy way to end an era.'

Moore at once sent a telegram of condolence and encouragement to Ramsey. Later he sent a letter saying:

'I am not so much sorry that you have left the job, but for the manner in which it happened. We had great times together. You made it great for the players. Best wishes in the future.'

It was simple and truthful. That May, Ramsey emerged from hiding from the media he detested and replied to Moore in kind:

'My wife is of the same opinion as yourself...a blessing in disguise.

'I will conclude by thanking you for all you have contributed to English football and myself, no-one could have done more.'

A long, reflective year after he received Ramsey's letter, Moore was summering in South Africa, financing another exotic holiday by making guest appearances for Hellenic, the Cape Town club, who were being managed by his old sparring partner from West Ham, Johnny Byrne.

One slow evening, like good old friends, they stood together on the long brow of Signal Hill, sharing a can of lager, and feasting their eyes on a huge sunset which transformed the sea into an ocean of rippling flame.

'You know something, Mooro. The players may have been lucky to have Alf but he was even luckier to have one or two of you.'

'How do you mean?'

'Tactics. Fine points. Corner kicks and the other set pieces. He'd ask your opinion and always defer to you. I can hear his team talk now. The same old team talk.'

'Yeah, Budgie, so can I. You know I could give Alf's team talk to any side right now. A bit about the opposition's pattern of play, a few of their strengths and weaknesses. Not much but enough to do his duty. Then on to: "They're more worried about us than we are about them. You're the best players in the world. The fittest. The strongest. Go out and win it."'

'Let's face it, Bob. He didn't hold a candle to Greenwood on knowledge of the game. Not in the same street. Between them they'd have made a good manager. Ron's knowledge and Alf's way with the players.'

Moore pondered a marriage of his two managers. The huge,

darkening sun dipped behind velvet folds of night on the horizon.

'Not bad,' he said. 'But not a patch on you and me, old son. Not a patch on you and me.'

CHAPTER FIFTEEN

Read All About It

Neither Sir Alf nor Ron Greenwood will be overjoyed to read that their prize pupil now considers himself to be their master.

Yet no man easily acquires such absolute belief in himself as Bobby Moore revealed that musky evening in South Africa. Each layer of self-confidence is tempered in the heat of crisis. And in 1970, a year which was in many ways the axis of his life, the tests of character came hard on each other's heels.

The leaden feet of Colombian justice dragged from one development to another long after the World Cup was lost. Then a fresh drama checked Moore on the brink of a new English football season.

It was August and the time for sweating away the indulgences of the summer was almost over. Long days spent pounding the practice field had flattened the most stubborn of West Ham's stomachs and that tell-tale sheen of fitness was back on Moore's skin. The final polish was applied in light training on the morning of the day West Ham were due in Bournemouth to sharpen their skills in a friendly match.

At 11 a.m. the coach was warming its engine in the car park when the telephone rang in Greenwood's office. The local police were in possession of a letter posted in Birmingham to the London *Evening Standard*.

Yes, it was anonymous, like most such correspondence. But no, this time it did not look like the work of a crank. This time it was a warning, not a threat. Tina Moore was about to be kidnapped, perhaps with one or both of Bobby's children. The ransom would be £10,000.

The team coach awaited the arrival of the police and gave Bobby time to read the letter 'Before I picked up that piece of paper I believed it would be just another nutcase. You get them all the time. But this one was different. The writer said he couldn't give his name because he was wanted by the police on another charge. But he'd heard the kidnap plot through his underworld contacts and felt we'd had enough troubles and

138

wanted to tip us off. He was posting his letter on the way out of the country. It was sensible and legible and I knew at once I couldn't go to Bournemouth.'

As the rest of the team set off for the South Coast, Moore was hurried to his Chigwell home by Bert Wickstead, a detective who was promoted later to heavier dramas with Scotland Yard's murder squad. Wickstead posted a 24-hour watch at the front, the rear and inside the house. For the second time that year, Moore was living under police guard.

This time it was for his own protection and this time it was not only Bobby but also his wife and children who could not set foot outside the house without a bodyguard. 'Everytime I went training one of the guys came with me. Whenever Tina went shopping she had a policeman to carry her basket. The kids had detectives to take them down the road to the sweet shop For the first forty eight hours it seemed very strange having a procession of policemen coming through your own home. There were nine of them a day. But again they became part of the family. You start making tea for six without thinking. They're playing football with the kids in the garden, they play cards with youand watch television with you and drink your lager. One of the night duty lads took to sleeping in a hammock and in the early hours you'd hear him fall out, crashing to the floor, screaming and cursing. They always answered the door. When Tina or I answered the phone, they picked up the extension simultaneously.'

The kept it all secret for the first five days, the period the police deemed to be the most dangerous. There was not a whisper to the Press until after Bobby had played the first League match of the season.

For that occasion, on 15 August 1970, West Ham were required to make the short journey across north east London to Tottenham Hotspur. They made the trip without their captain. 'The police forbade me to travel down to West Ham and then over to Spurs on the team coach. So we all went across in my car. Me and three bodyguards driving into the Tottenham car park. During the game one stayed with the car, another sat in the dressing room and the third fellow was out on the track round the pitch. Then we went for a drink with the rest of the team and they loved it. Best job they'd had in a long time.'

At home in Chigwell, Tina had come to terms with the problems of feeding a small private police force. She says: 'At first it was a shock to realise we had been singled out for something horrible like that. But trying to feed all those hefty fellows gave me something else to worry about right from the start. Most of them had enormous appetites and I ran up a huge catering bill during the ten days they had us under guard.

On top of that, while they were stopping someone making off with one of the family, they went and kidnapped our nanny.'

Like most women, Tina fondly believes that her female intuition and belief in astrology make her half way to being clairvoyant. She continues the story with relish. 'One of the detectives on duty outside in the garden was a nice-looking boy called Jeff and I said to Pauline: "See that feller out there? You're going to marry him." She laughed, but sure enough a couple of days later he asked her out to dinner. Pauline refused but I told her not to be so silly and so she went. Even when she came back from the first date she said he was too old. She was eighteen and there was six years difference. But he asked her out again and, lo and behold, they were married inside a year.'

Tina's instinct was put to a more serious test later that year. Bobby had left the house at lunchtime for a Saturday afternoon match at West Ham when the telephone rang and Tina answered.

'Mrs. Moore?'

'Yes.'

'I just want to tell you that your husband is going to be shot during the match today.'

Again the tone of the communique was flat, unexcited, unlike the usual babbling of the cranks who force star footballers, like most public personalities, to keep changing their ex-directory phone numbers and only ever answer 'Hello.'

Quickly, Tina dialled the ground only to be told that the match had already started. At once, she rang the police and again a squad car was sent hurrying to West Ham. By the time they arrived, Bobby was already leading the team into the second half. He played out the game, unaware of the uniformed and plain clothes men fanning out round the pitch. But at the final whistle he was suddenly surrounded by police in the middle of the pitch.

Bobby looked round them and said: 'Look lads, I've probably played better but I wasn't that bad. Surely Ron Greenwood's not having me arrested.'

He had been bustled to the dressing room before he was told: 'Sorry about that, but your wife received a phone call saying you were going to be shot from the stands.'

'Oh,' said Bobby. 'Well if he tried it he must be a worse shot than I am. Who's coming to protect me at the Black Lion?'

The police settled for seeing Moore safely away from the ground once the crowd had dispersed. Yet, like the kidnap threat, the incident left its mark. In a quiet corner of herself, Tina is almost as relieved when Bobby returns from a match as when the children come home safely from an outing. She says: 'All these things prey on your mind a little. You've got to accept that Bobby's got his life to lead and his job to do. But I'm always very cautious with the children now. For a long time I would never dream of letting Roberta or Dean go to play in the park like other children. They didn't go out of the house without I knew their movements exactly. I let them visit other children's houses but I always insisted there must be a grown up to keep an eye on them. Every time a new au pair arrived she was told about the kidnap threat. I'd frighten her a bit to make her realise that the children must never stray away from the house or garden. It was confining for the children but better than the alternative.'

The Moores accept that fame brings penalties as well as rewards. They remind themselves that for every problem there is a pleasure, like going to Buckingham Palace in the New Year of 1967 to receive Bobby's O.B.E.

That is one of his more treasured experiences. 'There were about 150 people there to get their awards that morning and I don't think one of us knew any of the others. You're all shown into this grand ante-room and told what to do when you file into the hall. You come in from one side. Stand in front of the Queen. Bow your head. Take two or three paces forwards and she pins the medal on you. Two or three paces back. Bow your head and file off the other side.'

It was less than a year since Bobby had collected the 1966 World Cup from Her Majesty. This time his hands were scrupulously clean and he remembered the conversation.

'Well done on winning the World Cup. I saw the game and enjoyed it very much. It was wonderful for us.'

'Thank you very much indeed.'

Not quite up to the standard of debate at the Oxford Union, perhaps, but Moore was suitably impressed. 'The Queen is a stunning woman. When she smiles she really does light up. It can't be easy to light up for 150 people a morning and remember the right remark for each one of them. I mean, what if she congratulated some professor on winning the World Cup Final?'

There should have been no worries on that count. For Bobby stood out not only as the youngest and fittest man in the company but as one of the few wearing an ordinary lounge suit. He recalls: 'All my life really I've liked to dress as casually as any occasion will allow. That's always been my style and the Palace requested you to wear morning suit or dark lounge suit. So I just put on my best suit. When I got there, though, the vast majority were in morning dress and I regretted not wearing a morning suit. I felt not quite right.'

Improperly dressed or not, Bobby and Tina posed happily for the newspaper photographers waiting eagerly outside the Palace gates.

That in itself was an event. For, like most leading sportsmen, Bobby Moore lives uneasily with the Press. As a body, footballers resent the intrusion into their private lives, react to adverse criticism by doubting the right and the technical knowledge of the journalist to sit in judgment, lose respect for any writer who misplaces or exaggerates praise, and withdraw trust at the first hint of betrayal.

As one who spends his working life walking that tightrope, I can be no more objective than Moore himself about the problems of co-operation and communication between professional players and professional writers.

Simply, he expects the right in these pages to express his subjective view of a conflict which has for too long been damaging the game.

Perhaps sadly, it is not the inspired Scottish rhetoric of *The Observer's* Hugh McIlvanney which sticks most clearly in Bobby's mental cuttings book, nor Geoffrey Green's lilting appreciations in *The Times*, nor Bernard Joy's cautious and complimentary analyses for the *Evening Standard*. What then? No, not my own contributions to the *Daily Mail*, not even the ghosted columns of his own views in the *Daily Mirror* which were a labour of love for Nigel Clarke.

Rather, Moore remembers the words which wounded his pride or aggravated his problems.

'Certain people,' he says, 'will never qualify for co-operation from me. Tina would have me row with them but I choose to give them nothing without being rude. Sometimes I'm amazed that writers who have slagged you off, written unkind things that have really hurt, have the cheek to walk up to you as if nothing has happened. I don't want to know them. But I won't give them the satisfaction of knowing I'm upset. I just fob them off. They never have the chance with me of going back to their editors with a story that the England captain lost his temper with them or refused to talk to them.'

Brian James, who in 1971 was football correspondent of the *Daily Mail*, was as close as any journalist to West Ham for several years yet incurred Moore's displeasure 'for being the first to blow up the Blackpool affair'. Moore says: 'Seeing something like that hit the headlines was to me unbelievable. Then there were so many contrasting stories in different papers. Quotes from the hall porter that we were supposed to have come in at three in the morning with hostesses and drinking champagne. I had to ring Tina and tell her not to believe half what she read in the papers.

'It still put a strain on the marriage. At the time Tina was due to take Roberta on a skiing holiday and I drove them up to Luton airport. All the cameras were there. They could chase me as much as they liked but I didn't think it was fair to hound my wife and daughter.'

Mike Langley of the *Sunday People* is on the blacklist 'mostly for digging up whatever facts he could on some financial difficulties of mine, without speaking to me. I only talked to the man at the time Fulham were having that cup run to Wembley as a personal favour to our manager, Alec Stock.'

David Miller, once of the *Sunday Telegraph*, more latterly with the *Daily Express*, is marked down for minimal co-operation 'for gloating over my mistake in the World Cup match in Poland.'

Moore's attitude to the national Press owes something to the suspicion of journalists which is latent in his West Ham club manager Greenwood and blatant in his England manager Ramsey.

Even as Moore's biographer, I cannot be certain that he holds me in any higher esteem than simply the writer he believed to be the best available to collaborate on this book.

Some of Moore's pet hates are rooted in 1966 'when none of the Press believed we could win the World Cup until after we'd beaten Argentina but then they all started waving Union Jacks'.

Others concern his front page exploits 'when people came on strong with the headlines without trying to understand my feelings and very often without knowing the true facts'.

All that illustrates the inevitable conflict of interests between footballers and football writers. The men on Moore's proscribed list were all doing their jobs to the immense satisfaction of their newspapers.

One or two of them have contributed to an improvement in the standards of football journalism which is evident to most of us in Fleet Street and to which even Moore will admit.

Ironically, Bobby might even have gone into the print himself. 'It was the best paid trade open to me even at the time I got the opportunity to become a footballer.' And among the trophies he covets most are the Footballer of the Year award bestowed on him by the writers association, and an exquisite Capi de Monte clock presented to him in Turin in 1973 by those of us who reported his record 107th international appearance.

'Both those gestures,' he says, 'brought a lump to my throat.'

It had been with very different feelings that Moore had observed the Press chronicling and criticising England's grudging decline from the heights of Mexico to that milestone in Turin.

CHAPTER SIXTEEN

The Descent of Superman

In their last four years, Ramsey's England were men running on the steep and shifting slopes of a giant sand dune, at times driving themselves unsparingly to hold their ground, yet doomed, finally, to slump exhausted into the enveloping pit of failure.

By the end of that scorching summer in Mexico, England were still within touching distance of the World Cup summit. At first their decline was almost imperceptible. Goals gradually became harder to come by, especially at home, but the first real shift of ground beneath their feet was delayed until April, 1972. Then West Germany returned to Wembley with a new star and, with a sickening lurch, the blond Gunther Netzer dumped us out of the European Championship.

Still, it was the 1974 World Cup which really mattered, wasn't it? And the draw was kind for the qualifying groups. We always beat Wales when we really wanted, didn't we? And who were Poland when it came to world championship football?

Sir Alf seemed impervious to football's winds of change, even though the sand was flying in our faces as the other great nations of Europe and South America kicked off in pursuit of Brazil's more adventurous tactical lead.

Bobby Moore and his contemporaries managed to sustain Ramsey's illusion through the first match of the new World Cup challenge, riding Colin Bell's goal to 1-0 victory over Wales in Cardiff, on 15 November, 1972. Two months later, England were so shocked by John Toshack's goal near the start of the return match that all they could muster was a pot-shot equaliser by Norman Hunter. One point was lost. Questions about Ramsey's negative strategy began to be asked more intently but Poland lost in Wales in March 1973, England scythed through the other British teams in the Home Championship and that first jangle of alarm was drowned by the clamour of expectation.

Moore admits that even England's most experienced men were guilty of undervaluing the importance of the Welsh draw. 'At the time we were just delighted with Norman's great goal. We knew we should have beaten Wales but, as always, we'd struggled for goals at Wembley because yet another team had come to defend. So we weren't all that concerned about dropping a point. We didn't realise the importance until later.'

Moore was one of many nursing a dangerous belief in the invincibility of England. For in Katowice, a grey and forbidding city of mining and industrial workers, the Poles were getting ready for us.

It is to Katowice, a place far removed from the culture and comforts of Warsaw, that the Poles always take the toughest of the matches they feel they have to win. It is a city where you acquire a taste for smoke, where you can almost reach out and touch the hostility of the natives to any visiting Soccer team who threaten to sour the odd ninety minutes relief from their interminable working lives.

Ramsey tried to give his players a fresh feel of the Iron Curtain atmosphere by playing a friendly in Czechoslovakia in the May of '73. He succeeded only in giving himself a fright. For it took a late, late shot from Allan Clarke to save England a draw in Prague.

On June 6, confronted by 100,000 glowering inmates of Katowice's granite Chorzow stadium, Sir Alf reverted to type. The manager turned to experience and cold English steel, dropping potential match-winner Mike Channon in favour of reliable match-saver Peter Storey and charging Moore with getting his defensive formation out alive. Instead of finishing with a draw, England ended the match without Alan Ball and with question marks appearing against the names of Ramsey and Moore.

The match was still in its infancy as Poland answered a roar for English blood which seemed to move the air within the walls of Chorzow. They won a free kick out by the left corner flag and speared it low towards the near post of Peter Shilton's goal. To the eyes of the world in the Press box and on the television rostrum, it looked as if Gadocha achieved the vital deflection. Moore now confesses to a virtual own goal. 'The ball came in low and fast and their No.7 and me went for it, him looking for a deflection and me trying to block it. But he didn't make contact. In fact I barely got to the ball but I did get a touch. It spun into the ground and flew up inside the near post off Shilton's shoulder.'

Still, there was plenty of time left. England inched their way into the game and at half time Ramsey said: 'Gentlemen, if we keep plugging away we'll get some sort of result. A draw at least.'

Moore, of all people, punctured that theory in the first moments of the second half with a solitary, sickening error for which the price was soon to be the end of his international career. 'My confidence was still running high and right from the restart I demanded the ball off Roy McFarland. I had plenty of time but that guy closed me down very quickly, you know, what's the fellow's name, oh yes...Lubanski. No matter where you are, a good player carries on playing the game by his usual instincts. I did what I always do in those situations. Its not my way to stick the ball in the grandstand. I looked up to see where I wanted the ball to go and I pulled it across him with my right foot to go wide into space. It was something I've done a million times before, something I've done a million times since and something I'll keep on doing until I pack in. And I'll always do it successfully...except that once. Lubanski just got a touch to the ball and it spun behind me. Perfect for him. The momentum of his run carried him past me and then he proved himself a great striker. He stuck it in perfect, just inside the post as Peter came out. Everything about it was right for them and wrong for us. It was a bad goal at a terrible time. No-one reacts well to giving a goal away just after half time. It put them two up and knocked the stuffing out of us.'

Poland's gamble on the fitness of the brilliant Lubanski, their outstanding player of his time, had paid off even though he collapsed under his recurring knee injury only minutes later. McFarland tackled him at the end of another long run and this time Lubanski did not get up. There was an unconscious minute's silence from the great crowd as an ambulance came around the running track, swallowed up their hero and sped to the hospital. Moore recalls: 'Watching the way he went down and seeing him go off in the ambulance I thought at the time that goal would be his last kick in a World Cup. I felt a twinge of pity for him because he was a fine player and a nice guy. But then I didn't know it would be my last kick as well.'

There was now a desperation about England's efforts. Martin Peters became embroiled with Cmikiewicz, Poland's hard-man in midfield, their answer to Peter Storey. Alan Ball thought Peters was about to be attacked, went to his team mate's defence and was ordered off by the referee, who thought he was assaulting the Pole. Ten men were never enough to recover two goals lost by a full England team.

Ramsey reminded himself the home game was yet to come, walked into the dressing room and said: 'Right. We're going back to the hotel together. We'll have a few drinks together.'

Then he tapped Moore on the shoulder and said: 'That means you, especially.'

That was Ramsey's only reference to the biggest mistake of Moore's footballing life.

As was their habit, Moore and Ball were sharing a hotel room. They sat, sick, on the end of their beds and Ball said: 'Well, Mooro, whatever happens we're going to make the headlines tomorrow, one way or t'other.'

Other players came knocking on the door, seeking the relief of sharing the depression with the team's leading characters.

At 11. p.m. Ramsey walked into the room, reminding the players they faced an early morning flight to Moscow and starting to suggest they got to bed. He was still there, with his captain, five hours later. 'We had a couple of beers in the room,' says Moore, 'and Alf started insisting on taking the blame for the first goal himself. He said it was his fault that he'd failed to warn us about the way they took free kicks from out wide. We argued black and blue that it wasn't his fault and although it hadn't really felt like an own goal I told him it was down to my last touch. A few of us sat there 'til about four o'clock trying to talk it all out of our systems.'

That World Cup tie was in fact the first match of England's summer tour and British Airways sent a charter plane next morning to take the party on to Russia. The crew brought the morning newspapers with them, which gave the players their opportunity to let off steam.

In times of distress, footballers are prone to finding someone else to blame. Sometimes they point the finger at their team mates, often it is the manager, occasionally the conditions, the referee, the crowd. When, as was the case with Ramsey's England, they are tied by mutual loyalties and expected to overcome adversity, they blame the Press. And there was plenty of critical fuel to pour on those flames in that morning's editions of the daily papers.

A cloudy mixture of hurt and anger came over Ramsey's face as the headline on my report in the *Daily Mail* sank in: 'Ramsey betrays England.' Storey, at least for the duration of that emotive flight, took as a personal slight my criticism of Ramsey's tactical decision to play him as a ball-winner in midfield instead of Channon as a goalscorer in attack. Ball singled out Desmond Hackett of the *Daily Express* for abuse during the remainder of the tour. A whole group of players were laughing and applauding as immigration police at Moscow Airport ordered Frank Clough of *The Sun* back on to the empty charter plane home to England because his Russian visa was out of order.

It took Moore, who accepted without demur his rather large share of the blame and criticism, to restore some semblance of diplomatic relations between the players and the Press, even though, as he says: 'Russia was hardly the place to go for light relief.'

Bobby's particular problem, insomnia, was aggravated by the weather. June 1973 was particularly hot and humid in Moscow and while The Metropole Hotel appeared to be a rather delightful English anachronism overlooking the splendour of Red Square, it was certainly not air-conditioned.

'It was no place to sleep for any of us,' says Moore, 'let alone me. On the second night of it I got sick of tossing and turning and walking around the room and standing by the window, so in the early hours I took a stroll. It was cooler outside and I found a park bench, put some newspapers over myself and actually got to sleep. They were Russian newspapers. I wasn't reading the English papers after my ricket in Katowice.'

Bobby woke up to see the sun shining and two members of the F.A.'s Senior International Committee expressing their surprise as the figure they took to be a tramp came out from under the newspapers to reveal himself as England's captain.

If that incident in Moscow helped ease the tension, then another suggested to the journalists that they were dealing with footballers of rather undeveloped intellect. It is more charitable to interpret as group loyalty to their manager, the refusal of the England football team to attend a last-night command performance of Sleeping Beauty at the Bolshoi. In preference to that majestic night at the ballet, Ramsey arranged for his party to attend the screening of an old Alf Garnett film at the British Embassy Club.

The mind boggled. Frankly, so did Moore's: 'One or two of us wanted to take the opportunity of going to the Bolshoi but we stuck by the majority decision.'

Bobby paid that debt to his own sense of occasion almost three years later, attending one of the farewell performances of Margot Fonteyn and Rudolph Nureyev at the Royal Opera House, Covent Garden.

England at least rose to their own occasion, the day after missing the Bolshoi. Bell had flown home because his wife was unwell in pregnancy and Ramsey had to leave out Ball because he would be suspended from the return match against Poland, the next critical objective. Still, the USSR were beaten 2-1 in the Lenin Stadium by virture of a goal by Martin Chivers and a luckless own goal by Khurtsilava, the Bobby Moore of Russia's defence. So England took flight in better temper for the brighter lights of Turin and the match on June 14, in which Moore would establish a record of 107 full international appearances.

Ramsey had the decency to announce Moore's inclusion as captain ahead of his normal team declaration, giving Bobby time to give interviews with his familiar dignity.

The players and the Press made their respective presentations of Capi de Monte treasures and Bobby went out to face Italy for the first time in his career. 'It was very odd that in all those years and all those games I'd never played against Italy. I think because we had no tradition against Italy the occasion wasn't noticed by them. There was no presentation from the Italian F.A. They didn't even have the decency to lose.'

One of the goals, scored by local Juventus idol Pietro Anastasi, flew in through Moore's legs on the goal line and suddenly Ramsey was talking darkly about gaps on the left side of England's defence, between Bobby and Emlyn Hughes.

It was the first hint of a fracture in the bond of loyalty between Alf and his established players and this time when Moore and Ball were in our group which sat up drinking all night, their manager was not with them. Moore and Ball were still holding court in the hotel foyer at 6.15 a.m. when the England amateur football team, who were also on tour, came down for the start of a long journey by road to their next engagement. Bobby saw them on to the coach with the gift of three bottles of champagne and went to his room to pack for the last flight of his final England tour.

After the forced gaiety on the plane, Bobby got home to Chigwell and unwrapped his mementoes. 'I felt quite choked up about those presentations and I have a great deal of affection for them. I knew it hadn't been a good tour. For the first time I felt fairly sickened by it all. Normally I'd always done well abroad. I'd enjoyed the different environment, the travel, getting the right amount of rest, the training, the spirit among the lads. But this time I knew I hadn't played well and all the disappointment over Poland made me depressed.

'I tried to decide if I was slipping, losing anything from my game. The odd thing was I figured I was playing well against Poland until Lubanski punished that mistake. I told myself that I couldn't go on for ever, even though in my heart I didn't want it to end. But then again I didn't feel I was on the slide. All my life I'd sweated on the letter arriving from the F.A. and then on the team being announced. But at that point I didn't see why I shouldn't still play for England.

'I asked myself if I was still helping the players around me as well as doing my own job. Perhaps I wasn't doing so much sorting out of situations that weren't really down to me. Maybe I was less positive in committing myself to help someone else, in case I couldn't recover and exposed us to worse problems.

'Had Alf picked me out of sentiment? It had been suggested he only played Bobby Charlton at the end so that he could break Billy Wright's record of caps. I didn't want people thinking that about me. But Christ, I'm not ready for the knacker's yard yet.'

The doubts whirled through Moore's mind for three months. Then, in September, England were due to play Austria at Wembley in a friendly preparation for the last, decisive qualifying battle with Poland. Moore noted that Ball was also in the squad. even though he could not play, and was encouraged to realise that Ramsey was still including all the players he hoped he would need in the World Cup Finals in West Germany the following summer.

To Bobby's dismay, the blow came in much the same way as the start of his fruitful liaison with Alf. After a morning's training at the British Aircraft Corporation sports ground at Stevenage, Ramsey singled out Moore to sit next to on the coach journey back to the team's headquarters, the Homestead Court Hotel at Welwyn Garden City.

'Bobby, I've got a disappointment for you.'

Moore knew it then, choked back the bile of dismay rising at the back of his throat.

Ramsey hurried on, embarrassed: 'I'm not playing you. I know how much you want to play. I can assure you its nothing to do with what happened in Poland. But Norman Hunter's been tremendously loyal and I've seen him play very well two or three times already this season and Leeds are in a tremendous run and Norman has been tremendous and there's his loyalty and the manner in which he's playing at the moment is – er – well, tremendous. And, you see, I've got to get a settled side for the next game against Poland which is so important and I have to try one or two things which will be best for the team…'

He tailed away. Bobby thought: 'Settled side? Try things? When did he ever have a settled side without me? And when did he ever try things without asking me?'

He asked Ramsey: 'Does this mean I'm no further use to you?'

No answer.

'Look, Alf. If I'm a liability and an embarrassment and you can't use me any more then say so. I'd rather know and we can call it quits.'

Ramsey: 'No, no. If we qualify I will need you. I expect to qualify and I'll need you to captain the squad in Munich.'

'All right. That's fair enough. I can't ask for any more. I'll battle to get back in the side.'

He remembered his respect for Hunter, sought him out at the first opportunity and said: 'Good luck, Norman. You've waited a long time and you deserve it.'

The England performance against Austria rendered that battle to get back into the side redundant. Martin Peters captained them on a seven goal spree. Moore: 'Many people thought I would be recalled against Poland for the sort of challenge I'd always risen to in the past. The Poles beat Wales the day we were playing Austria so we had to win against Poland and everyone seemed to think he couldn't leave me out.

'But after those seven goals went in it began to dawn on me that he couldn't change the side.'

Moore joined the playing members of the squad in their post-match celebrations, sharing in the lagers, taking the perfumed night air of La Valbonne club and steeling himself to miss the big one. Not even Bobby, in his personal disappointment, doubted that in this form England could overcome Poland without him.

Poland were due at Wembley on October 16. Ramsey walked up to Moore in training the day before and said simply: 'Norman's in.' As usual on the eve of a big match, the England party took in the early evening show at a local cinema. For once it was not a Western. They saw Jane Fonda playing a prostitute in *Klute* and some newspapers were moved to debate whether such a sexually stimulating movie would waste some of the players' previous nervous energy.

Again Ramsey spoke to Moore on the coach back to the hotel. 'When we get there I'm afraid there's bound to be a lot of fuss with the Press and TV because you're not playing. I don't want it to happen to you but there's nothing I can do about it so you'll just have to face up to it.'

Moore's self-imposed dignity withstood the strain of television and radio interviews and a host of phone calls from newspapermen. But when I spoke to him he said: 'Everyone keeps asking me how I feel about it, Jeff. How the hell do they think I feel?'

Whereupon I had to ask him how he felt.

The answer was unprintable in a daily newspaper.

Twenty-four hours later the whole of England felt even worse. Bobby Moore, a most distinguished addition to the substitutes' bench, had to sit, watch and suffer with the rest of us.

The earlier results had simplied the issue. England had to win and were confident they would do so, Poland needed a draw and half-expected to lose.

Moore remembers the game more sharply than many in which he played. 'It was a nightmare. Even I couldn't believe it when Norman gave them a goal with the same mistake I made in Poland. It was right in front of the bench. Again it was after half time. They cleared the ball down the line and nine times out of ten Norman would have clattered their player and the ball into the fence. But he tried to pull it back inside his man, same as me. And lost it, same as me. Roy McFarland was left with two men and Domarski was played clear through on his own. Even then Peter Shilton might have got it but he was a fraction late going down and the ball brushed the underside of his arm on its way in.

'One down. It was a joke. We were paralysing them. The TV lot were trying to work out whether their goalkeeper, that Tomaszewski, was a genius or a clown. He was like a cat on hot bricks, making some great saves but sometimes rushing so far out of position that our crosses were dropping between him and his goal. Never seen anything like it. Shots were hitting their posts and hitting bodies on their goal line and our lads couldn't have given any more effort than they did. We poured down on them.'

Moore sensed the need for fresh legs and a change of the attacking pattern. With fifteen minutes left there was a break for treatment to an injured player and Moore bent forward on the touchline to reason with the immovable Ramsey:

'It's getting desperate, Alf. Don't you think it would be a good idea to get a left-sided player on?'

Alf: 'I've pushed Norman forward.'

Allan Clarke recovered the lost goal with a penalty. Wembley's 100,000 knew it was not enough and tried to lift England to victory on a wave of sound. By now all England was looking for substitutes, still none were forthcoming from Ramsey.

Down below the Royal Box, out of earshot of the watching world, Moore pressed Ramsey again, still privately, more urgently.

'Stick a left sided forward on, Alf. We might get 'em down that side.'

Ramsey said it again: 'I've pushed Norman forward. I don't think we can do any more. How long to go?'

He had lost track of the time. Someone said: 'Five minutes.'

Ramsey: 'Too late now.'

Moore: 'It's never too late. Get Kevin Hector on for two minutes and see what he can do. Come on. Come on. Just get him out there.'

Ramsey nodded, transfixed, his world collapsing before his eyes. He sent on Derby's Kevin Hector for the shortest international career on record, just ninety seconds left to win his first and only cap.

Moore remembers: 'Once Alf agreed I was tearing at Kevin's track suit trousers. Someone else trying to get his top off. You could feel the

152

seconds ticking away. Racing the clock. We almost threw him on the pitch. And in that ninety seconds he nearly got Alf another knighthood. Alf ended up taking stick for forgetting the time and sending on a substitute so late. Yet Kevin knocked a ball only inches past a post, just before the final whistle. He might have put us in the Finals with his only touch of the ball for England.

'I think Kevin might have saved us if Alf had acted sooner. It was obvious we needed a left sided player to go through them. Emlyn Hughes was doing his best from left back but as usual he was cutting the ball back on to his trusty old right foot and losing the angles and the chances.'

Then it was over. The eyes of the Poles were glassy and staring at each other in disbelief. Wembley slumped into mourning. It was the beginning of the end for the entire Ramsey regime. Sir Alf rose, numbed to walk towards the dressing room. England's best had not been good enough. Moore echoed the sentiments of most observers of that freakish night's football as he walked alongside the manager across the familiar turf and said: 'I'm terribly sorry for you but it just wasn't meant to be.'

Ramsey said nothing much, neither then, nor in the dressing room, perhaps pondering his fate.

It was quieter and emptier in La Valbonne that night. Hunter sped for the haven of home, crucified by his error on the one night on which he had taken Moore's place by right, only to be asked by his son: 'Daddy, is it right you lost us the World Cup?'

Moore knew exactly how Hunter felt.

Poland went on to the World Cup Finals and justified that result, playing attacking football to get within one match of the Final itself before losing to West Germany, the host nation. Yet Moore insists: 'They were a long way from being a good side at Wembley that night. It was overcoming England which gave them all their belief in themselves and encouraged certain players to go on and prove themselves. England might still have done well in '74. Holland were the outstanding side in the world but they lost the Final partly because of Germany's fanatical support and partly because they hated the Germans so much that they wanted to take the mickey after their early goal instead of just pressing on to win.'

The Poles left Wembley with all that drama ahead of them. England had to return within a month, oddly enough to play Italy in another friendly. That outstanding fixture was one of many circumstances which conspired to give Moore a bonus cap, his 108th, and permit him to finish his England career at Wembley. Hunter was in the squad again but was handicapped by an injury which simplified Ramsey's selection. Moore led England out for the last time, but again no-one told Italy they were supposed to lose. Where England had squandered chances against the Poles, this time they failed even to turn pressure into opportunities and once more the Italians caught them on the break to win 1-0.

The evening was memorable only as Moore's farewell, even though there was no announcement to that effect. He says: 'It was nice to be back but I knew at the time, although noboby told me, that it was the last England game. I wouldn't play again.

'In many ways I'd been lucky. I'd started young and kept fairly free of injuries. We'd had good runs in two of my three World Cups, which meant extra games. I thought about that night against Italy...108 caps...difficult for anyone to pass me. Franz Beckenbauer ought to do it with Germany but I doubt if anyone will ever do it for England. The game's getting harder. I knew people would think I'd had enough. Even if I was still the best man for the job, they would be looking for new players now because for the first time England had failed to qualify for the World Cup Finals. They would be building for another four years on. So there was no need for old Mooro. But it was nice to finish at Wembley.'

Sure enough, Moore was missing when Ramsey, thrashing about in a desperate attempt to prolong his term of office, named a new, young squad to go to Portugal in February, 1974. All for nothing. The Football Association finally plucked up the courage to sack their silent knight.

A golden age of English football was at a tarnished end.

CHAPTER SEVENTEEN

Why the Man Called Chelsea Went to Fulham

So much of West Ham had been woven into the fabric of the England team that, in retrospect, it would have been surprising had Bobby Moore's club not fallen into decay in tandem with his country.

Like England, West Ham had been missing out on the trophies since the middle Sixties. Like England in that European Championship match against West Germany, the gradual erosion of West Ham's great team was given a savage, accelerating twist by a major cup-tie in 1972.

In the club's case, the tie was a League Cup semi-final, the opponents were Stoke City and not even a rare glimpse of Moore's versatility was enough to take West Ham back to Wembley through a contest which occupied these two clubs for seven hours spread over four matches.

The first two games were the scheduled home-and-away legs of the semi-final and West Ham had begun well by winning 2-1 at Stoke. The Midlands club drew level at Upton Park, however, to push the second match into extra time and on to the first of its many dramas.

The team were still deadlocked in the last minute of extra time when West Ham were given a penalty which brought two of England's World Cup heroes face to face. Geoff Hurst faced Gordon Banks in a one-shot showdown at twelve paces. And lost. Stoke's master goalkeeper defied West Ham's murderous goalscorer and Moore set his jaw towards a replay. 'As Geoff placed the ball I felt certain we would go to Wembley. That's what a penalty ought to mean in the last minute of a semi-final. Geoff went for power and blasted away at the roof of the net. Gordon flung up his right arm in a reflex action and the ball flew over the top. Everyone acclaimed a great save and it was a marvellous piece of reaction by Gordon. But really, for my money, it was a sickening miss.'

West Ham and Stoke went to Sheffield Wednesday's Hillsborough ground, went into extra time again and still could not conjure up a decisive goal. So, on January 26, the scene shifted to Old Trafford, home of Manchester United, a grand stage for the finale.

It was one of those intense football nights when the pitch is slicked with water to favour the most skilled attackers and the crowds mass in the shadows of stands and terrace, drawn like moths to floodlights focussed on that glittering green rectangle.

West Ham were in smooth control until Bobby Ferguson, their goalkeeper, plunged down among the flying feet, took a kick on the head and for once failed to rise. The crowd sighed its relief when Rob Jenkins, the trainer, at last got Ferguson to his feet. It was clear that Ferguson, lurching about his goalmouth and staggering into goalposts, was barely conscious.

Clyde Best, the Burmudian centre forward, was the player briefed to take over in goal in just such emergencies. Moore looked towards the tall, dark man 'All right Clyde?'

The occasion was too much for Best. He made a nervous gesture with his eyes and looked away, saying: 'No, man. Not me.'

Moore surveyed a team of averted eyes. He thought about the two other occasions in which he had taken over in goal, first in a reserve match against Crystal Palace, then during a first team game with Chelsea. At least he had never let in a goal. 'I'll go in.'

Within minutes he was facing a penalty. 'I'd hardly handled the ball when it happened. John McDowell underhit a back pass and committed a desperate foul to try and make up for the mistake, Mike Bernard stepped up to take the penalty and it must have got to him that he ought to beat someone like me who wasn't a proper goalkeeper. I took a guess and dived to my right and the ball came that way and I went to push it round the post. But it was such a bad penalty that it was closer in to me than I expected and I was all tucked up when I made the save and could only palm it down. Mike followed up to smash in the rebound.

'Again I was sick. For the first time I had that foul feeling of picking the ball out of the back of the net. The other couple of times I'd quite enjoyed the fun of a spell in goal. But this time there was too much at stake. I was in goal for fifteen minutes and they were the longest fifteen minutes of my life. Billy Bonds equalised while we were still down to ten men but all the time I wanted to get out into the real match and do something about winning it. That goalmouth seemed the loneliest place in the world. Goalkeepers must get accustomed to it but I felt like a prisoner caged in by the edge of the penalty box.'

Down the tunnel, West Ham were working with a frenzy to get Ferguson back into the match. The goalkeeper was propped against a wall as they threw footballs at him. For ten minutes they just bounced off

156

his unco-ordinated, rag-doll body. For a few minutes more he could not count the fingers thrust inches from his face. Then they sent him back out, teetering into goal to allow Bobby to return to the fray. Almost at once he failed to see a long shot from Peter Dobing. Two-one down.

'Again we managed to equalise,' says Moore, 'but the psychological burden was too great. We were too conscious of trying to protect Fergy, so Terry Conroy got a winner near the end. All I could think about going down the tunnel was the penalty Geoff had missed, not the one I almost saved.

'That was the beginning of the end of an era. A lot of players had already left and that summer Geoff went to Stoke. That would never have happened if he'd put his penalty past them. West Ham would then have gone to Wembley to meet Chelsea and we would very likely have been in Europe the following season. Instead the team was breaking up.

'We'd already lost Budgie Byrne, Ron Boyce, John Bond, Peter Brabrook. Martin Peters had gone to Tottenham in exchange for Jimmy Greaves and then Jimmy had packed in the game. You can't keep on losing players of that calibre. Two or three of them were world class and there aren't many of them around. You couldn't replace them just like that, however promising the youngsters. Then Geoff went off to Stoke and they had to get on with rebuilding.'

Increasingly, Ron Greenwood was turning to his assistant to perform that task. John Lyall had been a hard, uncompromising wing half before injury had curtailed his playing career. Greenwood had schooled him through the club offices and reserve teams, as his own successor. Moore: 'You could see Ron finding it harder to bridge the age gap between himself and the players. In the good days he'd got to know the lads by playing with them in the five-a-sides, larking about in the baths and showers, chatting in the changing rooms.

'That's not easy as you get older and it was obvious John would be given more and more control. That was all right by me because I liked John and he added some of his own toughness as a player to the team. But it seemed to me that I was part of the past, not the future.'

That feeling grew as two unsuccessful years slipped by. Moore pressed in vain to be allowed to join Brian Clough at Derby County. His dispute with Greenwood flickered on through England's troubles into the New Year of 1974. Then, in a third round F.A. Cup tie against ambitious little Hereford United, the worst injury of Moore's career intervened. Bobby twisted his knee ligaments, limped on for another twenty five minutes which aggravated the damage, and was out for eight weeks. The barely-known Mick McGiven took over the celebrated No.6 shirt and as if to prove Moore's point that his time was up at West Ham, a series of good performances took them clear of relegation trouble.

'Ron had agreed at the start of the season,' says Moore,'that they would let me go on a free transfer at the end of the season. Everyone knows that if a good player can get away for nothing, he has a better chance of securing a good contract for himself. Well, West Ham were out of relegation trouble and they'd found a replacement for me. So I was pretty pleased when Ron called me in and said I could go. But suddenly he was saying they wanted a fee for me.

'I couldn't believe it of them. That was disappointing after everything we'd been through together. They'd signed me for nothing and had years of service from me and now they were using me to help balance the books. After all, what was £25,000 to them against everything we'd achieved in my time there? I had a right go at Ron but he kept saying the board were insisting on a fee. And they wouldn't let me get to speak to Reg Pratt, the chairman, So I was stuck with a price on my head.

'What made me angrier was that I knew they had to let me go if they really were going to build a new team. Whether they care to admit it or not, the team was Bobby Moore-conscious. They took their lead from me and looked to give me the ball to start everything from the back. I was a complex to them and if some of the other lads were going to blossom out and express themselves I had to get out of the way. But West Ham wanted their pound of flesh.'

The word hummed along Soccer's grapevine that Bobby Moore was going cheap; an England captain for £25,000. Stoke and Leicester were among the First Division clubs to show interest but the positive moves all came from the Second Division. Norwich made a bid to reunite Moore with their manager, John Bond. Portsmouth chairman John Deacon saw Moore as the cornerstone of his rebuilding programme. Both offered Bobby good contracts and both were prepared to let him live in London, train at West Ham and travel to join them on match days.

'That would have been necessary because of my businesses,' he says, 'but I knew in my heart it would be better to break the ties with West Ham completely. For fifteen years I'd been putting the car on automatic pilot and it had taken me to West Ham. I needed a total change of environment, surroundings, atmosphere. Something fresh to get me going again.'

Throughout the negotiations, Moore nursed the hope that the fresh challenge would come from Crystal Palace and his old instructor in the defensive arts, Malcolm Allison. 'I could have sworn Palace would come in for me. I felt Malcolm would have wanted me and I'd seen their chairman, Ray Bloye, on holiday in Portugal the previous summer when he'd talked round the subject of me going to play for them if it ever proved possible.

'That was what I really wanted. I'd played fifteen years for my pride, motivating myself, rarely getting any praise. I believed Malcolm could give me the lift and the appreciation I needed to go on playing well, raise my game again. I wanted Malcolm to tell me where I went wrong and to pat me on the back when I did well. No matter how long you're in the game, you need that just like you do when you're a schoolboy.

'I wanted to play for Malcolm so much that I'd decided in my mind that if Palace were a bit tight for money I would take £5,000 less on my contract to go there instead of any of the other clubs. Truly. But Palace didn't come in.'

Fulham did. Their manager, Alec Stock, had been an acquaintance of Bobby's down the years and he understood enough about the man to time his move and gauge his approach to perfection.

Moore had given himself until that season's deadline day for Football League transfers, March 14, to make his decision. Stock made his bid on March 13. Stock knew that conversations with Johnny Haynes, George Cohen, Johnny Byrne and Alan Mullery had given Bobby a soft spot for Fulham. To a man, they enjoyed their football at Craven Cottage and the phone call to meet Stock and his directors was like a door opening to let light into a darkened room. Moore said he would sleep on their offer, but Stock knew he was hooked.

Next morning, Stock made sure of landing his catch by sending Mullery with Graham Hortop, the secretary, to Upton Park to complete the signing.

When Moore came out of an early, self-imposed training session, Mullery strolled up and said: 'Glad you're coming, Bob. You'll love it at Fulham. When I was leaving Tottenham I wanted another First Division club, just like you do. But when I got the opportunity to go back to Fulham I couldn't wait. The atmosphere's different class and all the lads are dying to learn from you. They'll do anything for you.'

It was the perfect boost to Moore's wavering self-confidence. Fulham's raiding party went home delighted to have Bobby's signature drying on the transfer documents. They might have had some qualms about their image had they seen Moore's birth certificate. His full name is Robert Frederick Chelsea Moore, the Chelsea being a hand-me-down from some distant and forgotten uncle on his father's side. Fulham had signed a player named after their closest neighbours and most intense rivals.

So the last of the World Cup winners left West Ham. He did so after

159

sixteen years and an impregnable record of 642 first team matches, 544 in the First Division and 98 in an assortment of cups. And he walked away without so much as a backward glance or a twinge of regret. 'It had come to the stage at West Ham where I couldn't do any more for them. I know from the letters I received after my move that the crowd appreciated me. But I couldn't surprise them or even satisfy them any longer. They'd seen it all before and they knew I couldn't go on forever. They wanted a new team and I needed a new challenge. It was as simple and final as that. From that day I was a Fulham player, 100 per cent.'

A bucket of cold water in the face could not have revived Bobby any more sharply. Stock, an old fox at the management game, knew what he wanted: a team with pace and style that spread a little enjoyment. He knew how to delegate. Stock had been first to spot the potential of Billy Taylor and appoint as coach the young Scotsman who then established himself as a part-time assistant to Don Revie, the new England manager.

At Moore's first team talk, Stock said: 'All right fellows. Let's push it about, plenty of movement. Hmmm. Show 'em we can play. Enjoy yourselves. I'll leave the rest to you, Bill. I'm off for a few gin-and-tonics in the board room. Can't be bad at fifteen grand a year, can it? See you later on.'

In his unusual fashion Stock had created a helpful atmosphere for Taylor to go happily through the details of the match plan of the day and Bobby felt at home from the start. 'The mood was so light hearted that it was like a ton weight being taken off your shoulders. It was very different from West Ham where it was always deeply technical, highly involved...and sober. But I knew Alec was no fool under the chatter. Unexpectedly, in a very unusual way, he provided just the boost I was looking for.'

His enthusiasm survived a disastrous debut for Fulham. Moore's first appearance doubled the Craven Cottage crowd to 18,000 for the visit of Middlesbrough on the night of Tuesday March 19. In the midst of all that eager anticipation, Fulham were thrashed 4-0. Bobby recalls: 'They had some injury troubles at the time but the defence was fairly settled so I agreed to start off in midfield. From the off it was obvious to me that Middlesbrough were an outstanding Second Division side and would go on to win promotion and do well for Jack Charlton in the First Division. Which they did. We were hammered out of sight. Yet in a way it excited me. Middlesbrough exposed all Fulham's shortcomings in the first night and although the crowd were disappointed, I knew all that information would be invaluable if I was going to make a contribution. I started try-

Away Games

An impromptu training session on the beach at Acapulco.

GaLa
BUSH TV

13856

umultuous welcome in Malta.

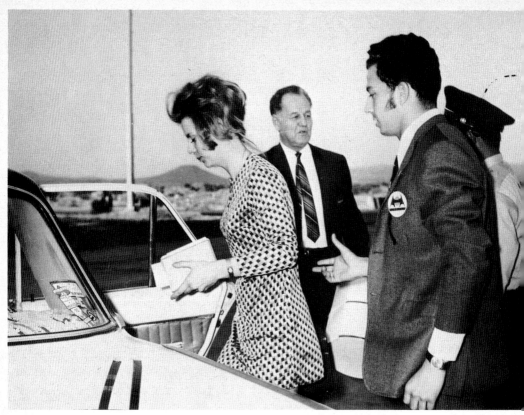

The Bogota bracelet affair. *Above* Tina is hurried to a car at Mexico City airport. *Below* Bobby and Jimmy Greave
(left) with Bobby's hosts at a British Embassy safe house. *Opposite* How Jon, the Daily Mail cartoonist, saw the affai
FOTOSPO

" ALL THIS-A TROUBLE JUST TO GET HIS AUTOGRAPH "

Above Bobby meets the oil sheiks . . . and *below* the children on the beach at Copabanca.

by Moore — cricketer.

TERRY O'N

Bobby Moore today, with the scars of battle. *Inset* Bobby at age eleven.

ing to help out a bit here and there. The lads were so eager to learn and it was lovely watching them mature around Mullers and me.'

Within a month Moore was facing Allison's Palace, the team he would have given £5,000 to join, and suffering 'the second great embarrassment of my career'.

He recalls: 'It was almost as bad as that early day when Johnny Quigley gave me a roasting at Nottingham Forest. It was Good Friday and Palace came to Fulham and gave us a good hiding, 3-1. I hated it because Malcolm was watching and I wanted to show him what he'd missed in not signing me. My pride was hurt so much that I went off up-field and scored one of my few goals.'

He really must have been upset, because goals from Bobby Moore were as rare as caviar in Canning Town. During his 108 international matches he scored only twice for England, oddly enough within the space of twenty four days in the significant year of 1966. Both came during the warm-up for the World Cup, the first giving England a 1-1 draw with Poland at Goodison Park on June 5 and the second contributing to a 6-1 win over Norway in Oslo on June 29.

The goal against Palace, however, was a futile gesture in the face of defeat. The chance for revenge was only four days away. The next Tuesday, Fulham went to Palace for the return Easter fixture and won 2-0, virtually dooming Allison to relegation to the Third Division. Busby and Barrett scored the goals but Moore, in his rightful defensive position for the first time for Fulham, produced the killing performance. He says: 'There were 30,000 people in Selhurst Park and I always love a big crowd. On top of that I had a score to settle. I played from the heart and felt great. Full of myself. As I walked down the tunnel Malcolm came by and just said "Well done." I'd killed his chances of staying in the Second Division but he showed me his respect. I'd played the way he taught me. Oddly enough I didn't see him for a while after that, too long after to say what I wanted to say to him: That's the way you told me. How did I do?'

Bobby, in fact, continued to do all right for Fulham. By the following season, Moore and Mullery had imposed enough of their class and experience on the team to launch them on an F.A. Cup run which not even they dreamed was possible.

To begin with, they needed replay after replay to dispose of Hull City and Brian Clough's Nottingham Forest. Moore says: 'By the time we finished we'd played enough matches to have put us in the Final of the European Cup Winners' Cup the following season.'

Oddly, for every ounce of strength drained from the players by those marathon ties, they received a double injection of experience and team spirit. 'By the end,' says Moore, 'the atmosphere in the club was fantastic. We had built up almost overnight the community spirit which had been so important in the mid-Sixties with West Ham. Really, I suppose football teams are like grown-up schoolboys the way they like to do things with their mates. But without that togetherness we could never have got to Wembley with the quality of players we had at Fulham. We had to accept our limitations and try to play to our strengths and all those replays gave instant experience to a lot of young lads.'

The critics were convinced the run would end at Everton, who had been top of the First Division for much of that season. Yet Viv Busby scored both goals in a 2-1 win which was startling not only as a statistic but because Everton were completely outclassed. 'The odd thing was that I thought we could do well at Everton,' says Moore. 'They were very negative the way they played every game and I couldn't see them scoring many goals against us. Everyone got the jitters in the dressing room when they thought about all their big money players. Our younger lads began to worry that the job was too big for them to handle. But Alan and I went round chatting to them and when we got out there we played them off the park. Fulham were tremendous and Everton were a disgrace for a team who looked like they could win the Championship. No flair. No nothing.'

The ride home on the team coach that evening was a liquid affair and Bobby continued celebrating at BBC TV's *Match of the Day* studios. He fell into bed late and awoke in the morning to find his new house had been burgled.

A first glance downstairs told him that many of his caps, medals and trophies were missing and he steeled himself against the loss of some of his most beloved mementoes. After telephoning the police he went sadly to the front door to collect the milk and the Sunday papers and found his treasures in a tidy pile on the lawn.

'There had been a lot of robberies in the area,' he says, 'and it was the turn of our house. But the fellow must have been a football fan. When he realised whose house it was and what he had taken, he stacked them up for me. In a way it was touching. I thought then it must be our year to go to Wembley.'

First Fulham had to travel to a quarter final on another First Division ground, Carlisle. 'The team had hardened up by now,' says Moore, 'and we hung on and hung on until Les Barrett got us a goal out of the blue and we were through to the semi-final.'

Again the opposition was First Division, this time in the shape of Birmingham, but on neutral Hillsborough. Moore's defensive performance

162

in the 1-1 draw earned ecstatic praise from Don Revie down to the youngest spectator. So Fulham survived for another replay. At Maine Road, Manchester they hung on and hung on once more until, just minutes from extra time, John Mitchell snatched a goal from nothing.

Bobby Moore was going back to Wembley. By the most delicious, improbable irony, so were West Ham.

CHAPTER EIGHTEEN

Last of the Glory Days

The West Lodge Park Hotel at Hadley Wood is one of those watchful country houses which it is impossible to approach undetected. The crisp crunch of gravel beneath tyres and the tell-tale crackle of fallen leaves beneath the feet signal the end of a modest journey from London, past the northern extremity of the Piccadilly Underground line, to the Hertfordshire hillside which has become a fashionable retreat for football teams pausing for breath on the way to Wembley.

We are there on Saturday, 3 May 1975. Bobby Moore's new team will play Bobby Moore's old team in the F.A. Cup Final and, as such, the occasion is unique. For the veteran of so many glory days, however, the exceptional has become nothing unusual and for once he is still sleeping on the dawn of a gala performance.

By contrast, Alec Stock is to lead a team up that tunnel of dreams for the first time in English football's longest managerial career. At 6.30 a.m. he is walking through the wet grass and gentle mists of a country morning, anxious to know if his show will go on.

One company of football boot manufacturers who claim to have Fulham under contract are seeking a High Court injunction on this, of all days to prevent Stock's men wearing football boots manufactured by another company who claim to have Fulham under contract. In fact, as at most clubs, Fulham's players have painted the trade markings of the highest bidder on to their favourite footwear. But the more lurid of the morning headlines hint that the great game could be off and Stock's fragile nerve is more frayed than usual. Already, there has been a whiff of scandal about players selling tickets to the touts.

Nature chooses to be kind to one of her gentlemen. The sun rises behind trees whose branches spread their leaves in welcome. The dew glistens for a long moment before evaporating into crystal air and Stock feels good enough to illuminate the day with his own philosphy. 'Fulham are the first Cup Final team playing just for their pride and the glory. That's how I want it. That's how it should be. Wembley is about dreams, not contracts. The players have had their rewards for getting Fulham back on the map and into the black. They don't need another penny to make them give their all today.'

By 7.30, despite the sleeping drugs which have become a faintly worrying part of most footballers' routine, the younger, more nervous players are coming in search of their corn flakes. As a star with no particular ties to any of his new team mates, Bobby has a room to himself and in fact it is quarter to ten before he wakes to a day filled with sunshine and looks out across lawns dappled bright with expectation. He arrives downstairs by 10.20, declines breakfast and helps Alan Mullery, Fulham's captain, calm the youngsters.

Bobby raises a hand to his shoulder, turns his head to stretch the muscles and says: 'Nothing to worry about today. Slept so well for once that I've got a stiff neck. What time is this match, anyway?'

The kick off is still the best part of five hours away but the Cup Final has already started. Moore and Mullery smile with their lips while their eyes scan other faces for the first signs of tension. Peter Mellor's grin is nervous so they poke fun at the husky goalkeeper's pansy-yellow shirt.

Moore, as is his superstitious habit on Wembley mornings, sets off to walk the hotel grounds. A blue silk shirt is his gesture of individuality on a day for wearing the club apparel. It is so warm that he leaves the grey jacket behind as he picks his way between the television cameras, across the cables and over the putting green towards the pond. Prophetically, he says, 'Hope Peter Mellor's okay. No good if the keeper's got the shakes.'

He strolls back into the packed foyer to find Les Strong, the injured full back, returned from representing the players at the High Court hearing and reporting that the Cup Final will proceed if they black out all the trade markings on all their boots. A typical British compromise on a day steeped in British tradition. The tension lifts and Moore and Mullery set the mood for a jokey interview with BBC television. The outside world are advised that Fulham seem relaxed and confident and the players mock West Ham's players when they appear on the screen in the hotel lounge.

'Look at the state my old mob are in,' says Moore. 'So much for the First Division.'

Out in the gabled doorway, Stock is dealing with the last unpleasantness before settling down to enjoy his day. He tells young John Dowie he has lost the last vacancy, that of substitute, to the experience of

Barry Lloyd.

'Not a pleasant job, that,' says Stock. 'But it's my job to do the rough bit and knock him down and it's up to Billy Taylor and Bobby and Alan to pick him up.'

Lunch is however much of an omelette you still feel like eating which, as usual in Bobby's case, is very little. They pile on to the team coach, jokes still flying for the benefit of their own nerves and London Weekend Television cameras riding with them to Wembley. Martin Tyler, the interviewer, has to conquer his own nerves and announces: 'All right, lads. We're going live...now.'

Mullery shouts down the coach: 'Get the lagers out, Mooro. What sort of a coach outing is this?'

Les Strong may be out of the match but he's still playing for Fulham. Viv Busby, the goalscoring hope, has been too quiet for too long. Strong says: 'Come on Viv, don't lose your bottle now. Give Mooro his repair kit, poor old sod.'

Tight faces crack into smiles. Stock sits at the back, tense and upright. The TV men cannot persuade the bubbling players to stop waving girlie magazines at the cameras. But the closer to Wembley, the quieter the journey and the drier the mouths. One street seems just like another and the surprised faces of High Street shoppers are a blur. Around a corner to see the first glimpse of Wembley's towers. They are reconstructing the approaches to the stadium and those players making the trip for the first time are saddened that they cannot drive up Wembley Way. The driver picks his way around the back to the dressing room tunnel, through the throng of fans in their scarves and favours. The players wave jerky hands at Fulham fans beating, barely heard, on the sides of the coach. They plunge for the echoing quiet of Wembley's north dressing room.

Moore glances round the familiar cavern: 'Nice to be home again.'

He forgoes the traditional inspection of the pitch for more important business, gaining a psychological edge over West Ham. Bobby's former team-mates arrive to find him waiting in the tunnel, ready to smile them in the back: 'Come on, Bonzo, give us a laugh...where we going tonight, Frank...you all right, Trevor? Truly? The old voice sounds a bit croaky.'

Moore's ego tells him that his presence among the opposition will be West Ham's biggest mental block. At their moment of arrival, West Ham need Bobby like they need a broken leg. He jangles as many nerves as possible as they dive for their own dressing room.

The rest of Fulham come back down the tunnel. Aerosol cans of black paint are dug out of the kit baskets and passed round for the players to spray out the white flashes on their boots. laughingly complying with the

166

High Court ruling. Seconds later the smiles are wiped from their faces. Somebody forgot the shinpads. Billy Taylor reaches into his back pocket for money and sends a police motor cyclist racing to a corner shop in Wembley to replace the missing equipment. When they arrive the pads are too big and cumbersome for the players' liking. A stadium official finds a hacksaw and Taylor feverishly cuts them down to size.

The atmosphere is steamy with nervous sweat. In a discreet corner, physiotherapist Ron Woolnough gives Stock an anti-asthma injection. Through it all, Moore and Mullery are moving quietly from team-mate to team-mate with calming words of advice and encouragement.

Moore tells Busby: 'They're the First Division side. They're the favourites. Let them worry about us.' He is dressed in shirt, boots, socks and athletic underpants. Everything but his shorts. As usual, they will go on last. Partly superstition, partly because the greasy embrocation is drying on his legs and he is as meticulous as ever about his appearance.

Taylor, the coach, appears confident but confesses a private concern. 'The build-up has drained some of them. It doesn't matter what you do, stay or home or go to a hotel, let TV in or keep them out, the pressure will get to a few of them. You know which ones it will be but you still can't do much about it.'

The battle plan has been discussed and decided days ago. The last team talk is short. Stock tells his mandatory joke: 'See this old suit? Had it sixteen years. Haven't been able to buy a new one. Remember the old fellow and go out and do it.'

Taylor jogs a few tactical memories and exhorts them: 'We haven't come all this way to fail now. Let's go out and play our football.'

Stock says: 'Remember lads, enjoy yourselves. This is it.'

Moore replies: 'And you remember, Alec, tall and proud up the tunnel. Stride out there and show 'em we mean business.'

Up the tunnel to face the world. Bobby knows that roar. Not so much a wall of noise for him, more a warm welcome. West Ham can still hear Moore firing jokes at them. The players warm up, coaxing the nervous stiffness from their legs. The officials settle on the touchline benches. No space between the crammed Fulham and West Ham shoulders. No malice, either. Alec Stock and Ron Greenwood embrace. Billy Taylor and John Lyall time the kick-off.

Strong, the full back Moore believes might play for England but whose injury ties him to that bench, wipes away the first of many Fulham tears this day. Then he settles among men who might be watching any game, anywhere. That bench is a professional vantage point on a carnival day. Down here the pace seems more deliberate, the physical contact firmer the marking so tight that you think Wembley's wide open spaces must be in the car park.

The audience of 100,000 hardly know the game has started but Moore's psychological warfare is working and he and Mullery are already in control of the game. They set up a chance for John Lacy. He heads just wide and on the bench Stock and Taylor slowly relax fists clenched in premature celebration of a goal. Greenwood and Lyall put it out of their minds. If a 6ft 3in centre half comes up in attack, you can only try to stop him, not always succeed.

West Ham are more worried about the balance of their team. Lyall shouts to Holland: 'Get out right, Patsy. Go long and check out. Run him.'

Strong's injury has forced Fulham to move the right-footed John Fraser to left back and West Ham go to work on a man playing out of position. Holland, then Brooking, now Bonds, all come to test Fraser. Each time Moore is on hand, advising and encouraging quietly. Fraser's temperament holds as firm as his tackle. Moore and Mullery are masters of the first half. The opening roars give way to respectful applause for two craftsmen. Even Lyall and Greenwood nod their heads in approval.

Fulham want to capitalise on their command. Taylor calls for more effort from Les Barrett, who looks like he might win the match from outside left. Stock berates Alan Slough for running too much with the ball, interrupting the flow of the team's movement. Kevin Lock, Moore's young successor at West Ham, has grown out of early nervousness and is holding them up. But only Trevor Brooking is worrying them. Once he cleverly plays Bonds in for a volley and Strong says under his breath: 'Christ, he can play.' Moore heads for the dressing room at half time demanding more action from the forwards to make it count. Taylor tells them: 'They're more worried about us than we are about them. Keep playing. It'll come.' Moore agrees. They are mistaken.

Across the tunnel, West Ham are deciding to switch their pressure to the right of Fulham's defence, on to John Cutbush who has come in to Fraser's place. Almost at once, Cutbush gives the ball away to Holland, Jennings shoots, Mellor palms the ball away and Alan Taylor slaps it back through his legs.

Silence from Stock and Taylor. All the West Ham bench are on their feet except Lyall and Greenwood. They hold a private brains trust into the incident, Greenwood with eyes screwed up, Lyall chewing and smoking. That is West Ham's way.

Five minutes later, a worse error. Mellor drops Paddon's shot and Taylor picks up the pieces once more and puts them in the roof of the net. Moore thinks: 'Bloody goalkeepers.'

This time, Greenwood lets himself go. He puts one congratulating hand on Lyall's shoulder. You could almost believe they smiled.

For Fulham, the dream is over. Moore and Mullery flog them in to reprisals. Mitchell is foiled by Day a second time. Lyall senses West Ham are flagging. 'Come on, Patsy. Run, Trevor, run. Get hold of them, Frank.' Bonds is seizing up and Frank Lampard is now captain in all but name. Moore knows that but for Lampard they still might crack, and curses out of respect for the man he believes has developed into West Ham's best and most consistent player.

Just for the moment, Lampard seems to be playing Fulham on his own. Taylor mutters on the bench: 'Get us extra time. They're dying. We'll kill them in extra time.' But when you're two down at Wembley, you know you've lost the moment the police come up the tunnel and fan out around the pitch. Moore sees them emerge, like undertakers, and experience tells him they are into the last eight minutes. There is time for one last gesture. He draws the infuriating Lampard deep into one corner, flicks the ball over his head, pulls it down and strokes it smoothly away. A masterly touch in the face of defeat. Then it's over. West Ham lift the Cup, Moore is barely conscious of climbing the steps to receive his medal. Back in the dressing room he refuses a drink, waving away the cup of champagne and saying: 'It's a new experience, losing. You live and learn.'

Stock tries to lift drooping heads, singing: 'If I could live my life again...I'd come to Wembley every year.'

Someone says: 'Hell, two mistakes. And that Taylor only kicked the ball twice.' Moore sees Mellor smile nervously, bites on his tongue and walks sternly to the showers. The goalkeeper says: 'Well, someone's got to be the fall guy at Wembley. I wish I hadn't watched Bob Wilson's preview on the television. He was on about how goalkeepers could lose finals. John Lacy told me to go in the bathroom instead of watching but I said it couldn't happen to me.'

Moore comes out of the showers as the overflow of reporters and cameramen clustered round West Ham's door wash through the losers' dressing room. The attendants are sweeping up the debris of plasters, tie-ups, mud and plastic cups. A bottle of champagne stands half empty on the square white table, against a stark white wall in that bare white room. It is the only bottle taken from its crate.

Bobby is last out of the dressing room. The others walk up the tunnel, across a corner of the pitch and into the entrance beneath the Royal Box. They turn into the bar. But Moore pays a courtesy call on the West Ham

169

dressing room then walks directly on to the team coach. Had they won, he would have staked claim to one end of the bar and held court for his admirers. Like most winning sportsmen, he is a bad loser. On the coach, he signs programmes pushed by loyal fans through the narrow air-conditioning slits beneath the plate windows. One by one the others come aboard and the coach bounces away. At thirty-four, Moore knows the odds are against him ever returning as a player. For most footballers, one appearance would be the realisation of a dream. For Bobby, Wembley has become a way of life.

He does not look back. Instead, he starts opening the mountain of good-luck telegrams. It helps pass the journey to the West End hotel where Fulham's Cup Final night banquet will be held regardless. As the coach pulls to a halt outside the Dorchester, Bobby is met by Tina and his two children, all dressed in Fulham's black and white and biting their lips to keep back the tears. They rush to give Daddy a hug before the au pair takes them home to Chigwell.

That night, no more than one hundred yards along Park Lane at the Grosvenor House, West Ham have the Cup. But at Fulham's function they are mostly happy again and proud to have gone to Wembley. Bobby pays lip service to the celebrations.

James Mason, the actor, is staying at the hotel and begs entry to the banquet. He picks his way through the revelries, seeks out Moore and says: 'As one artist to another, I would like to shake your hand.'

Moore relishes the compliment but is only partially shaken from his depression. Tina despairs of James Mason, the lagers or even herself improving his hidden mood and retires early.

Bobby follows in the small hours, sits on the foot of the bed, velvet dinner jacket over one shoulder, bow tie hanging loose down his shirt front.

Slowly, he fishes in a pocket, opens a small box, looks blankly at his loser's medal and says to no-one in particular: 'I'm glad I didn't get many of these.'

CHAPTER NINETEEN

England,
My England

Even by insomniac standards, he had a bad night. If, in the last moments before death, one's entire life really does trip across the mind's eye, the Cup Final defeat at Wembley is the nearest Bobby Moore has yet come to extinction.

Five stars above the hotel entrance may well be a guarantee of creature comfort, but they do nothing to still a fidgeting brain. There was little rest, even though the warm darkness of his suite at The Dorchester was perfumed by the presence of his wife, stretched sleeping beneath silken covers.

He thought about his father back in Barking, no longer able to take active interest in his career because of a stroke which was also applying crippling pressures to the loving bond between both parents. He tangled with the problems that only money can bring. And he worried like any ordinary footballer about what would become of him the day his legs could no longer keep pace with the players of the future.

Bobby had given up counting sheep long ago. Instead, that night, he started flicking players through his mind. Great men, pictured for an instant on grand occasions. Footballers with strength of character, subtlety of mind and sleight of foot; men with whom he had felt honoured to play. By the time he was standing at his window, watching the damp emerald of Hyde Park shimmering a welcome to the rising sun, he had selected the team he would have been proudest to captain in the name of England.

The choice was restricted to men with whom he had shared a football pitch. They would have lined up in this formation:

1
Gordon Banks (Leicester & Stoke)

2	5	6	3
Paul Madeley	Roy McFarland	Bobby Moore (Capt.)	Ray Wilson
(Leeds)	(Derby)	(West Ham)	(Huddersfield & Everton)

8	4	11
Johnny Haynes	Alan Mullery	Bobby Charlton
(Fulham)	(Tottenham)	(Manchester United)

7	9	10
Tom Finney	Geoff Hurst	Jimmy Greaves
(Preston)	(West Ham)	(Chelsea & Tottenham)

Substitute: Martin Peters (West Ham & Tottenham)

Many of the arguments which will be triggered by that selection, raged through Bobby's mind. Finally, the key to 'my England team to beat the world' was found in a half-forgotten virtually meaningless match played by a Football Association XI on a tour of Australia and New Zealand in 1961. Moore was gaining experience as a twenty-year-old member of an English party who were ambassadors rather than competitors. The gentle, exhibition nature of the football tempted the great Tom Finney to come out of retirement. The term 'great' is not misapplied, as Moore's memory of that occasion bears witness.

'Tom had been one of the giants of the game when I was a boy and had hung up his boots at Preston eighteen months before. As a brash young lad I couldn't understand all the fuss about bringing the old chap out of retirement on that tour. Then we kicked-off. It was as if Tom had never been away. That lovely, easy control of the ball, the appreciation of the game, the finishing, much of the change of pace, it just unfolded in front of me. I'd never played with a winger like that and I never would. I was amazed by Tom Finney. He remains the last great England winger and without him I wouldn't be able to pick a 4-3-3 formation.

'A stack of wingers were tried in my time: Peter Thompson, John Connelly, Terry Paine, Bryan Douglas, all good players but all failed at England level. Finding Finney in my memory makes my team work. To partner him up front I'd have to play Greaves. Simply, one of the best goalscorers of all time. To start with, I'd try supporting them with Hurst's running.

'But if they didn't blend I would replace Geoff with Bobby Smith. Him and Greavesy were magic together at Spurs and I remember them playing together for England in Czechoslovakia. in '63. Magic. Jimmy got two, Bobby one and Bobby Charlton got another in a 4-2 win. When you watched Smith from the stands you tended to think he was just a brute who put the fear of Christ up the defenders and goalkeeper. But when you played with him you realised how much skill and vision he had to offer. Geoff would have to do well to keep him out.

'Behind them, the key to the midfield is Alan Mullery. A lot of people opposed the way Alf Ramsey picked ball-winners, tacklers, in midfield. But without an anchor man you can't pick the class of Haynes and Bobby Charlton. Teams are all about blend and Alan is the best of three candidates for that role because he can also offer you more constructive qualities than Nobby Stiles and Peter Storey.

'Around Mullers you have Haynes, the perfect passer and the perfectionist, and Charlton. Now Bobby could be inconsistent and exasperating but he was one of our few truly world class players and was a bigger force in the game in midfield than on the wing, where he started.

'I know that picking those three will have Alan Ball hammering my door down. Ballie's a pal of mine and he's done great for England, Everton and Arsenal. He's so intense about the game that he'll take it to heart. But he could only get in the team if we were playing it tighter with four midfield men and one less forward. If it's a choice between him and Tom Finney, then Ballie's out.

'Jack Charlton won't be too happy about Roy McFarland playing centre half. But although Jack's exceptional in the air and a good character to have in your team, Roy is a much more complete player, not only tough but capable of helping us play a lot more football out of defence. At the end of the day I suppose Big Jack and I still agree to differ about the way he liked to whack the ball away.

'Picking the left back wasn't easy. Leeds converted Terry Cooper from a winger and by the time he came into the England team he was a tremendous attacking full back. But before him, Ray Wilson was no slouch going forward and he was world class at defending, which is where your judgment of full backs has to start. So Ray's in, with Paul Madeley as his partner. Paul is not only one of the most versatile players but also one of the quickest, strongest and most intelligent. He's a player you always want in your side and he comes to the rescue at No.2 because we've had a terrible shortage of class right backs.

'For goalkeeper, it's enough to say there's only been one Gordon Banks. And Martin Peters is perfect for substitute because he's a class performer who's played in every position during his career, and played well in all of them.'

So only five of the 1966 World Cup Final team make Bobby's selection. More pointedly, only two players, Madeley and McFarland, survived the transition from the old England of Ramsey to the new England of Don Revie. That stands as a question mark against England's future and against the individual young hopefuls of the mid-Seventies. Moore says: 'When Revie took over he found himself in the same position as Ramsey, at the start of a ten-year cycle. It's like that with football teams. One lot grow old and you have to start again. Looking back, a lot of our team of the Sixties were a long way from being world class players when we started but we grew out of experience. The problem for the future is that the players' skills don't look so sound and their potential is not so exciting. The more you look at each one the more you worry.

'Perhaps because me and Norman Hunter were in the way, Colin Todd took a long time developing at Derby and once he came through I understand he turned down the chance to reach out and grab the captaincy. So where's his ambition? Trevor Francis looked to have all the ability in the world when he burst into the limelight at Birmingham but it seems to have taken him forever to break through into the England team. If he was going to be another Bobby Charlton he should have been playing international football as young as Bobby Charlton.

'Then there's this lad Kevin Beattie at Ipswich. Ballie came back from one England trip telling me: " I've found one for you. You'd love this boy Beattie. A real character and tremendous player." Then the next thing you know he's failing to turn up for an under-23 match because of the pressures. Pressures? Who's had more pressures than me? Yet if Don Revie wanted me to play as an over-age player in the under-23's, to guide the youngsters along a bit, I'd be there at seven in the morning. If I was manager, I'd be worried all my life that Beattie was going to let me down when it mattered, bang in the middle of a World Cup Final or something. He's a brilliant player but it's nonsense to talk about him yet as another Duncan Edwards. With his physical assets he ought to be a Rock of Gibraltar in your team, yet you can't rely on him.

'Kevin Keegan is another exciting player who raised a question mark against himself. Because he wasn't picked for one match, he went running home to Liverpool. If you're going to be a great player you've got to take the kicks in the teeth. You are in top football for one thing, success. If you just want an easy existence then run away to mum and stay there.

'Revie's had to forgive that sort of behaviour because of a shortage of top class players in England. But I doubt if he's forgotten and his day will come when someone breaks through to demand a place. Like Ballie and Martin Peters did in '66. Meanwhile, you find yourself still hoping that Colin Bell can fulfill his potential. Watching Colin play for Manchester City you figured he ought to become the white Pele. Two good feet, good in the air, unbelievable stamina and power. Could run anyone into the ground and then kill them off with a hell of a shot. Yet he so rarely comes out of his shell for England to show his regular club form.

'So if Colin's not going to run the game for you, who is? Ballie's too old. You know Alan Hudson could conquer the world but there's no guarantee he's going to conquer his temperament. It's only in goal that we seem to be all right. Ray Clemence, Peter Shilton, Phil Parkes. We're still the best nation in the world for keepers. But when I go to watch England now I'm looking for someone to win the game for me. We're talking about competing at the highest level, where being just good is not good enough.

'When have we looked like producing a player to compare with Pele or Johan Cruyff? Pele was the best in the world for a long time and then Cruyff proved himself the best for a period with Holland, Ajax and Barcelona. the little Irishman should have been up there with them but the English game seemed to have a destructive effect on him as well. George Best ran away in his own way.'

That judgment is based partly on an extraordinary first hand experience. Bobby, Tina and George crossed paths in Johannesburg in the summer of 1974. At a party given in his honour Best flirted with Tina: 'If you ever get a divorce, let me know.' Now, jealousy is a powerful element in the make-up of the Moores, as several women will bear witness after flirting with Bobby at various functions and feeling the full blast of Tina's wrath. But this time Bobby said: 'I wasn't angry. I just felt he should still have been proving himself on the football pitch.' That is where Moore judges men. the teams he has most admired were as strong in character as they were rich in class: Brazil in '58, '62 and '70; the European Cup-winning teams of Real Madrid and Ajax; and, at home, the Spurs League and Cup double-winning side of the early Sixties; and the consistent Leeds United of the late Sixties and early Seventies.

The real clue to Moore's fear for English football lies in his preference for the sheer exhilarating class of Real and Spurs over the brilliant Dutch strategists of Ajax and the arch professionals at Leeds.

He says: 'I accept the game has become more difficult to play in, because the preparation of each team has become more and more thorough. A lot more thought goes into the organisation of a side now. But with the exception of one or two entertaining and skilful teams like Derby County, we have got to face the fact that football has deteriorated as a crowd-pleasing spectacle.

'Basically, there is a chronic shortage of top class players. the changing environment is at the bottom of that. I don't remember television being a big deal in our lives when I first started playing football. All me and my mates used to do was go out in the streets and kick a ball about. The first holiday I ever had was a couple of days with a relative in Hainault, which I thought must be miles away but was really just a bit nearer the Essex countryside.

'I see the difference in my own kids. Roberta and Dean will start playing with other children but within a few minutes they're huddled round the old colour TV. Even when they can tear themselves away, there are so many more distractions. For me it was football or nothing. For them there are swimming classes, riding lesson, anything they want. Where I grew up, roller skates were few and far between, a real status symbol. My lad's already moving on from bicycles to mini-cars.

'Then those who do become players don't work at the game. Again it's a question of distractions. When I was a young pro there was the billiard hall, which didn't particularly appeal to me but which ruined a few players' lives, the cinema, which you couldn't go to five days a week, sitting in a cafe, which soon wore thin, or going home, which was boring. So we went back every afternoon and worked on our ball skills. The top players would be there as well, taking real pleasure from simply kicking a football, even though they were only earning £20 a week. That was how West Ham became something of an academy of football. It produced future managers from players who loved the game.

'Now it's as much as some players can do to fit training into their business and social lives. That's okay once you've mastered the craft. But the young lads are getting too much, too soon, too easy. Then most of them find themselves under managers who are governed by fear: the fear of defeat, the fear of losing their jobs.

'The Arsenal team which did the double in '71 proved that success is the yardstick for judging the game. A lot of people I know are Arsenal fans and at the start of that season they could hardly bring themselves to watch the sort of negative football their team were playing. But by the end of the season they were all rolling up because Arsenal were going for the League Championship and the F.A. Cup. It was still the same, boring football.

'Trouble was it was no good for the other managers, playing bright stuff, getting beat, and getting the bullet after uprooting their families to take the job in the first place. Long contracts might be the answer, but I still wonder about the quality of managers. I learned a great deal from Ron Greenwood and I would like to have played for Malcolm Allison but other than them there were probably only two managers I would really have given anything to work under. I'm sure it would have been an education to play for Don Revie at Leeds or Bill Shankly at Liverpool because they were so consistently successful. Greenwood, Allison, Revie, Shankly, they all made the business something more than mere survival, which is all it has become for a lot of managers.

'The pressure on the managers comes from bad directors and administrators. Too many of the men in the boardrooms treat the whole business as a hobby. Too many of the men at the F.A. can't live up to their responsibilities for the welfare of the game. Look at the old International Committee. For a good many of the years I spent as England captain, I was addressed as Ron by certain committee men because they thought I was Ron Flowers, who also happened to have fair hair and played at wing half.

'A lot of club directors are totally out of touch yet they come down occasionally from on high and expect the dressing room to go all quiet and respectful and all the players to call them Mister Chairman, or Sir, or Mr. John. What a joke, when they don't even know their job. When Jimmy Hill got appointed managing director of Coventry City it was a step in the right direction. Football is a big business and should be run that way. The game should have paid directors, who would be out of a job if they weren't working properly for the club.'

The class barriers in football, which are still enthusiastically manned by many boards of directors, are blamed by Moore for the shortage of opportunities for the talented showmen among the ranks of the players.

'Because those amateur directors can't stand losing matches,' he says, 'managers are wary of the ball players who don't work as hard as the team men. They know that if they pick a Peter Osgood, a Rodney Marsh, a Stan Bowles or a Charlie George, they are taking a gamble on the result. So they play the percentages and shy away from the type of player who can entertain the crowd. They feel that the best way to get success is by stopping other people playing and by nicking the odd goal.

'One or two managers have been trying to change the system more recently. Dave Mackay is telling good players to get on with the game at Derby. Tommy Docherty's got Manchester United attacking. Queens Park Rangers play some tasty football under Dave Sexton. That's good, because it's ludicrous to try to change great individual players into robots. You wouldn't catch me complaining if Jimmy Greaves was doing nothing else in my team except scoring two or three goals a week.

'My whole game has been built around doing the simple things quickly and efficiently, playing to my strengths and only pulling out something extraordinary if that was the only avenue left open to me. No doubt the right attitude to coaching is to get people doing the right thing at the right time. But I would always want one player in my team capable of doing the unusual and the unexpected. An Ossie. A Rodney. A Stan Bowles. Any half-way decent team should be able to cater for one luxury player. Look at Trevor Brooking – a fabulous luxury for West Ham to have in their team. If his name was Netzer or Gerson or Rivera we would all be crying out for an English player like him. But because he is English we complain that he doesn't run about enough or tackle hard enough.

'As long as a luxury player is doing his thing – getting goals or laying them on – it's one of the duties of a manager to live with his own sense of frustration that the player could be doing more. If I'd been manager of Martin Chivers at Tottenham, I would have been tearing my hair out watching him stroll about. But I'd have done it quietly. Because players like that really believe they are giving one hundred per cent. And without a player like that to score goals for them, Tottenham would have been relegated on about three successive seasons.'

Bobby's concern for football is rooted in the suspicion that there are more bad managers than good, just as there is a majority of bad players, and that bad referees also outnumber the good. He says: 'We should have tried professional referees years ago. They should be fitter, sharper and more involved with the players and coaches so they know what is going on in football and recognise what's going wrong. For most of my career, players and referees only seem to have been annoying each other. This is a professional game in which the referee's job should be on the line against his efficiency, the same as the rest of us.'

Above all, Moore despairs of the administrators. 'The emphasis should be on producing a game which the players can enjoy because they are encouraged to express their skills. That would automatically entertain the public and keep them coming through the turnstiles.

'Instead of worrying themselves silly about trivialities and their own private jealousies, the men at the F.A. and League should be looking for some way of improving the game. For example, there could be a simple rule change which might tilt the balance in favour of right in football.

'By and large I'm not in favour of tampering too much with the laws. I once went to Canada with Gordon Banks and Jack Charlton for an experimental game which had, among other things, goals ten feet high. That might not sound much for a fit man who can jump. But even Gordon Banks was not the same goalkeeper in a ten-foot high goal. The score was about 9-7 even though we only played twenty-five minutes each way. Now that's a joke. Goals should be precious because their rarity value is what makes them so thrilling. But there are many ways of encouraging a better mood and a better style in the game.

'For a start, we could consider banning players from passing back to their goalkeeper from outside the penalty area. To underline that, it would also be an offence to run with the ball back into the box and then give it to the keeper. At a stroke you would reward the skilfull players. It would make defenders try to play their way out of trouble and punish the men who lack the skill to do something creative in a difficult position.

'How about improving the mood of the game by borrowing a rule from Rugby Union? There is so much nastiness, embarrassment and wasted time in our games while referees try to force defenders to retreat the regulation ten yards from a free kick. In Rugby, if the defending players are not ten yards away by the time the kick is ready to be taken, the ball is moved ten yards nearer the goal. If you still don't move, another ten yards. In soccer, a harmless free kick on the halfway line could quickly become a scoring chance from the edge of the box. That would stop players arguing with referees.

'Why be afraid to try anything that might improve the game?'

These expressions of anxiety about the state of soccer and proposals for its improvement are made out of a deep and abiding affection for the game.

Football has, after all, been the vehicle for conveying Bobby Moore to fame and fortune, albeit a somewhat smaller and less secure fortune than his lifestyle might suggest or his public might imagine.

CHAPTER TWENTY

The Reckoning

Jack Turner used to have a room midway along the office corridor at Upton Park and the sign on the door said 'Property Manager'.

Nobody was quite sure what that meant, except that Turner could be responsible for nothing or everything at West Ham United according to how the mood took them. In Ted Fenton's time, the Property Manager found himself dealing with every problem which was either too trivial or too delicate to involve the team manager.

Turner is solid and square, of physique and character. In his sober grey suits, slim ties and shoes polished to reflection, the young footballers found him a comforting figure, full of sound advice and calm reassurance. Most mornings, they could be found queueing at that door for an answer to their troubles. Jack Turner could be relied upon to fix a mortgage, complete a tax return, even offer fatherly advice on the most intimate domestic problems. But the part he liked best was helping out with the scouting.

One raw winter day in 1955 found him on a wide-open touchline alongside Flanders Road, East Ham, gloved hands jammed deep into coat pockets, eyes watering in the wind, answering Fenton's request to 'go and watch a kiddy called Moore who's been recommended.' When that cup-tie was over, Leyton Boys had drawn 3-3 with East Ham and Turner went home to write neatly in his report: 'Whilst he would not set the world alight, this boy certainly impressed me with his tenacity and industry.' He proved to be a better judge of character than he was a prophet. Still, there was something about that fair-haired, fifteen-year-old wing half which roused Turner's curiosity and he went to watch the replay, a game won by one of Moore's rare goals. This time he pressed Wally St. Pier, West Ham's chief scout, to make a personal check. Bobby Moore was earmarked for the West Ham ground staff.

So began a partnership which bridged the generation gap and was to earn them both a small fortune.

Not that there was any cake to cut at the start. Bobby's starting wage was £6.15s. 0d. and from where he came from he counted himself lucky: 'It wasn't a bad wage for a school-leaver. On top of that, you could get a bonus of £1 or £2 for playing for the reserves in the Football Combination. And when you played away they would give you five shillings tea money. To the boys, that seemed the best bit of all. Maybe because you could win on the deal. If you stopped for a sandwich and a bottle of pop on the way to somewhere like Newbury, you could make a three bob profit. That was invaluable. You'd give fifty bob to your mum and set so much aside for your fares and your Saturday night out. Your wages were spoken for and that tea money was the little bit of extra in your pocket. Sometimes you could persuade them to give you three games a week with the reserves and the youth team, and that meant three lots of five bobs. Handsome.

'And all the time the work you had to do made you all the more determined to make the grade and turn pro. Today's apprentice professionals just do the same as the senior pros, train and play. Perhaps that's why too many of the young lads are undisciplined, and not enough of them are hungry footballers. We didn't have any breath to spare for answering back.

'First thing Monday morning we would start sweeping the terraces and cleaning out the stands. We'd break off from that in time to get the dressing rooms and the kit ready for the pros when they came in for training. You'd do some running and ball work yourself for the rest of the morning, then clear everyone's kit away and go back to sweeping the terraces, maybe cleaning the toilets, painting the back of the stand. Anything that needed doing.

'To get to your little match on Saturday, you'd have to get through Friday. There'd be the usual chores with the kit and the boots for training. Then you'd set about getting the pitch in shape for the first team game. When you had a pitch like West Ham's used to be, with such bad drainage, that meant three or four of us spending three hours pushing and pulling the heavy roller. Flattening it out. Backwards and forwards until you couldn't wait to go back to the dressing rooms and start polishing the taps on the baths and the showers. You'd stagger home at six and be up and out by nine next morning ready for an eleven o'clock kick off. When you look back at that, it's laughable to think we're called full time professionals when all we do is train a couple of hours a day.'

Those hours spent slogging at the heavy roller stored up the muscle power, willpower and indirectly, the earning power on which Bobby was to call at the high points of his career. More immediately, he was rewarded by his first professional contract. In April 1958, shortly after his 17th birthday, he signed for £12 a week, the maximum wage for his age at that time.

As a young man, he took no more than a distant interest in the struggle by Jimmy Hill's players' union to secure the abolition of the Football League's maximum wage. But by 1961, when that iniquity was swept aside, Bobby's single-minded concentration on securing a first team place at West Ham and launching his international career with a string of apprearances for England's under-23s had put him in a powerful bargaining position. 'I'd not been on the £20 maximum all that long and for a while I'd been happy with that. But when it became clear that the maximum wage would go, I sat down and worked out what I thought I was worth to West Ham. And I decided I was worth £30 a week.'

The figure reached by that self-evaluation became a point of principle in Moore's first financial dispute with West Ham. By sticking to that principle, he began accumulating his reputation as a hard-headed, commercial man. When the last of his team-mates settled for £28 a week, Moore stood his ground alone for six weeks, a period which affected his political standpoint for the rest of his life. He had never been much interested in politics, nor filled with the ideological zeal which grips many young men. He simply decided that any individual had the right to profit from his own talent and initiative. He was twenty. By the time he came of age, this working class lad from a staunch Socialist background had grown into a committed Conservative voter.

In that fight for an extra £2 a week he learned to look after himself and first sensed the intrinsic worth of his talent. 'Looking back, it's laughable that Ron Greenwood and I should have had such an enormous disagreement over £2 a week. West Ham were quibbling over £100 a year when they would soon be wasting £100,000 on a new player. I had made up my mind that as an under-23 international and a player already being linked with other, bigger clubs, I was worth that £30. Ron offered the whole squad £28 a week and at first none of us signed the new contracts. Then one or two gave in, then a couple more signed. Two days before the deadline the last half dozen signed. If you didn't take the £28 a week, they simply retained you on the old contract of £20. But I held out for another six weeks. And I won the battle for all the players who had backed down. Finally, the club decided to put everyone's wages up to £30, so they could settle the whole business. To be fair to them, they back-dated my rise so that in the end I didn't lose any money. I think, in the end, they accepted that I had held out for what I believed was right. If they

182

had offered me £30 a week at the start I wouldn't have started asking for £35. I would have signed at once.'

At the first possible moment, Moore had hardened himself for the new procedures of contract negotiation. Then, in order to minimise his personal embarrassment in forthcoming pay battles, he sat down and thought out a personal income policy. 'From then on there was going to be a lot of tough talking every time the contract was renewed and a lot of clubs were getting players to accept lower wages with high appearance and bonus money.

'That was okay if a season went well. But what if you were plain unlucky? Or out with injury? And what happened in the summer if you had adjusted your life style to a good income and suddenly you were back on a low basic? So in every financial settlement I insisted on a high basic wage, never mind the ifs and buts. Then I always assessed my value to the club according to the service I had given them and what I had achieved in football during the previous couple of years.

'Too many players want paying big money on a promise of what they are going to do in the future. I would never base my argument around what I might or might not do in the next four years. Let's face it, you could get run over or cop for a bad injury or simply hit a long patch of bad form. What I insisted on was a reward for what I had done in the past and recognition of my value as an asset to the club. As a man good enough to captain England, I was obviously of some value to West Ham as a player and as an attraction to the crowds.

'That might sound cold and hard, but you had to have some basis from which to negotiate. I learned in that first battle with Ron Greenwood how damaging the whole business might be to a manager and a player. We were in violent disagreement over £2 a week. It was ludicrous that we would end up the afternoon resenting each other yet next morning we would have to get out on the training pitch and try to get the best out of each other.

'The system has always been wrong in this country. Clubs expect a manager to come in from the seven-a-side, splash about in the bath with the lads, then put on a collar and tie and become a businessman. It's obvious that we should operate on the same lines as the Continentals, with a working director handling the finances. The team manager would be freed from all the bust-ups with players over contracts and when it came to transfers he would just tell the financial man which player he would like to sign and let him get on with fixing the deal.

'It is just as ridiculous that the League forbids a player to instruct an agent or representative to negotiate on his behalf. That's a throwback to the dark old days when they didn't think the players ought to earn much money, anyway. And they seem to think it's one way of putting the brake on the demands by the players.

'Everyone thinks players are money mad, but the fact is I don't know one professional footballer who enjoys negotiating for his money. Not one little bit. It's embarrassing. It's very difficult to sit there and tell someone how good you are. It would be much better for all concerned to have an agent go in there and do the talking for you. If golfers can leave all that to their agents and concentrate on playing, why shouldn't we? I would have gladly left my salary negotiations in Jack Turner's hands.'

As it was, Turner was falling from grace at West Ham under Greenwood's management and he began to interest himself in Bobby's earnings outside the game. The first man to toy with that potential had been Bagenal Harvey, the London-based agent to a veritable Who's Who of sporting, journalistic and television personalities. Harvey rushed in with a two year contract when Moore returned from his first World Cup, in Chile in 1962, and started well by securing a £450 payment for a Brylcream poster advertisement. But almost at once, the flow dried up and Moore asked Turner to arrange his release from the contract.

Turner had already helped establish Bobby in a sports goods shop, making available a small house directly opposite the main entrance to West Ham's ground which he had been using as a warehouse for an unsuccessful venture into football boot manufacturing. When Bagenal Harvey agreed to waive his hold on Moore, Turner immediately launched Bobby Moore Ltd., the biggest money-spinner in both their lives.

The sports shop was already progressing well. Under the expert management of Tina's mother, Elizabeth, and with the help of Bobby's frequent attendance behind the counter, the fans flocked in. Consistently, down the years, it made Bobby as much as he was earning from his football, doubling a salary which was itself constantly increasing as his reputation grew.

Meanwhile, Turner was after bigger money. Under the umbrella of Bobby Moore Ltd., he pushed his man's name at the media, the major companies, the advertising agencies. His first coup was a weekly column with Titbits. It paid £80 a week over a 26-week run. After paying £15 a week to his ghostwriter, Roy Peskett, Bobby was left with £65 profit, from half an hour's chat. He was earning £35 a week from football.

By 1964 he had pushed his West Ham salary above £60, even though many of his colleagues in the team which beat Preston in the F.A. Cup Final were earning less than £30 a week.

The real boom took another two years to materialise. Then Moore captained England to victory in the World Cup Final and suddenly money seemed to be growing on goalposts. Bobby returned to Greenwood's office to resume discussions which had been temporarily suspended by that dramatic signing of a one-month contract in the England hotel on the morning of their first World Cup match. He knew he was talking from an unprecedented position of strength. 'I was well aware that they couldn't afford to let me go to Tottenham or anywhere else after that World Cup. I also knew I was worth a great deal to them as England captain.'

Moore remembers the nub of the conversation quite clearly.

Greenwood began: 'How can you give your best for West Ham if you really want to leave us?'

'I've only thought about leaving in order to better myself. We've gone into a depression here but I won't dispute that we might be able to achieve things again. Let's concentrate on negotiating the right sort of figure.'

'What figure are we talking about?'

'Let's settle on £150 a week.'

'That's almost double your old contract. I don't know about that.'

'If you match my demand I'll sign a six-year contract to prove my loyalty to West Ham.'

'The club will have to think it over.'

West Ham agreed within a week and Moore signed a three-year contract with West Ham holding the option to retain him for a further three years after that. He says: 'I'm sure it made me the highest paid player at West Ham at the time. But it wouldn't have worried me if I'd found out that Geoff Hurst and Martin Peters had come back from the World Cup and got better deals than me.

'I never discussed my money with anyone else and all that concerned me was getting what I felt to be a fair deal, I don't suppose I was the best paid player in the country. There were a lot of stories about big money being earned by Bobby Charlton, Denis Law and George Best at Manchester United. But they were getting 60,000 people for games at Old Trafford and I felt that on West Ham's gate of around 30,000, my money was fair. Also I was able to stay close to my business interests and didn't have to move away from my side of London, my own environment.'

Moore and Turner also realised that although England's £1,000-a-man bonus for winning the World cup was in itself a pittance, it was only the first drop in an ocean of opportunity. The Golden Age had dawned. Footballers were not only social darlings but also sure-fire sellers of everything from cars to corn flakes and the faces of those World Cup winners beamed out from nearly every packet in every household.

Bobby Moore Ltd., became a seven-day-a-week, 18-hour-a-day business. The newspapers became as clamourous for columns as the magazines and his signed articles for the *Daily Mirror* and *Shoot*, the football weekly, were grossing £160 a week, plus expenses.

The ad-men fought to have Bobby Moore smile into the camera and endorse their clients' product. By the time of the next World Cup, in 1970, Kellogg's were paying him £3,000 for a single corn flakes commercial.

That was when the boom hit its peak. Bobby Moore Ltd. was grossing £22,000 a year, even though Turner was careful to turn down offers which might tarnish the solid image of his star. In fact, partly to help reinforce that image, Moore did not charge for one anti-smoking commercial for the government.

Through it all, Turner was strictly Mr. Ten Per Cent. He says: 'Other agents expect fifteen or twenty per cent but I believe Bobby is something special and it's better to have ten per cent of a lot than twenty per cent of nothing at all. And apart from all that, I love the involvement. I could have made a lot more money for myself in other walks of business. But I'm happy.'

A house not far from Moore's in stockbroker Chigwell is an aid to that contentment. Nevertheless, Turner is the one person Bobby trusts completely, apart from his own wife. The only time Moore felt that Turner let him down concerned the loss of his entire playing career's collection of newspaper cuttings. That record of his life was bundled into a sack one evening and left, carelessly, in a corner of Turner's offices in Manor Park. The cleaner threw out the sack with the rest of the rubbish next morning. A more emotional man might have wept at such a loss. Bobby counted it a small price to pay for Turner's unquestioned loyalty and integrity.

It has been outside Turner's sphere of influence that Moore has made his mistakes.

In the boom years, the acquaintances came thick and fast with their propositions for jumping on the Bobby Moore bandwagon. Hatton Garden jeweller Peter Younger begged permission to launch Bobby Moore Jewellery in 1968. Net proceeds: Nil.

That same year, clothing retailer David Walker set up Bobby Moore Shirts and Ties as a London outlet for goods being marketed in the north of England by Manchester City footballer Mike Summerbee. 'It might have worked,' said Bobby, 'if they could have produced enough gear to satisfy the orders on the books.' Net proceeds: A dozen monogrammed silk shirts and ties.

Again in 1968, Moore involved himself in a more substantial venture with Freddie Harrison, a manufacturer of suede and leather wear for ladies, and Morris Keston, fanatical supporter of Tottenham in general and football in particular, as well as a successful gown manufacturer.

They decided to attack the suede and leather market for men.. They formed Harrison-Moore Ltd., and this time Bobby had to invest £5,000 as well as his name. He has yet to recover a penny.

For a start, they used a factory in East London and opened a West End showroom in Percy Street. Then Keston withdrew because of personal differences with Harrison. They expanded into a larger factory at Wickford in Essex but when the government met a power crisis by declaring a three-day working week, they were forced to close down and sub-contract their work to outside manufacturers. Harrison then purchased a small factory in Cyprus which had only just settled to producing a regular flow of quality goods when the Turks invaded the island. They again contracted their work outside the company. They re-opened operations in Cyprus at the end of 1975 but Harrison went bankrupt in March 1976, having already passed on his share of the company to his brother.

Still, Moore hoped Harrison-Moore Ltd. could be a strong plank of his economy at the end of his playing days. 'Every penny I might have taken out has in fact been ploughed back into the business and it could still be a success, given a longer period without major problems.'

At first, the problems with Harrison-Moore Ltd. seemed incidental. Even the football itself became lucrative. Moore returned from the 1970 World Cup in Mexico to make arrangements for his testimonial match, a privilege for which every footballer becomes due after ten years with one club. Celtic provided the opposition to West Ham at Upton Park, Esso secured some publicity for themselves by sponsoring the event, 26,000 people came through the turnstiles and by the time Bobby left to host a reception at The Sportsman Club, he was assured of a tax-free benefit payment of almost £20,000.

That sum did not compare with the £40,000 testimonials of Denis Law and Bobby Charlton at Manchester United and Billy Bremner and Norman Hunter at Leeds United, but it was a killing by southern standards. Two years later he was negotiating yet another new contract with West Ham. 'To be fair,' he says, 'they had improved on my £150 a week during the period of my six-year contract. Without much prompting from me, they accepted that times changed and came up with rises accordingly.'

In 1972, however, he pushed his basic wage well clear of the £200 a week milestone by agreeing a contract 'comfortably in excess of £10,000 a year.'

After another two years, he harvested the proceeds of his transfer to Fulham. At that time another of Moore's acquaintances, the Bill Larkin of roasted peanut fame, organised a whipround among businessmen fans of West Ham to keep Bobby at Upton Park. Between them, they promised to cover the £30,000 extra which Bobby could expect to earn from a three year contract with Fulham. However touching, it was an impractical gesture and the transfer went through.

By 1974, Moore was becoming in need of that injection of extra capital. 'You get used to a certain standard of living.' The lifestyle of the Moores had progressed apace. The humble semi in Ilford was bought for £3,600 and sold for £6,500. The mock Tudor residence in Chigwell cost £11,500 and brought in £41,000. Morlands, the new mansion, comes to £80,000 worth of purpose-built luxury.

The move to Fulham coincided with the sale of the West Ham sports shop to one of Tina's cousins. 'There didn't seem much point keeping it on since I was leaving the club.'

Besides, he was by then up to his neck in a much grander enterprise which for a time threatened him with bankruptcy and which even in this Spring of 1976 promises to prove a very costly self-indulgence.

The nightmare has a name: Woolston Hall. It identifies a charming manor house set in a cleft of Essex countryside between Chigwell and Abridge. It seemed perfect for a country club. Del Simmonds thought so. A car dealer and yet another of the fraternity of Chigwell businessmen, Simmonds was on friendly terms with two star names who could front the operation, his golfing partner Sean Connery and his favourite footballer, Bobby Moore. He could also count on financial aid from Lou Wade, his and Bobby's mutual friend, Wade's businessman son Michael and a seventh partner, East End publican Kenny Bird.

Together, in 1971 they agreed the project was a winner. Jack Turner strongly opposed Moore's involvement but Bobby and Tina were taken with the glamourous nature and apparent potential of a country club. Bobby says: 'It seemed perfect for the area and the deal seemed tremendous. We had the house valued at £½ million and the total cost of the project was only £250,000. There were twenty six acres of land only twelve miles from London and we all knew we lived in a rich area where you had to queue up to get a table in the local restaurants. What we didn't know, between us, was the slightest thing about catering or organising a club of this kind.'

That did not deter Moore from investing £5,000 cash and encouraging the confidence of the group's backers, the Dunbar Bank in Pall Mall, by becoming a director and freely giving the use of his name. Even before the refurbishing work was completed, Bird, the publican, had withdrawn from the project. Before the club could open, there was an underworld attempt to burn down Woolston Hall and a shotgun was fired at Simmonds' home from a passing car. The five remaining partners duly accepted Simmonds' resignation.

They pressed on with the opening of their exclusive £100-a-membership country club which embraced a restaurant, discotheque, cocktail and lounge bars, sauna, golf driving range, swimming pool and tennis courts.

'The great problem, ' Moore now acknowledges, 'was that with the exception of the restaurant, discotheque and bars, we spent a fortune on facilities which did not bring in a penny piece. And we had bought the best of everything, from the teaspoons upwards.'

The debts mounted. Moore's agents took on increased guarantees at the bank. They changed the style of the Woolston Hall operation, sacrificing exclusivity for a more popular appeal. They cut prices. They increased the share issue. In vain. The club had opened for business in August 1972. By early 1974 they decided to cut their losses and sell out. They were left with an outstanding debt of £100,000.

The following year, Moore found himself in the embarrassing position of being sued under an alleged guarantee for a six-figure sum. The subsequent lengthy litigation is still causing Bobby and Tina a great deal of unexpected worry.

By the standards of many of the world's leading sportsmen, the entire sum of money involved might have been an acceptable sum to risk in business. Jack Nicklaus, Gary Player, Muhammad Ali, Jackie Stewart, Lew Hoad, all could stand that sort of racket without long-term grief. So could Pele and Johan Cruyff, but unlike his Latin American and Continental contemporaries, Moore is no millionaire.

The financial crisis has served to confound the cynics who predicted that the Moores would go the unhappy way of so many celebrity marriages. In fact, the crisis has strengthened their ties. At Christmas 1975, when Bobby lapsed into depression as he felt his playing days running out and the financial furies at his heels, Tina took his hand and said firmly: 'Don't worry. We'll prove them wrong. And then to hell with all the people who said we were on the skids.'

Bobby was in more optimistic mood by his 35th birthday on 12 April,

1976. The problems had given Moore a new sense of purpose and direction. For a long time he had been fidgeting with the thought of giving up football completely when he retired as a player. He said: 'I was lucky enough to be around for the best years professional footballers have ever known in this country. From now on, there will be a handful of top men still earning good money. But by and large the economy of the game is becoming much tighter.'

The sudden, sour taste of commerce came as a sharp reminder of his appetite for big time soccer. 'Hell, I'd like my playing career all over again. Every minute of it. Maybe I've got nothing left to prove as a player. Maybe I proved myself the best at my business for twelve years non-stop and you don't have to go on proving that forever. but I wish I could go on playing forever.'

As if on cue, rich American clubs, headed by San Antonio, materialised with offers tempting Moore to join Pele and other distinguished names in giving the world game a fresh and exciting impetus in the hitherto unconverted United States. The money and the challenge were ideal and again he felt the spurt of adrenalin through his veins.

Beyond that, he began to hunger for a chance to show what he could do in management. 'I never thought much about running my own team but now that prospect excites me as well. It would have to be right. I wouldn't want to start at the bottom all over again, scuffling about in the lower divisions. But the right challenge at a good club, great.'

Right on schedule, like most events in his well-ordered career, Bobby's character has been unbending in time to accommodate the extrovert sporting mentality of America and the more varied demands of management.

A twinkling wit and warmth of nature have been allowed to surface slowly through the dignified image he deemed suitable for an England captain.

Whether his long-term future lies with the eager Americans or the suspicious brethren of English managers, he will come among them a richer, rounder, more open personality with all the more to offer for his later, sobering experiences. Not that any of those expanding qualities will weaken his basic stiffness of resolve and hard edge of competitive spirit.

As Ron Greenwood was saying when it all began, Bobby Moore is a very ambitious young man.

Index

191